Theories of Women's Studies

Theories of Women's Studies

Edited by
Gloria Bowles and Renate Duelli Klein

Routledge & Kegan Paul
London, Boston, Melbourne and Henley

First published in 1983
by Routledge & Kegan Paul plc
39 Store Street, London WC1E 7DD,
9 Park Street, Boston, Mass. 02108, USA,
296 Beaconsfield Parade, Middle Park,
Melbourne 3206, Australia, and
Broadway House, Newtown Road,
Henley-on-Thames, Oxon RG9 1EN

Set in Journal 10/12pt. by
Columns, Reading, Great Britain
Printed in the United States of America

Library of Congress Cataloging in Publication Data
Main entry under title:

Theories of women's studies.

Bibliography: p.
Includes index.
1. Women's studies — Addresses, essays, lectures.
1. Bowles, Gloria. 2. Duelli-Klein, Renate.
HQ1180.T48   1983   305.4'2'072   82-19512

ISBN 0-7100-9488-4

Contents

We dedicate this book to the coordinators of the first National Women's Studies Association meetings at Lawrence, Kansas, 1979: Emily Abel; Shirley Harkess, Debby Rosenfelt and Peg Strobel; to Dorothy Brown, who teaches the senior thesis seminar in Women's Studies at Berkeley; and to Maresi Nerad for her joyful energy and effectiveness in creating an international feminist community.

Acknowledgments

The original version of *Theories of Women's Studies I and II* was published by the Women's Studies Program at the University of California, Berkeley. We would like to thank Melitta Beeson and Kathy Gallup of Special Programs for their help throughout the publication and distribution of the original version. Eric Mills has typed the manuscript speedily and thoughtfully. And Taly Rutenberg has edited the editors — many thanks!

On the other side of the Atlantic, our gratitude goes to Philippa Brewster of Routledge for her encouragement and support in making this book possible and to Dale Spender whose ideas and friendship are an immense benefit to both of us.

Notes on contributors

Gloria Bowles and *Renate Duelli Klein* met at the University of California, Berkeley in 1978, where Gloria Bowles is Coordinator of Women's Studies. They collaborated on *Theories of Women's Studies I and II*, originally published by the Berkeley program, and are presently working together on the *Women's Studies International Forum*, a bimonthly feminist journal edited by Dale Spender, and the *Athene Series*, an international series of feminist books published by Pergamon Press. They have experienced that people from very different disciplinary and cultural backgrounds can work well together: Renate Duelli Klein is Swiss and holds a MSc in biology; Gloria Bowles is a mid-westerner with a PhD in Comparative Literature. Both have been 'student' and 'teacher' to each other and have exchanged these roles many times over the years.

Gloria Bowles's research is on Women's Studies as an academic discipline and women's poetry. She is writing a monograph on Louise Bogan. Renate Duelli Klein loves to discuss theories and strategies for a feminist future and feels very strongly about women's needs to know about the ideas of our foremothers. She now lives in London and is writing her PhD thesis on the theory and practice of Women's Studies. With Maresi Nerad and Sigrid Metz-Gockel she had edited *Feministische Wissenschaft und Frauenstudium* (1982) and she hopes to contribute with her work to the growth of an international feminist network.

Sandra Coyner is Director of Women's Studies at Kansas State University in Manhattan, Kansas. Her PhD is in history but she considers herself a Women's Studies person now. She is the Editor of *Program Network Notes*, the newsletter of US Women's Studies coordinators, which is one of the best sources of information on what is really going on in US Women's Studies.

Barbara Du Bois is a psychologist, feminist theorist, psychotherapist, teacher and spiritual seeker, now living in Vermont.

Toby Epstein Jayaratne is completing her PhD dissertation in psychology at the University of Michigan. She has been involved in Women's Studies programs at the University of Michigan, Washington State University and the University of Oklahoma.

Mary Evans was one of the founding members of the MA in Women's Studies at the University of Kent at Canterbury where she teaches sociology and Women's Studies. Her research is in the area of Women's Studies and literature and she is the author of a forthcoming book on Simone de Beauvoir.

Maria Mies is a Professor of Sociology at the Fachhochschule Köln, West Germany. She spent many years in India as a lecturer and a researcher. From 1979 to 1981 she worked at the Institute of Social Studies in The Hague, Holland, where she set up an MA Program on Women and Development. This program – the first of its kind – gives Third World Women an opportunity to qualify in Women's Studies. Maria Mies is the author of two books on Indian women: *Indian Women and Patriarchy* (New Delhi, Concept, 1980), and *The Lacemakers of Narsapur: Indian Housewives in the World Market* (ZED-Press, London, 1982). She is a founding member of the German Feminist Association for Social Science Research and Praxis. Since autumn 1982 she has worked as a co-editor of the *Beiträge zur feministischen Theorie und Praxis*.

Shulamit Reinharz is an Assistant Professor of Sociology at Brandeis University. She wrote the present paper while an Assistant Professor of Psychology at the University of Michigan. Having this interdisciplinary orientation, she feels right at home in Women's Studies, where she also teaches. She has written *On Becoming a Social Scientist: From Survey Research and Participant Observation to Experiential Analysis* (Jossey-Bass, 1979), co-authored *Psychology and Community Change* (Dorsey, in press), and is co-editor of the journal *Qualitative Sociology*. Her research and publications are in the areas of feminist methodology, women's individual and collective competence, and social gerontology.

Taly Rutenberg is a graduate student in Social Welfare, at Berkeley. She wrote 'Learning Women's Studies' as an undergraduate in Women's Studies at UC Berkeley. During the next few years she will be struggling to translate her feminist vision into a livelihood.

Dale Spender is an Australian who lives in London. A practical theoretician, she has for the last decade pursued the question of *how* male power is brought into existence and she has written and edited books and articles on *how* men take control in language, education, literature, history, and knowledge in general. She believes passionately that the control of knowledge is one of the crucial sites of feminist struggle and is a committed member of the women's resistance. She is involved in projects to encourage the development of women's knowledge and to make it readily available. Her books include *Man Made Language*, Routledge & Kegan Paul, 1980; *Men's Studies Modified*, Pergamon Press, 1981; *Invisible Women*, Readers and Writers, 1982; *Women of Ideas and What Men Have Done to Them*, Routledge & Kegan Paul, 1982 and *Feminist Theorists*, The Women's Press, 1983. She is also the editor of the *Women's Studies International Forum*.

Liz Stanley and *Sue Wise* live together in Manchester, England. Sue Wise works as a social worker and Liz Stanley as an academic sociologist. The 'Stanley and Wise' order of names is an alphabetical one only and signifies nothing about who contributes what and to what extent. They have jointly written *Breaking Out: Feminist Consciousness and Feminist Research* (Routledge & Kegan Paul, 1983) and are presently working on a book on sexual harassment.

Bari Watkins is the Director of the Program on Women at Northwestern University and a lecturer in the department of history. She received her PhD in history from Yale in 1976. Her special interest is nineteenth- and twentieth-century women's culture. With Cynthia Patterson she is currently preparing for publication a documentary history of the women's movement since 1963.

Marcia Westkott is an Associate Professor of Sociology at the University of Colorado, Colorado Springs. She has spent the last two years as an assistant dean of the College of Letters, Arts and Sciences. Her essay on 'Feminist Criticism of the Social Sciences' is a classic in the field. She teaches courses in Women's Studies and social theory and dreams of a woman-centered university.

1

Introduction: theories of Women's Studies and the autonomy/integration debate

Gloria Bowles and Renate Duelli Klein

'We may get lost in our transformation' (Elaine Reuben, 1981).[1]

1 The autonomy/integration debate

This publication has its origins in the first National Women's Studies Association conference in Lawrence, Kansas in 1979.[2] By then Women's Studies in the US was ten years old. As feminists in academe, we had spent the first ten years creating our programs, and surviving. We had embarked on the journey of doing research from a feminist perspective and our new scholarship inspired by our classroom experiences came into being rapidly. At Lawrence, in a number of independently conceived sessions, we found ourselves asking whether the different questions we asked which led to growth and innovation in both content and method in our teaching and research meant that Women's Studies was forming itself as an academic discipline, a study in its own right.

The papers in *Theories of Women's Studies* document this evolution.[3] They ask questions about the nature of Women's Studies in higher education and, by extension, they ask how Women's Studies as a discipline is different in content, in form, in aims and objectives from the traditional disciplines. Although we did not plan it that way, we now see how the papers in this volume provide the information and the background for that crucial debate which will shape the development of Women's Studies throughout the 1980s: Is Women's Studies a

1

discipline of its own, that place in the university where radical, women-centered scholarship grows, develops and expands? Or shall feminist scholarship, according to the integrationist model, be incorporated into the disciplines so that eventually Women's Studies as a separate entity will become obsolete?

The advocates of each approach have different views on how *change* takes place. The integrationists encourage 'The Powers That Be' to include women in the curriculum; they think that acts of convincing, informing, consciousness-raising are the path to the transformation of our present one-sided education. Those who believe in the existence of Women's Studies as a study in its own right have their doubts about this approach. They maintain that the structure of knowledge can be changed only by radical, innovative feminist scholarship that is given a chance to grow in a setting where there is vibrant exchange and debate among autonomous feminist scholars who have control over their knowledgemaking.

However, few feminist scholars would want to take an either/or stand on the autonomy/integration issue. Many factors influence our strategies for promoting and expanding feminist thought within academe. The nature and size of our particular university or college, the presence or absence of a Women's Studies program, local cutbacks or federal monies for integrationist projects — all of these material realities have a profound impact upon our visions and even more so on our day-to-day actions. Indeed, under the given circumstances on a particular campus integration might seem the wiser road to take. However, we believe that all decisions in favor of integration should be informed by our awareness of its potential danger to autonomous Women's Studies and feminist thought in general.

In the following pages, we hope to bring into focus the major assumptions and differences between the two approaches, the points where their arguments meet and the strategies of each.

2 Integrationist definitions and strategies

Initially, Women's Studies students and teachers expected that within a few years we would have succeeded both in creating courses on women and in integrating that knowledge into the general curriculum. We soon found out that 'adding' women was not enough. Ultimately, the questions we asked and the answers we began to formulate did not fit into the framework of Men's Studies,[4] because Women's Studies shares neither the assumptions of the dominant cultures, nor do we find the present compartmentalization of knowledge adequate to pursue our questions. To introduce feminist insights means to challenge radically the generation and distribution of knowledge; it means changing the whole shape of the course, or the problem − or the discipline. Such a concept of Women's Studies demands more than having a course 'on women', more than remedying the curriculum by inserting some women poets into a course on 'great poets of . . .'. It goes beyond demanding that women be 'equal' to men, for, as we know from women's history, such an equal rights approach still accepts androcentricity − the value-set of the dominant culture − as the norm into which women must be fit.

Autonomous Women's Studies, as we define it, has the potential to alter fundamentally the nature of all knowledge by shifting the focus from androcentricity to a frame of reference in which women's different and differing ideas, experiences, needs and interests are valid in their own right and form the basis for our teaching and learning. Within such a conceptualization of Women's Studies *every* issue is a Women's Studies issue: women are no longer subordinated to the power and control of male-defined knowledge. *All* existing knowledge needs to be examined for its adequacy and usefulness for women and men.

We are skeptical whether the present structure of education (and the nature of societal institutions at large) can ever accommodate feminist claims because its very existence depends on the perpetuation of patriarchal assumptions and values. Advocates of autonomous Women's Studies and integrationists thus work from different assumptions: the integrationists hope to achieve the transformation from within the very framework which we believe needs transforming.

At this writing, there are 49 integrationist projects in the US (McIntosh, 1982). These projects vary greatly, depending on the program administrators and the institutions in which they find themselves. Each integration project has its self-conception, its own image. For example, at Montana State University, the project 'proposes to develop strategies for reducing sex bias in higher education curriculum, through a two-year faculty development program' (Schmitz, 1981, unpaginated). Although this language subtly points to male bias it makes no great claims, saying only it will attempt to reduce sex bias. Does such a stance seriously challenge the androcentric nature of the present curriculum? At Stephens, a small private women's college in Columbia, Missouri, a Women's Studies Program was already in place before the onset of an interdisciplinary project whose goal it is to bring Women's Studies closer to the center of the whole curriculum, because 'the dignity and equality of women' is the uppermost aim of the college (Stephens College, 1982, unpaginated). Wheaton College, a small women's college in Massachusetts, hopes for a 'more balanced curriculum, reflecting the experiences and accomplishments of women as well as men' (Spanier and Schmidt, 1981). Such a balanced view of human existence, however desirable as it is, seems unrealistic – to say the least – in our unbalanced world, where half the population dominates the other half and 'balance', in the eyes of many, equals women becoming like men. In their publicity materials, Wheaton further argues that 'the development of separate Women's Studies courses and programs has so far produced only a minimal impact on the core of the liberal arts curriculum' (Spanier and Schmidt, 1981).

This assumption that Women's Studies is something 'separate' or apart, a kind of ghetto, is repeated in other integrationist documents. Indeed, feminist scholarship is not known by many outside our own circles. But is this the responsibility of Women's Studies or a result of the very resistance that we have to expect from the educational system and society at large? Why do we seem surprised by this resistance? For in fact what we are about is nothing less than an intellectual revolution: we challenge the dominant culture at its source. As Elizabeth Minnich puts it (1982, p. 9): 'What we [feminists] are doing, is comparable to Copernicus shattering our geo-centricity, Darwin shattering our species-centricity. We are shattering andro-centricity, and the change is as fundamental, as dangerous, as exciting.' And we are surprised that we are not welcome in the academy?

Other integrationist projects share Wheaton's optimism about 'balancing the curriculum' by adding Women's Studies. Judith Walzer, a Princeton administrator, writes that 'Women's Studies does not constitute a new discipline but a new subject with a special perspective that can help to change the old disciplines' (1982, p. 22). For her, integration wards off the possibility of being 'cordoned off from the mainstream of the university.' She says that this 'has sometimes been the case with Afro-American Studies and other enclaves for special interests and purposes which the university as a whole may ignore while supporting these enterprises financially' (Ibid., p. 22).

Here we have the ghetto idea again. We think, however, that there is another way to look at this. We see it as the attempt of a minority culture (such as the Afro-American people in the US) and a minority/majority culture (such as women world-wide) to reclaim the past, to alter the present, and in so doing to challenge the continuation of white male hegemony. Why should Women's Studies and ethnic studies programs be seen as ghettos and enclaves for 'special interests' rather than represent a move away from the present oppressive culture of the dominant few — white men and their values — towards a more inclusive structure of knowledge validating and reflecting the differing experiences and interests of a wide range of people? For sure, Women's Studies, as it presently exists, has its own problems with heterosexism, classism and racism in its predominantly white programs — all inherited from patriarchal culture. But within Women's Studies there is an awareness of these problems and we are working hard to overcome them.

Mary Ruth Warner, who teaches Black Studies and Women's Studies at the University of Massachusetts at Amherst, says, in describing the goals of the Women's Studies program: 'While one of the goals of the Program is to foster the mainstreaming of Women's Studies into the university curriculum, our primary focus has been the development of Women's Studies as a discipline.' And she continues: 'Another important aspect of our efforts has been the mainstreaming of the subjects of black women and racism into the Women's Studies curriculum' (Dinnerstein, 1981, unpaginated). Thus for Warner — and we would hope for many other Women's Studies practitioners — the focus is on making Women's Studies a complete study in its own right and inclusive of and for all women.

3 What future for Women's Studies?

The idea that Women's Studies as a discipline is an enclave for special interests is also the centerpiece of Carolyn Lougee's call for integration. Lougee voted against a course in women's culture at Stanford and worked instead to infiltrate the required western civilization curriculum. She writes that:

following the dominant pattern for course development in women's studies, a separate course on women's culture was proposed as a corrective for those students who might have a special interest in women. This proposal was turned down on the grounds that it was inadvisable to have a separate compensatory core curriculum for those with special interests. This would reaffirm the marginality of women's studies and in a perverse way relieve teachers in the mainline course from the obligation to deal with women's issues (1981, p. 5).

Of course, both Walzer and Lougee are worried that the traditional disciplines will be let off the hook if we do not mainstream the malestream. But in fact, as they devote their energies to changing the hearts and minds of the education establishment, they build up obstacles to the development of Women's Studies as a study in its own right. If we put our efforts into changing 'them,' will we have energy left to develop 'us'? If all the womanpower and financial resources go into faculty development seminars, integration workshops, and curriculum development in the existing disciplines, when is the overworked and underpaid Women's Studies 'expert' going to do her own research and teaching *in Women's Studies*? Moreover, once the integration of the study of women into the disciplines has been declared to be the central goal, why should the university or college support the existence of autonomous Women's Studies, especially when short of funds?

There are feminist scholars who talk openly about the eventual demise of Women's Studies. Writing to an audience outside Women's Studies in *Change Magazine*, Florence Howe, whose pioneering work in establishing Women's Studies has been invaluable and who deserves every possible credit for it, characterizes Women's Studies as part of the passage towards integration, or transformation. She writes that 'It is, in my view, impossible to move directly from the male-centered curriculum to what I have described as transformation of that curriculum into a changed and coeducational one — without passing through some form of women's studies' (Howe, 1982, p. 18). She adds: 'In short, there is no way around women's studies, if by that term we mean a deep and richer immersion in the scholarship on women' (Ibid.). Does Howe want to have it both ways, as she tells those who dominate academe that we must have Women's Studies but promises that eventually, and what we are all working for, is the withering away of Women's Studies? Does Nancy Cott take a similar line, when she is quoted as saying that 'I hope that in the long term, Women's Studies will not be necessary as a separate perspective because the perspective that it suggests will become the normal one, that is, a perspective in which women are as much recognized as men are. But, when I say in the long term, I think it's going to take fifty years or so' (1982, p. 3)? Is this a strategy to avoid announcing our intention to be around for a very long time or a real, felt goal? We think the distinction is crucial.

Up to now we have been speaking primarily of those who have been in Women's Studies for several years. But of course there have been and are many feminist scholars who are studying women within the disciplines. This is quite different from doing Women's Studies. A feminist scholar working within one of the traditional disciplines must write to the audience in her field; she has to ground herself in the structure and ideas set up by that discipline and to be knowledgeable about it. In order to survive, the feminist disciplinary scholar must tactfully take apart brick by brick the ideas of her forefathers. And, unlike the Women's Studies scholar who is supposed to do the integrating of Women's Studies into the disciplines, to give her energies to 'balancing' the curriculum, the feminist working to change her discipline will not find it advantageous to support and work in Women's Studies. Most probably her participation in Women's Studies will not add to her chances of keeping her job or being promoted. In either case — whether of the feminist disciplinary scholar or the Women's Studies person redirecting her efforts to integration — it is the old, old story of women taking on double burdens: women must be experts in the 'old' Men's Studies *and* in the 'new' feminist ideas on the traditional academic disciplines.[5] The autonomous Women's Studies person, on the other hand, has the possibility of continuing her feminist work (relatively) free from the interference of patriarchal belief-systems.

No matter what decisions individual women make about the nature of our feminist work and commitment, we think it is essential that we are aware both of the long range implications of our choices and of the necessity of understanding in detail our different points of view. Most importantly, women who have chosen either approach must keep informed about our work and support each other. The divide-

and-conquer mechanisms of separating women from each other — as for instance in juxtaposing autonomous with integrationist Women's Studies — is all too obvious. Without support from outside our own circles autonomous Women's Studies may wither away; but without the existence and support of innovative and radical autonomous Women's Studies the feminist disciplinary scholar and those integrating Women's Studies into the existing disciplines may have more and more difficulties in justifying their work to those in power in their disciplines.

If we do not join forces and work together we may all disappear! Does history inevitably have to repeat itself? Do we need to go away — if only to surface again fifty years later and thus to repeat what Dale Spender has convincingly demonstrated has been happening with women's protest for centuries (1982)?

Some feminist scholars working for integration see the pitfalls of overwork and narrow disciplinarity and the necessity for autonomous Women's Studies. Peggy McIntosh, Director of the Faculty Development Project at the Wellesley College Center for Research on Women points out that the integrationist projects 'absolutely depend on the work of scholars in Women's Studies.' She says' 'We need to be careful not to wear out our womanpower, not to spread ourselves too thin, not to allow superficial change, not to dilute the radical work of Women's Studies as it enters what used to be called the mainstream' (1982).

And in their report on 'How to Integrate Women's Studies into the Traditional Curriculum,' Myra Dinnerstein, Sheryl O'Donnell and Patricia MacCorquodale of the Southwest Institute for Research on Women (SIROW) write:

> It should be made clear from the beginning that intergration is an adjunct and not a substitute for Women's Studies courses and that these courses need to continue to provide the depth and breadth not possible in mainstream classes (1981, p. 22).

The SIROW report also acknowledges that some Women's Studies scholars are sceptical of their new strategy. They state that

> Interestingly enough, some of the resistance to curriculum integration comes from dedicated Women's Studies scholars and teachers

who worry, quite legitimately, about what will happen to the
feminist perspective in the classrooms of non-feminist professors.
They believe that mainstreaming will result in only token and
sometimes inaccurate additions to the curriculum and would pre-
fer that students be exposed to this material in Women's Studies
classes (Ibid., p. 19).

We share these concerns and in the following summarize what we see
to be some of the problematic issues in the integrationist approach:

Who is the primary audience for integrated Women's Studies? Is it
an audience of academics who wish to reform the disciplines but
see no need to challenge the existing structure of knowledge based
on the dominant androcentric culture? Or is it a feminist audience
committed to changing society on a fundamental level including
change in the content and form of what is considered 'knowledge'
and 'education'?

What happens to a body of feminist knowledge that is distributed by
non-feminists because they have to incorporate it into their course?
And what happens to the student who gets her or his feminist
education from such a teacher?

What do integrationists mean by integration? Does their aim of
'balancing the curriculum' mean to fit women into the present male-
defined framework of knowledge: by whose definition and for
whose benefit is this 'balance'?

Through integration, will the radical potential of feminist scholarship be diluted? With its gained respectability and legitimacy will it
become just as dogmatic, rigid (and boring) as much of the present
Men's Studies is? What will prevent the feminist mainstreaming
scholar from becoming co-opted and colluding with those in power
in order to keep her job? And what will prevent women from
becoming invisible again within the existing disciplines?

What precisely is being integrated? Is it the study of white, heterosexual middle-class women into the study of white, heterosexual
middle-class men? How will the integrationist efforts influence the
already fragile alliances between women of various colors, sexual
orientation and classes outside and inside formal education?

Turning to the influences of integrationist Women's Studies on autonomous Women's Studies, the following questions might be asked:

Is there a relationship between calling Women's Studies (and Ethnic
Studies) 'ghettos' and 'for special interests and purposes', as some
integrationists do, and the ongoing misogynist and racist devaluation of all 'non-male' and 'non-white' people as 'other' which
feminism is supposed to oppose in the first place?

Many integrationists insist that autonomous Women's Studies
Programs within higher education are necessary too. But what
exactly is being done to secure the future of autonomous Women's
Studies? In times of financial restrictions how are administrators
to be prevented from declaring Women's Studies obsolete in the
light of seeing women become integrated into the existing disciplines? What will convince them to fund separate Women's Studies
Programs?

Women's Studies scholars are urged to become involved in mainstreaming Women's Studies. If they take on the task — and in many
instances they won't even have the chance to say no — how can they
simultaneously continue to do innovative cross-disciplinary research
and teaching *in Women's Studies*? And it is not only the sheer work-
load with which we are concerned but equally the disturbing need
to constantly change one's frame of reference: from telling 'the
unconvinced' (and encountering all sorts of familiar responses from
ridicule to intellectual exploitation) to coping with the problems
among 'the convinced': internal and external constraints on Women's
Studies practitioners.

Finally, why is it that after only ten years of autonomous Women's
Studies there is this impetus to tell 'them' rather than develop 'us'? The
parallel to women taking care of ('men's?') emotional needs comes to
mind: why do women do it? Isn't integrationist Women's Studies
premature? Doesn't entering into mainstreaming reflect a 'giving-in'
to the perpetuation of patriarchal power? And why is it that rather
than acknowledging economic hardships which may indeed necessitate
this decision under the pretext of 'true concern', women mediate,
and translate and nurture trying to make 'them' understand 'us'? We
think that women should continue our women-centred study of women

and men without feeling guilty for catering 'to women only'? And we hope that our work will prove that women need not always turn against each other and thus weaken our joint feminist impact upon the Powers That Be?

With these reflections it is to that compelling field within Women's Studies — women's history — that we turn to make some final comments on the autonomy/integration debate.

4 Herstory's lessons: female autonomy and power

How does this change take place? Does it occur by trying to convince those in power to give up their power voluntarily? Or does it happen when the powerless empower themselves? These are not new questions nor can we pursue all their dimensions in a few pages. But contemporary feminist scholars have recently addressed them as they look back upon the history of women. In *Women of Ideas and What Men Have Done to Them: From Aphra Behn to Adrienne Rich* (1982) Dale Spender argues that 'men either use or lose' women's ideas and that they have done so for centuries. We do not know the names and the theories of the radical thinkers of our past and we are made to believe that women have no intellectual heritage. How many of us know about Mary Astell or Harriet Martineau or Matilda Joslyn Gage or Hedwig Dohm or Mary Ritter Beard — to name only a few of our feminist foremothers? Compared to their ideas, ours are neither original nor radical.[6] Now that feminists are (again) unearthing our heritage we can start to draw upon both the experiences and the theories of these women for our work. But have we learned from them? The present developments make it not unreasonable to believe that our ideas too will be used or lost, appropriated or absorbed, diluted or distorted. Dale Spender advocates 'that women withdraw their labour, that they go on knowledge strike, for if women cannot control the knowledge they produce, at least they can ensure that it cannot be used as evidence against them.' Our worst fear is that 'integration' will make women invisible once again.

The integrationist trend opens up some additional disturbing questions that are difficult to raise even within our own circles. Why are some women backing away from independent women — power in academe, as they abandon the central goal of establishing Women's

Studies programs and work instead to change the disciplines? From whom does the idea of Women's Studies as a 'separate' study and as representing 'special interests' come? Why is the reality of a female culture so frightening? Why indeed do some of us seem wary of asserting the need for a women-centered education?

Perhaps most of us still need male approval. And are we afraid of being perceived as 'man haters'? These dilemmas were apparent in the early 1970s as the current wave of the women's movement began: it is strange to see those fears surfacing again in the 1980s. We think this perception comes from the outside. No doubt there are some men for whom it is advantageous to argue that we have hateful motives, others are simply confused or frightened by women who believe in a women-centered education. Still others — a few — indeed attempt to change. It is not 'man-hating' that motivates us but rather 'woman-loving'; our passionate opposition to a system of domination which does not allow women to work and be together for a better future in ways that *we* choose.

Our sense of the need for autonomous Women's Studies is based on our own experience and on our reading of women's history. In 'Separatism as Strategy: Female Institution Building and American Feminism, 1870-1930,' Estelle Freedman (1979) shows vividly how doomed is the attempt to forsake a female sphere in order to pursue an idea of 'equality.' She argues that the 'private' domain of the female sphere, and the bonding which took place within it, led to public power. A *Feminist Studies* symposium on 'Politics and Culture in Women's History' points to, among other things, the differences between a self-created women's culture and a male-imposed 'separate sphere' (Walkowitz, 1980, p. 26). And Gerda Lerner's years of work in women's history has led her to understand the threat of women-centeredness not only for men but also for women:

> The move of women from marginality to the center shatters the system. That is too dangerous a thought for most women to contemplate. . . . We abort our thought in order not to lose the spiritual safety provided for us within the patriarchy. . . . Without our co-operation it could not exist. [And] against the enormous weight of patriarchal thought, valuations, and the thousands of years of institutionalized disadvantaging of women, there stands only the reality of the female experience of self and community, the *actuality* of women's historical past (1980, pp. 21-2).

We need autonomous and independent Women's Studies programs or departments within universities so that feminists from a variety of backgrounds and interests can engage in active dialogue among themselves in order to build feminist scholarship and to bring it to the classroom. Moreover, it is crucial for feminist scholars wherever they might be and whatever their chosen field within the academy to actively support autonomous Women's Studies. 'We may get lost in our transformation' if women give all their energies to changing the disciplines. In the US we will no longer have a professional organization if women decide to devote themselves exclusively to their disciplinary groups rather than to the National Women's Studies Association. For, as Estelle Freedman notes, 'Without a constituency a movement cannot survive' (1979, p. 515).

Of course autonomy in itself does not guarantee a radical restructuring of knowledge. If Women's Studies were to follow the example of the traditional disciplines, then a separate Women's Studies entity might be the road to elitism: writing and thinking time for the privileged few, this time for white middle-class women. Some autonomous Women's Studies programs and departments may indeed turn that way. In others — and we are optimistic that this will be the majority — the links between the feminists inside academe and the women's community outside will be strong enough to prevent this from happening, as they point our research and teaching in the needed direction. Because indeed, an academic Women's Studies without connections to our own roots — the concerns of all women that started the women's liberation movement — could not fulfil the expectations and hopes that inspired its beginnings.

We believe that autonomous Women's Studies programs, in constant interaction with the community, hold the potential for contributing to changes in the present power relationships in society at large. If knowledge is power — and we hold on to this belief — then we must carefully scrutinize the roads we take in our quest for knowledge — the way we make our revolutions — and ask whether they are indeed suited to making our visions come to life. Despite all the good intentions of the integrationists, we are worried that women may end up being invisible again: buried in the existing disciplines and separated from each other.

We need autonomous Women's Studies because by exploring women's experiences and investigating our needs and interests in a context free from the interference of men we generate knowledge *for* women. We believe that women have just as much 'right' as men to have courses in which women are at the center of inquiry — and avowedly so and without apologies! In an unequal world, courses 'for women only' are of vital necessity. A women-centered education[7] will teach us about our heritage, make us strong with and for each other as we validate and acknowledge women's similarities and differences. We have to prevent yet another cycle of history in which feminist ideas will be buried and erased from the record of knowledge-making. Women's intellectual contributions must continue to be *available*. In autonomous Women's Studies programs we have (some) control over the knowledge we produce and we should treasure them as places where we can continue our feminist work in theory and practice.

The papers in this volume all subscribe to the need for strong women-centered feminist research and teaching. The authors are questioning the dichotomies of conventional research; we are creating women-centered theories and we are thinking dialectically and en-visioning. The cumulative effect and the relationship between our papers make us think twice about terms such as 'social science' and even 'inter-disciplinary.' There is some 'humanities', some 'social science' and some 'natural science' in these contributions but what they jointly achieve is a way of thinking which because it is feminist and thus women-centered, aims at dis-covering positive meanings for women and leaves behind patriarchal traditions. This exciting development is especially true for the notion of 'theory' and it is to a discussion of this topic and the contents of this book that we now turn.

5 Theories of Women's Studies

'There is nothing so practical as a good theory' (Kanter, 1977, p. 295).

Women's Studies programs and departments are crucial as centers for developing feminist thought. This is the place in the university where our ideas are taken seriously. Here we can build and test our theories, confident that critiques will be substantive and engaged. (This is, by the way, how the disciplines function for scholars in other fields.)

As we build our theories, we must confront women's unique relationship to theory. For some of us, theory is something we *cannot* do (it's what men do). Some of us are hostile to theory because theories have been used against women; some of us associate theorizing with elite educations which are not available to most women.[8] Through dynamic interaction with each other, we have learned that there is nothing inherently misogynist about theory formulation. Theories are useful, nothing more or less than tools for our work, and they change constantly, as our knowledge grows. Our theories must incorporate both facts and feelings in order to reveal the totality of women's experiences. And we theorize in order to act: we need women-centered theories to develop strategies for change. Of course such a definition of theory has little in common with the standard notion of theory as 'Supposition or system of ideas explaining something, esp. one based on general principles independent of the facts, phenomena, etc., to be explained' (*The Oxford Concise Dictionary*, p. 1201, 1979).

One of the first claims of feminist scholarship was that male theories about women were biased. So we declared that since everything is biased we at least would *state* our biases. In 'Theorising about theorising,' Dale Spender acknowledges, and accepts, the relativity of all 'Truths,' including feminist ones. In a meditation on becoming a feminist and a writer, she reminds us of the arbitrary nature of all meaning. Meaning is projected in retrospect on a series of previously unordered thoughts; it is socially constructed ('Theories and perspectives do not fall from the air ready made'). Our theories are always in flux, we must tolerate contradiction in them, and we must look to other women for validation of other theories, she says.

The papers which follow trace a question which for us several years ago was really a question: 'Is Women's Studies an academic discipline?' Gloria Bowles's article shows what Women's Studies has in common with the existing disciplines. But she is also wary of this appellation because she fears that Women's Studies will become just another academic discipline, 'academic' in the sense of 'useless' to the community and esoteric as well, so that only a new scholarly elite speaks the Women's Studies language. Sandra Coyner, however, is quite firm in her declaration that Women's Studies *is* an academic discipline. She gives us a complex view of the nature of the existing disciplines, and goes on to capture a vision of what ours could ideally be. She speaks of 'Women's Studies as an academic discipline: why and how to do it,' taking the unorthodox view that 'interdisciplinarity' as she defines it is not suited to Women's Studies. Both of these papers come to the conclusion that we must pursue the development of Women's Studies as a study in its own right. They recognize that we need analysis that makes use of established knowledge (e.g. Freudian or Marxist theory) but they also advocate the development of Women's Studies theory in and of itself. Feminist scholarship must go beyond the limits of received perspectives to develop our own theories and methods.

In 'Learning Women's Studies,' Taly Rutenberg shows how this new knowledge is brought into the classroom. For her, Women's Studies is a dynamic study which contrasts with her work in the established disciplines. The Women's Studies student is engaged in the classroom because the subject matter has meaning in her own life. Students are central to the process of creating Women's Studies theory; they are pioneers whose work is important.

Bari Watkins offers a slightly different angle on the relationship of Women's Studies and the established disciplines, arguing that the humanities have a good deal to learn from Women's Studies, if they will only learn. In 'Feminism: a last chance for the humanities?,' she points out that Women's Studies offers a 'model of intellectual revolution which may well prove to be effective for all of the humanities.'

Renate Duelli Klein contends that so far feminist scholarship has focused on the 'what' and neglected the 'how' of its research. In 'How to do what we want to do: thoughts about feminist methodology' she argues that the lack of feminist methodological development has contributed to research *on* women rather than research *for* women. Sexist bias in method has not been given sufficient attention; since methods are tools for translating theory into action, we must be certain that they reflect the experiences of women. In an example of feminist research from Germany, she describes some of the criteria feminist methods should meet and goes on to discuss strategies for developing women-centered methods.

Duelli Klein's essay is the first in a series of papers on feminist methodology.[9] At the heart of these methodological approaches is the idea that feminist research must be *for* women, that it should be useful in improving the daily life and the general lot of a diversity of women. The writers have different ways of going about this and if they had a chance to sit down together one evening to 'talk methodology,' there would be disagreements. Yet it is striking that this kind of thinking has been taking place simultaneously on the continent, in Britain and in the

US, although the writers had no contact with each other.

One of the major concerns of these scholars is the link between the 'researcher' and the 'researched.' How does the relatively privileged researcher, usually white, with a university education, reach out to the woman in the community? Isn't there something patronizing about formulating the relationship in this way? Do academic women and battered women or displaced homemakers share common ground? Or are these false distinctions — since in some kinds of ways we are all battered, can all use research tools? How is the researcher changed by the research process? Do we measure the success of a successful feminist research project by the extent to which these very dichotomies between researcher and researcher are broken down? And what about the implications of our findings for policy decisions?

It is the basic assumption of these articles that all women are oppressed and that we need to identify and understand both the similarities and the differences of our oppressions. Women researchers, then, must begin with our own experience. Maria Mies says that women, not men, are best equipped to undertake research for women: 'If women social scientists take their own subjective experience of sexist discrimination and their rebellion against it as a starting point and guiding principle for their research, they ... become critically aware of a number of weaknesses of ... established research.' For Liz Stanley and Sue Wise as well, our own experience must be our guide. They want to find out about the 'events and experiences in women's lives!' Dailiness is crucial: 'We must necessarily effect many small liberations in many small seemingly insignificant aspects of our lives or we shall never start the revolution, nor even recognize it happening around us.'

Of course, none of this is easy. First, women have been barred from experiencing our experience; it takes an enormous effort, an enormous consciousness to even be able to feel our own feelings and think our own thoughts, as Barbara Du Bois points out. The research processes described here try to find out how to find out what we do know. In devising ways to find out what women know, the researchers both borrow from existing approaches and depart from them. Toby Epstein Jayaratne shows how quantitative methods can be altered and used *for* women. Shulamit Reinharz points out how her 'experiential analysis' is related to existential and phenomenological thought. Liz Stanley and Sue Wise acknowledge their debt to ethnomethodology. It is important to know our relationship to existing thought and to the thoughts of each other since we do not have time both to re-discover the already known and find new knowledge for women. Acknowledging debts is one thing; but, as Wise and Stanley say,

> We're first, foremost, and last, feminists; not feminist-phenomeno-logists, feminist-marxists or feminist hyphen anything else. Our interest and concern is with feminism and feminist revolution. And because of this we believe that feminism should borrow, steal, change, modify and *use* for its own purposes any and everything from anywhere that looks of interest and of use to it, but that we must do this critically.

In their search to find out how to find out what we know about being women, several of the contributors to this volume experiment with new ways of writing. Barbara Du Bois invents a poetic prose, marking her essays by sections (I, II, etc.) in the way that many feminist poets today mark their poems; each section reflects upon the others. She calls her essay 'notes', a way of bringing these lofty topics into perspective rather than inflating them as some male philosophers do. 'Notes' also denotes thought in process: there is fluidity here, a sense that this is not final. Du Bois lets feeling, and poetry, into her prose; her method for knowing what she knows reminds us of Dale Spender's introductory essay on theorizing which reveals associational thought, the sense of a writer working things out on the page, coming to know through various permutations of language. Dale Spender's is associational thought; Barbara Du Bois writes 'notes.' But years of training, de-training, work, finding a way to speak of their own experience, stand behind these associations, these notes. All of the contributors to our volume are white, from different classes and of varying sexual preferences; they have had different levels of access to education. All of us who can write — who have the education, and now the time — are among the most privileged of women.

Marcia Westkott's piece is philosophical prose; there are echoes of the existential idiom in her lines: 'Individual freedom and the freedom of all women are linked when one has reached the critical consciousness that we are united first of all in our unfreedom.' But the sentences are jarring precisely because the existentialists *never* talked about women; Westkott has appropriated this prose for women and thus at once provided a critique of the old tradition and put women at the center of a new one. Hers is an act of feminist revolt. 'Feminism withdraws consent from the patriarchal construction of reality,' says Barbara Du Bois. A reinvention of language is one of the ways these authors withdraw consent.

In 'Passionate Scholarship,' Barbara Du Bois reminds us in very basic ways what we are about; this grounding is important to feminist scholars since we are dedicated to staying with our basic purposes. 'To address women's lives and experience *in their own terms*, to create theory grounded in the actual experience and language of women, is the central agenda for feminist social science and scholarship.'

For Du Bois, as for the other feminists writing in these pages, the challenge is 'To see what is there.' Du Bois thinks we cannot see women through traditional science and theory. Whether or not this is the case is crucial for Women's Studies; the writers in this volume offer a range of perspectives on this debate. Du Bois addresses as well the central issue of dichotomous thought, the female way of seeing things whole; she shows how language reflects these different ways of viewing the world. Like Liz Stanley and Sue Wise, she wants feminist scholarship to be both complex and contextual; and like all of the writers represented here, she wants it to be rigorous.

The first version of the article by Maria Mies, 'Towards a methodology for feminist research,' was given in a talk in Frankfurt early in 1977. 'Methodische Postulate zur Frauenforschung' ('Methodological postulates for Women's Studies') grew out of Mies's longtime involvement with action research, her work as a teacher and researcher in developing countries, especially India, and her involvement in the German women's movement, notably a project on violence against women. The German version has been revised for an English speaking audience. In 'Towards a methodology for feminist research,' Mies says that 'new wine must not be poured into old bottles.' We must reconceptualize all stages of the research process so that Women's Studies is in constant interaction with the concerns of the majority of women who are not among the privileged earning their living by doing research. Mies proposes seven methodological postulates: (1) the feminist researcher must openly state her biases, her conscious partiality, which is not to be confused with mere subjectivity; (2) the researcher's usual view from above must be substituted by a view from below; (3) the researcher must actively participate in the women's liberation movement, in order to avoid uninvolved spectator knowledge; (4) the starting point for the scientific quest must be a commitment to changing the status quo; (5) the research process must be one of 'conscientizaçao,' as Freire means it, and this research is pursued in order to act; (6) as part of the 'conscientization' process, women must study our individual and social histories in order to appropriate our past so that we can devise strategies for the future; (7) women must talk together about our experience and generalize from it in order to understand the social causes of our individual deprivations.

Mies goes on to discuss the application of these postulates in a project with battered women in Cologne. And in a postscript, she considers their application in non-western cultures. With this postscript, we are able to see how women's studies methods could be for all women, crossing cultural and material boundaries, how research has the potential to serve as a means to self-help and self-actualization instead of being a way for 'us' — women in academe — to impose models upon women out there — 'them.' Mies does not gloss over the difficulties in pursuing this kind of work, the conflicts which arise when women of different realities and priorities work together and the blocks which prevent researchers from breaking away from training which assumes a hierarchical research situation. Her goal is to document and analyze the many elements of our oppression in order finally to overcome it. This is a theme that appears often in this collection; in fact, it is remarkable how many of the ideas first expressed by Maria Mies in 1977 are the very ideas elaborated upon by feminist social scientists writing in 1981.

For some time social scientists have been engaged in debates about the virtues of qualitative versus quantitative research. Feminist researchers have also taken up this discussion, though with different emphases. Many feminist social scientists are actively hostile toward quantitative research because they believe that human behavior cannot be measured and that those who measure wish also to control. Toby Epstein Jayaratne, in 'The value of quantitative methodology for feminist research,' argues that quantitative research can be used *for* women; because feminists are often accused of bias, more 'objective' means of measurement can function to reinforce our beliefs about discrimination against women. While Jayaratne thinks there is no such thing as pure objectivity, she respects 'the guidelines, codes of ethics, and standards developed by quantitative research' but suggests some changes in that research process (specifically in survey research) which would make the approach more feminist. She does not see quantitative and qualitative research as mutually exclusive, but thinks both should be used to improve the lives of women.

Jayaratne says that often social science has not been used for people; rather we have been used by it. She urges feminists not only to do quantitative research but to make certain that this research is seen by policy makers. It is also Shulamit Reinharz's contention that social science has used people more than it has been of use to them. Her purpose in 'Experiential analysis: a contribution to feminist research' is to expand on ideas developed in her book, *On Becoming a Social Scientist*. Reinharz would agree with Dale Spender that knowledge is socially constructed, that there are certain things we are permitted to know. She shows how changes in approaches to knowing have taken place within her own discipline and how this critical perspective leads her constantly to question what she knows and how she knows it. This questioning eventually leads to new ideas, new methods. In an act of translation that is particularly useful for those of us not trained in the social sciences, Reinharz goes on to show how 'experiential analysis' is both grounded in and departs from other innovative, anti-positivist approaches in her field; she also sets up a contrast between traditional research methods and her own approach. Thus, the paper vividly illustrates how many steps academic feminists work through in order finally to establish the validity of their own sense of what is important to study and how one goes about studying it. Reinharz speaks in detail about how she does her research. She sees 'experiential analysis' as a 'collection of interacting components: assumptions, personal preparation, problem formulation, data gathering and stopping, data digestions and presentation, policy questions.' For her, the purposes of research are to 'represent growth and understanding in the arena of *the problem* investigated, the *person(s)* doing the investigation, and the *method* utilized.'

All of these writers want feminist social science to be for women but each one sees the working out of this usefulness in a different way. Toby Epstein Jayaratne is interested in influencing policy makers; Maria Mies wants to work directly with groups of women. In ' "Back into the personal", or our attempt to construct "feminist research" ', Liz Stanley and Sue Wise say that we must bring our research to our lives.

We do not have to wait for the revolution, if we make it take place in every minute of our life. For Stanley and Wise, 'what feminists spend our lives doing must obviously be the subject of feminist research.' The process includes researching the researcher; as women, we must become the focus of feminist research in order to know how we construct our realities. By examining the lives of women from within, that generalization 'oppression' will take on precise and particular meanings — and then we can devise strategies to overturn it. This comes close to Maria Mies's notion that we have to construct our social history in order to know the mechanisms which oppress women. As an example of these theories, Stanley and Wise discuss their research on the obscene phone calls they received while staffing a lesbian/gay crisis line in Manchester. The phone calls, and the responses to these calls from straight women and gay men, led them to change fundamentally their ideas of the nature of women's oppression and specifically lesbian oppression.

What can we learn from Stanley and Wise? What is a feminist methodology according to them? (And by methodology we mean both the tools we use and the overall conceptualization of research.) For Stanley and Wise, research should not differ from what we do in everyday life: we should use the same approaches and procedures in each. This concept challenges all traditional notions of 'research' and, though it might appear simple, it is in fact very hard to admit so much of life to research! Our strategies for survival in a sexist world are our method; we use this 'documentary method,' these interpretations of what is happening in our lives, whether we are trying to survive in academe, or shopping, or working in the corporate world, or living collectively with other feminists. In conducting research, then, we must start with the experiences of the researcher as a person in context. Wise and Stanley ask a great deal of the feminist researcher. How many researchers are willing to expose ourselves, to make ourselves vulnerable, in the ways that Stanley and Wise ask us to do and in fact carry out in their own research?

Marcia Westkott's essay, 'Women's Studies as a strategy for change: between criticism and vision,' brings us back to earth, to the Women's Studies classroom and to the radical purpose which informs our work. Westkott reminds us that Women's Studies is not a mere academic exercise but an educational strategy to induce change in a sexist world.

This goal means that we 'do more than describe or distill that world. We simultaneously understand and oppose it.' Westkott points out that coming to knowledge and making judgments are not separate processes; rather 'judgment is implicit in seeing and seeing is implicit in judging.' Here is an echo of the train of thought of Dale Spender, Liz Stanley and Sue Wise, who say that all knowledge is constructed through the interaction of self and world. For Westkott, the women's studies teacher/scholar rejects the male-defined intellectual tradition which pretends to separate seeing from judging 'not simply because it bores us intellectually, but also because it violates the vehemence with which we oppose the sexist world that devalues us' (p. 124).

'Women's Studies as a strategy for change: between criticism and vision' reminds us of the relationship between our scholarship and our teaching. The goals for feminist scholarship in this volume have their analogue in feminist teaching. The centrality of researchers, as well as the researched, receives its translation in the classroom as a valuing of the views of both teacher and student. In both the classroom and the research situation, we are trying to work against the domination of a few over 'others,' working to develop patterns of collaboration and cooperation. In both teaching and research, we must scrutinize who we are and for whose benefit we create knowledge. We must make sure that a diversity of women, a variety of experiences enter our work. Yet both of the processes in which we are engaged, research and teaching, show us how much we have yet to do to free ourselves from old patterns of thinking.

Finally, Mary Evans, one of the founders of the first MA Course in Women's Studies in Britain, ends this volume by reminding us of the importance of theory for the liberation of women. 'In praise of theory: the case for Women's Studies' responds to the claims of some movement feminists that Women's Studies is a sell-out and that theorizing is a masculine and elitist activity. Mary Evans gives us a sense of the complex position of feminists within the university as she asserts the usefulness of many different kinds of theory for women.

Her work draws us to two conclusions. First, it is quite clear that movement feminists and Women's Studies practitioners are still vividly engaged with each other, still committed to entering into these debates, no matter how dangerous and contentious they seem. As we have said before, we think that these connections are crucial to the dynamics — and the future — of Women's Studies in and outside the university.

Second, Mary Evans joins us in our concern that we must think clearly about the implications of any choices we make. In the case of the autonomy/integration debate — to return to the beginning of this introduction — material realities *do* shape our decisions. But we must insist on our right to have our own space and uninhibited time to work towards an understanding of women's past and present in order to envisage our future. Such an understanding is crucial for our practical choices: we need autonomous Women's Studies to create *Theories for Women* to create *Actions for Women*.

Berkeley and London, August 1982

Notes

1. Elaine Reuben voiced her concern about the future of Women's Studies in a talk given at the First Summer Institute in Women's Studies at Ann Arbor, 23 July 1981.
2. Three of the papers were presented at the first conference of the National Women's Studies Association in Lawrence, Kansas in 1977. Gloria Bowles and Sandra Coyner participated in the session, 'Is Women's Studies an Academic Discipline?' and Bari Watkins spoke at a session on 'Women's Studies: Issues of Renewal, Rejection or Creativity in Method, Language and Content.' The first version of this introduction was presented by the editors at the 1982 National Women's Studies Association meetings in Arcata, California.
3. The title of this volume is derived from the 'Theories of Women's Studies' seminar initiated by Gloria Bowles in 1978 and taught since then in the Women's Studies Program at the University of California, Berkeley. A syllabus for the course can be obtained from Women's Studies, 301 Campbell Hall, UC Berkeley, Berkeley CA 94720.
4. See Spender (1981).
5. Recently, Women's Studies became 'legit' enough to make the *New York Times* (see Bennetts, 1980). Other major American newspapers heralded the new Women's Studies majors at prestigious Yale and Stanford as though they were the first in the country. Regretfully, this new legitimacy has led to a kind of bandwagon effect; some people who have never done Women's Studies and do not have the foggiest notion what it is all about are now declaring themselves Women's Studies experts. For sure, Women's Studies does not want to be elitist; any woman who wishes to challenge all her old ideas and to try hard to learn to work with other women is welcome to join our programs. But one does not learn it all overnight.
6. In 1934, Mary Ritter Beard, most famous for her account of *Women as Force in History* (1946) in which she makes a case for women's strengths

and influences throughout history, wrote a 56-page syllabus for a Women's Studies course called 'A Changing Political Economy as it Affects Women' on behalf of the American Association of University Women. Discovering it, one cannot be but incredibly astonished, impressed and somewhat embarrassed, if one thought (as we did) that given all the other recurrences in the various waves of feminism at least Women's Studies was a unique and original development of our age. Another wrong assumption about originality: Women's Studies obviously is not original and of course before Ritter Beard, there were many others (see Spender, 1982). As Ann J. Lane describes it (1977) Mary Ritter Beard's syllabus is divided into four main areas: the history of the idea of sex equality and the actual status of women in the United States; the impact of international forces on the position of women; the role of nationalism in theory and practice; and the 'feminine determination of feminine destiny' which, as Lane states 'today would be called woman's autonomy' (p. 203). Lane goes on to say 'I have found no indication that the syllabus was ever used.' This at least *is* a difference to the present as we do use our syllabi!

7   Perhaps it might do us a lot of good to re-read Adrienne Rich's piece 'Toward a Woman-Centered University' (1973-4) and to remind ourselves of her passionate case for autonomous Women's Studies inside and outside formal education.

8   Responding to our discussion in the 'Theories of Women's Studies' seminar, Nina Nordgren, a graduate student from Finland, wrote a paper, 'On Feminist Fear of Science and Theory.' In it she asked,

But why should we let ourselves be afraid of theory? What we should be afraid of is the non-critical and blind acceptance of . . . theory. What we should be afraid of is accepting old myths as truths — and one of these old myths is surely that theory itself is the ultimate truth.

She further hypothesized that 'the feminist aversion . . . to theorizing can perhaps be traced to an uncertainty of the reliability and validity of our work.'

9   In the original publication, Renate Duelli Klein's paper concluded *Theories of Women's Studies I* and provided a starting point for the papers in volume II.

References

Bennetts, Leslie (1980), 'Women's Viewpoints Gain Respect in Academe,' *New York Times*, 2 December, pp. 5-6.

Cott, Nancy (1982), 'Women's Studies Major: A New Point of View,' *Yale Alumni Magazine and Journal*, February, pp. 3-4.

Dinnerstein, Myra, O'Donnell, Sheryl and MacCorquodale, Patricia (1981), 'How to Integrate Women's Studies into the Traditional Curriculum,' A Report of the Southwest Institute for Research on Women (SIROW), Women's Studies, University of Arizona.

Freedman, Estelle (1979), 'Separatism as Strategy: Female Institution Building and American Feminism, 1870-1930,' *Feminist Studies*, vol. 5, no. 3, pp. 512-29.

Howe, Florence (1982), 'Feminist Scholarship — The Extent of the Revolution,' *Change*, vol. 14, no. 3, pp. 12-20.

Kanter, Rosabeth M. (1977), *Men and Women of the Corporation*, New York, Basic Books, p. 295, quote attributed to Kurt Lewin.

Lane, Ann J. (ed.) (1977), *Mary Ritter Beard: A Source Book*, New York, Schocken.

Lerner, Gerda (1980), 'Placing Women in History: A Theoretical Approach,' paper delivered at the Organization of American Historians, San Francisco.

Lougee, Carolyn C. (1981), 'Women, History and the Humanities: An Argument in Favor of the General Curriculum,' *Women's Studies Quarterly*, vol. 9, no. 1, pp. 4-7.

McIntosh, Peggy (1982), 'Transformations within the Academy: Reconstructing the Liberal Arts Curriculum,' talk given at the closing plenary session of the National Women's Studies Association meetings, Arcata, California, 19 June.

Minnich, Elizabeth (1982), 'A Devastating Conceptual Error: How Can We *Not* Be Feminist Scholars?', *Change*, vol. 14, no. 3, pp. 7-9.

Reuben, Elaine (1981), talk given at the First Summer Institute in Women's Studies, Ann Arbor, Great Lakes College Association, Michigan, 23 July.

Rich, Adrienne (1975) 'Toward a Woman-Centered University' (1973-1974) in Florence Howe (ed.), *Women and the Power to Change*, New York, McGraw-Hill.

Ritter Beard, Mary (1934), 'A Changing Political Economy as It Affects Women', American Association of University Women, Washington DC, 56 pp.

Ritter Beard, Mary (1946), *Women as Force in History: A Study in Traditions and Realities*, New York, Macmillan.

Schmitz, Betty (1981), 'Seeking Women's Equity Through Curriculum Revision,' Montana State University project, xeroxed materials, unpaginated, February.

Spanier, Bonnie and Schmidt, Ruth (1981), 'Toward a Balanced Curriculum: Integrating the Study of Women into the Liberal Arts,' Massachusetts, Wheaton College, xeroxed materials, unpaginated, June.

Spender, Dale (ed.) (1981), *Men's Studies Modified: The Impact of Feminism on the Academic Disciplines*, Oxford and New York, The Athene Series, Pergamon Press.

Spender, Dale (1982), *Women of Ideas and What Men Have Done to Them: From Aphra Behn to Adrienne Rich*, Boston and London, Routledge & Kegan Paul.

Stephens College (1982), 'Liberal Education at Stephens College, Curriculum Revision,' xeroxed materials, unpaginated, Missouri, Stephens College, Spring.

Walkowitz, Judith R. (1980), 'Introduction, Politics and Culture in Women's History: A Symposium,' *Feminist Studies*, vol. 6, no. 1, pp. 26-7.

Walzer, Judith (1982), 'New Knowledge or a New Discipline: Women's Studies at the University,' *Change*, vol. 14, no. 3, pp. 21-3.

2

Theorising about theorising

Dale Spender

Theories and perspectives do not fall from the air, ready-made, and what I am trying to do here is to *reconstruct* how it is I come to 'know', and to 'theorise' in the way that I do. There is, however, a danger in telling a tale in retrospect, and it is the danger that everything appears ordered, purposeful, meaningful. Yet my understandings neither 'arrived' nor were forged in a chronological fashion: nor does what I know and use comprise more than a fraction of what I have been exposed to and have wilfully selected. What does not 'make sense' to me passes by as non-data, what does not fit the fundamental assumptions and the framework with which I begin often goes unnoticed, or else refuted. If now, for the sake of convenience — and comprehension — I reconstruct some of the influences and insights of the past in a linear and ordered fashion, it is not because that is the way they were experienced but because in retrospect I can impose and project meaning, I can create order out of the chaos of everyday experience of the past. The meaning is mine and I am still in the process of constructing it. This constitutes an evaluatory stop along the way and is by no means a destination.

There have been two factors, I think, in structuring the framework in which I work; one is, of course, the women's liberation movement, and the other is being socialised in one country and then living as a member of another. Both have enormous elements of challenging what was previously taken for granted, both have exposed ways in which I feel I have been 'conned' by social constructs and have accepted as inevitable and preordained elements which are within man's (*sic*) control. Both have made me vigilantly suspicious of everything I know and have provided me with the only security and meaning that I can tolerate . . . that everything I know is open to challenge, that there are no absolutes, that meaning is socially constructed and that human beings seem to have an enormous propensity for imposing order (and meaning) on chaos. This does not apply to everything else BUT feminism; I include feminism in it as well and I can distinctly remember one of the hardest lessons that I ever set myself was to 'prove' that feminism is as arbitrary as everything else I know.

If, however, we are going to construct meaning, I am committed to the idea of constructing meanings that do not require enormous energy (and denial) to sustain. If meaning is arbitrary in the sense I am suggesting that it is, then I will put my energies into constructing meanings that help to explain things that were inexplicable under patriarchal rules, and that help to show me, and women, in a positive rather than negative light . . . which has been the case while males have been in charge of constructing meaning.

Accepting the arbitrary nature of feminism (along with the arbitrary nature of everything else) has necessitated a reconceptualisation of right and wrong. If everything I know is 'wrong', that is, if there are no absolutes, no truths, only transitory meanings imposed by human beings in the attempt to make sense of the world, then 'wrong' becomes a meaningless category. Instead of being frightened that something I am arguing for as truth, as right, as logic, may in fact be wrong, I am starting from the other end and arguing that I know it is temporary and inadequate. I am then searching for the 'errors', the 'flaws' that will help me to refine. 'Mistakes' get revalued and become something to seek, to take on, not something to be dreaded and denied. Unlike many academics, I have a vested interest in finding the limitations of my thesis, not in having it perpetuated.

I do not subscribe to a static theory of society or knowledge; I believe everything to be in a state of constant flux and that any theory or conceptualisation is drilling a sample at an arbitrary point — try again tomorrow, or in another place and you will get a different result.

This has meant that I can tolerate ambiguity and contradiction. I find it 'logical' to accept that women have different life experiences and that this gives rise to different interpretations and that all are equally valid for those experiences. Trying to reduce the diversity of human experience and the creativity of human meaning to one solitary sediment seems to me not only wasteful and time consuming, but unnecessarily stupid and denotes enormous insecurity in being unable to accept any meanings other than one's own.

Why are people frightened to change what they believe? Are we so committed to meaning that having created one, we dare not let it go? Over and over again from psychology and anthropology I was confronted with the evidence that human beings had this enormous power to 'create' the world we live in but having performed our 'creation' we are loath to modify it in any way: infinite possibilities coupled with rigidity.

I can remember walking along Chelsea Embankment quite disoriented trying to come to terms with the idea that everything I knew I had 'made up' and so had everybody else; I even asked myself what was the point, if everything was MEANINGLESS, why continue? And then I realised that someone had had to make up the idea that meaning was necessary . . . who had said that we had to have meaningful lives?

I expect chaos, not order, absurdity, not meaning, and in a sense that is security and protection, for I am more often right than wrong in terms of what I encounter.

But feminism? Where does it fit in?

Looking at girls in the classroom through the lens of being judged wrong, NO MATTER WHAT THEY DO. Looking at language and knowing that women's language is wrong, NO MATTER WHAT THEY SAY. Coming to understand that sex is the fundamental category of meaning in our society, the basic axis on which we build sense; polarised − right and wrong, subjective and objective, logic and emotion, trying to evolve an acceptable framework for women's wrongness . . . in a society that does not care to acknowledge the existence of such an entity.

It was a fundamental shift to recognise that women are wrong, that they are the basic category of wrongness, of deviancy in our society while men decide. Discovering that men are right by virtue of their sex, and women are wrong, meant that it was impossible for me to go for being right. It seems such a limited and useless term.

Theorising about women theorising in a patriarchal world. Rediscovering the women from our past. Realising that what I had thought was fresh and new was debated centuries ago. Seeing with fresh vision the fundamental and radical claims of three centuries ago that women are men's intellectual equals: deploring that the standard against which they are measured is male. Acknowledging that I have a long way to travel before I can acquire and accommodate some of their insights and understandings: recognising my own conservatism in comparison: regretting the wasted years and the lost women.

Re-examining the concept 'progress' and suspecting that if it has any meaning it applies only to men: questioning the linear explanations when women's history reveals cycles. Watching women's protests bloom and die, theorising that every fifty years (or less) it buds again, flowers, and assumes it is the first of its kind. Reflecting on the past and contemplating the future, flinching at the understanding that we must struggle to catch up to where our predecessors stood, appreciating the vulnerability of our optimism, predicting that we will be as little known to future generations as past generations were to us; vowing that this time it will be different: assessing the odds.

Theorising about men's theories and wondering how to move outside them: they occupy all the conceptual space. Noting the looks of surprise and confusion at the suggestion that their logic, their truth, their reasons and their theories are but one version. Testing the limits, for those who rule have the ruling ideas; their version has become the social version: posing alternatives is heresy — or madness!

Knowing the many and varied prices we pay for living under patriarchy: beginning to appreciate the astonishing convenience of the concept of 'intelligence' in a hierarchical society — the ultimate justification for stratification, the 'inherent' and 'natural' quality over which human beings supposedly have no control and which explains inequality more satisfactorily, more legitimately and more sophisticatedly than the 'crude' class, ethnicity, or sex.

Developing a theoretical framework for this when the words aren't there and the concepts are shadows. Being brave . . . deliberately adopting positions that are legitimated as outrageous. Looking to women for validation . . . huge change when it is no longer necessary to seek male approval and confirmation.

Recognising that life cannot be separated from knowledge . . . that we are knowledge, nothing out there . . . who we are means what we know. My life, my biography inseparable from what I know . . . dispensing with male approval: not an intellectual decision. Finding new ways of understanding not learnt through books. Finding myself involved in processes and then trying to describe and explain what happens.

Pushing myself to the paradoxes: perceiving who put it on its present plane, recognising the ends it serves, knowing I will not subscribe. Wanting to endorse theorising and wanting to insist that it is open to all. The contradictions. The necessity of a new frame of reference. The reconceptualisation of theory in order to theorise.

3

Is Women's Studies an academic discipline?[1]

Gloria Bowles

Bertolt Brecht was a teacher of doubt, carried with him on his many forced travels a Chinese scroll representing the Doubter. He distinguished firmly between doubt and vacillation, and he seems to have thought that even doubt, or at least the expression of doubt, was politically undesirable at times. But his writings are unequivocal on this score.

Disbelief can move mountains, he wrote. 'What has not been altered for a long time seems unalterable', but 'a long time is not forever'; only doubt can make us see the possibility of alteration (Wood, 1980), p. 13).

1 The inner contradiction: Women's Studies in the university

Out of the initial 'fad' stage, Women's Studies is now compelled to prove that what we are about is serious academic work. We are in a position that is almost impossible. On the one hand, our continued presence in the university shows that we still believe in the value of that social institution. On the other hand, as feminists trying to create that new thing, 'Women's Studies,' we are opposed to the university as it presently exists. We are critics of the very institution of which we are a part. Like Brecht, we doubt.

All of us involved in Women's Studies have feminist friends who have given up on the institution. These are the people working to build the feminist community — the bookstore owners, the carpenters, the poets and painters. My friends in the Bay Area women's community think I am crazy to pursue feminism within the academy.[2] And at times I envy the world they have created to pursue feminist thought and action. It is not easy for Women's Studies scholars to be critics of the academy, to express doubt, since most of us are in highly vulnerable positions within it. Nevertheless, we have a basic belief in the potential power of the university, in the value of education for enriching individual lives and for improving society. As it exists now, society's institution, the university, lives outside society; since it has chosen not to study women and ethnic minorities, who are so obviously a part of the real world, the university has built an unreal world.

2 The origins of the academic disciplines

When called upon to prove that what we are doing is proper to the university, university-like, these terms are invoked: 'Well, is Women's Studies an academic discipline?' The attempt to answer this challenge has sent us down many a briared path. In the pages which follow, I want to outline some of the implications of this question.

First, Women's Studies scholars are proud to be engaged in research and teaching grounded in a social movement. Instead of apologizing for these political origins, we need only point to the early history of the social sciences. In a model of incisive scholarship, Dorothy Ross shows that the founders of social science were independent scholars and reformers as well as university people. The American Social Science Association (ASSA) 'had been founded in 1865 to extend social knowledge and provide a more authoritative basis for dealing with contemporary social problems' (Ross, 1979, p. 109). Universities were at first wary of these new social sciences; President Gilman of Johns Hopkins, for example, thought 'the desire of the ASSA not only to study but to advocate reforms made it incompatible with university education' (Ibid., p. 110). Like Women's Studies, the social sciences came into being in part as a response to great social movements and the need to understand those movements.

There is yet another lesson to be learned from the history of the social sciences. The founders of the ASSA were eventually replaced by those who began to develop the empirical methods which the new disciplines would use to study society. 'The ASSA was finally overwhelmed by the very wave of social change to which its founders had set out to accommodate themselves and society,' Thomas Haskell tells us (1977, p. vii). Then, as now, it was often a case of the outsiders (the immigrant scholars and those of the working class) challenging the insiders (the patrician professors). Ross calls this second group of social science scholars 'militants' and by that she means those who were devoted to 'their conception of modern science as a product of empirical investigation' (1979, p. 113). These 'younger militants had perceived a serious disjunction between the theories of their elders and the nature of reality as disclosed by their own empirical observations' (Ibid., p. 114). At the same time, they wanted 'to use their knowledge more directly in the solution of social problems than their social science precursers in the university' (Ibid.). 'The militants turned ... to professionalization ... the means by which they could force entry for their new programs' into the American university (Ibid., p. 116). Of course they met resistance from many quarters.

Certainly the late nineteenth century needed empirical observation to build scholarship; now a hundred years later, Women's Studies scholars and those in many other fields are critical of the extremes to which data gathering has gone. From a desire to develop a scholarship which would be linked with social progress to the founding of empiricism to the present-day critiques of that very empiricism — these are great shifts in the development of knowledge, great waves of revolution and reaction. Language study has known similar shifts; the Modern Language Association, for example, was originally founded to make the study of modern languages as legitimate as the study of the classics. Ours is a knowledge revolution of no smaller proportions than these, a revolution of content and method which we must see in historical context.

It is crucial for us to distinguish between the original versions of the academy, its development in the late nineteenth and early twentieth century and its present state. The basic belief of Women's Studies scholars in the value of education and our stance as critics of the university indicate we feel that somewhere along the way the academy went astray, that it deviated from founding principles. Originally, 'academic' had to do with the academy or the site of learning; and 'discipline,' as Florence Howe has written, 'was not used to describe a particular branch of learning, but rather the exercise of one's mental faculties' (1978, p. 2). Of course, at first only men could participate in this joy of learning. In 1980, to many of those outside the university and to critics within it, 'academic' means useless, as in 'that question is academic.' 'Discipline' used to mean good old-fashioned rigor, clear thinking; 'discipline' is now almost entirely synonymous with departments. Certainly I was moved to study comparative literature for some of the old-fashioned reasons. Talking about literature is one of the best ways in the world to begin to think and feel deeply. The tradition of reading and teaching has its Western antecedents in the medieval university. The study of the classics required, first, a study of language *per se* and then a basic study of the text and what it meant. From the Middle Ages until the twentieth century (I realize I am traversing centuries at a rather speedy pace) there were many debates among intellectuals and professors and writers (an elite) about how to read books; I think of Goethe and Eckerman or the French literary salons.

One gets the sense (from literary history, from the correspondence of these earlier periods) of dynamic discussions that were crucial in a very basic way to the intellectual and spiritual lives of the people participating in them. Public education has made it possible for more people to engage in these kinds of discussions and this is all to the good. Yet the discussions themselves, at least among academics, have taken on an entirely new tone in the twentieth century.

3 Scientism and the modern disciplines

Literary criticism as it is practiced today comes partly out of honest impulses — the wish to be more systematic and less impressionistic than, say, the nineteenth century in reading fiction and poetry and drama. We did need a more sophisticated literary criticism; now, like so much else in 1980, we are shocked to see how far it has gone. For modern literary criticism has been profoundly influenced by the scientific age. Critics of literature in the twentieth century felt misunderstood, believed that what they were doing was just as intellectually responsible as the work of scientists and mathematicians. Because their work depended not only on *ratio* but also on feeling it was less valued in a university newly dominated by science. So literary scholars set about to develop a more scientific (structured, precise) criticism of literature. Literary criticism now speaks in such esoteric ways partly because of these influences and because of the systems we have built up around it. Undergraduates, graduate students and professors must be sustained; the publication imperative has taken on a life all its own. This is the new business of literary criticism, very far indeed from the old ideas of the value of the text for stimulating and touching our lives.

Emerging social science has been under the same kinds of pressure as literature. University departments were formed after Science took over the liberal arts curriculum. Modern social science has tried to out-science science, so to speak. It has attempted to provide proofs, to be 'objective.'[3] Feminist academics have been attacking the God Objectivity ever since we entered the fray, but He is still very much with us, and will be for some time. Social science, inspired by a view of natural science as objective and value-free, has tried to build air-tight provable theories about human behavior. Humanists and the new feminist social scientists think people are too complicated and interesting to be divided into manageable categories. As a colleague of mine says, this kind of scholarship is proving the obvious, focusing on what is clear rather than upon what is not clear and important. This preoccupation with proving the obvious has far-ranging implications; in studying what is, bad social science also *promotes* what is, substantiates the status quo.

4 An enlarged critique of the academy: the doubters

Of course, there are brilliant exceptions in all fields — research that is original, pathbreaking. And, of course, my point is not new; it has, in fact, been with us since the 1960s.[4] But we must keep saying these things, expressing doubt, in order to make the academy a place that is alive for those of us in it and useful for those we serve. The critique of the academy is becoming increasingly widespread, both from without and within. One cannot pick up a major educational or intellectual journal without finding a piece on the crisis of the disciplines, usually written by a member of the academy.[5] Attacks on literary criticism for straying too far from the emotional value of the text, its preoccupation with theorizing and sign systems, surface again and again.[6] The decline of history is blamed on a tendency of scholars to write for each other. ('More and more, historians are writing for each other. We are becoming an incestuous profession. We are turning the public off history.')[7] The attack on traditional social science is no less furious. Several examples. A recent headline in the *Chronicle of Higher Education* announces that, 'Social Scientists, Unable to Explain Some Issues, Turning to Humanities.' The article goes on to report that the president of the Social Science Research Council says that 'social scientists are feeling "a serious and widespread uneasiness" over their inability to explain some of the important issues they study' (Scully, 1980, p. 1). Kenneth Prewitt's annual report to the Council noted that 'tracking down the source of this uneasiness is not simple, but at least some of it appears to be associated with the unfulfilled promises of quantification.' He suggests that introducing some of the insights of the humanities into the social sciences will be a way 'of effectively integrating quantification and narration into the basic methodologies of the social sciences' (Prewitt, 1979, pp. xx, xxi). Prewitt makes it clear that the social sciences are suffering a loss of public esteem and that these methodological problems must be resolved so that studies can have an effect on public policy.

Arlie Hochschild has pointed out that sociology has never developed a theory of feeling and emotions.[8] A new book by a woman scholar analyzes graduate education, concluding that the two major methods of social science investigation, statistical surveys and participant observation, ought to be replaced by 'experiential analysis,' which takes into account the experiences of both researcher and researched (Reinharz, 1979). Lillian Rubin sounds a similar theme in the introduction to *Worlds of Pain*, where she writes she is 'aware that both the methods of this study and the style of presentation are vulnerable to criticism from colleagues in the social sciences' (1976, p. 13). By method she means the small size of her sample which was not randomly chosen and her bias (she is from the working class and hers is a study of that group). By style she means the story-like telling of her findings.

It is no accident that many women are engaged in these evaluations; as outsiders within the academy, it is clear to us that there are great gaps in knowledge about women and inadequate methodological tools to study what we do know. The feminist scholars cited here want to build a social science which does not set apart researcher and researched and which substitutes a larger chunk of uncontrolled reality for controlled experiments of human behavior.

This enlarged critique, taking place within the academy, is extremely healthful. It is emerging from all quarters — from women and men, humanists, social scientists and natural scientists. Sometimes Women's Studies students and teachers imagine we are the only critics; this idea makes us feel a little lonely and a little self-righteous at the same time. The Women's Studies analysis does have much in common with this enlarged critique of the academy: to keep this in mind puts our own efforts into perspective. At the same time, we need to be clear about our differences. Women's Studies scholars are the only critics to demand that the study of women become a central focus of the university curriculum.

5 The potential usefulness of the disciplines

By now it should be clear that I do not want Women's Studies to be 'academic' in the sense of 'useless' and a 'discipline' in the sense of a department committed to a secret sign system. I want Women's Studies — and all the disciplines — to be 'useful,' by which I mean 'having an impact upon the world.' The universities are in trouble because they have cut themselves off from the rest of the world. At spring ceremonies for graduates in the modern languages at Berkeley, the professorial speaker, attempting jest, lamented that all the students had degrees that were useless. By that he meant those degrees could not be immediately translated into dollars or jobs. His remarks, which sent a shudder through the audience, hark back to the theme that the liberal arts are designed to make the 'man' whole, to make life richer. Indeed they do — but, properly taught, they also give students the skills that will make of them successes in the work world. What could be more valuable to an employer than a person who can think clearly and write well? Snobbishness, and an inability to make explicit the relationship between education and the world, has produced the professor's lament. We have become trapped by this vision of ourselves. If we could recapture our sense of the academic disciplines, we would no longer be compelled to parade our uselessness.[9]

Ultimately, when we are asked, 'Is Women's Studies an academic discipline?,' we are being asked by the unconvinced: 'What are you doing at the university?' I have suggested that if we know something about educational history and the contemporary critique of the disciplines, then we can ask the same question of the questioner. As we have seen, the academic disciplines have been defined in many different ways over time. What we must do is re-capture some of the older meanings in order to begin to make the university more useful in the closing decades of the century. Put it this way and it seems the simplest thing in the world: by leaving women and ethnic minorities outside of scholarly consideration, the academic disciplines are telling us only half-truths. 'Universitas' means the whole, the total. On every campus there is at least one building with 'Veritas' emblazoned upon it. We need only remind the colleague who asks, 'Is Women's Studies an academic discipline?' that the university needs Women's Studies to live up to its highest and oft-processed goal, the search for Truth.[10] This declaration will surely meet resistance, since many an academic career is built upon tightly webbed systems in need of thorough revision if the subject 'Woman' is brought to bear upon them. What we are about is a revolution in knowledge. Our revolutionary nature is at once our drawback (because we are threatening) and our overwhelming advantage (because we are exploring a new frontier).

6 A Women's Studies approach to knowledge

Besides the departmental attachment, disciplines are connected to a particular body of knowledge which has its own ways of finding out what it wants to know. Various disciplines have a different vantage point, a different perspective of a single problem. We commonly hear, 'Oh, he thinks like a political scientist,' or 'That guy has a sociological bent.' What do we mean when we say, 'She is a Women's Studies person'? Clearly, Women's Studies is concerned with that area of knowledge — women — that crosses all the disciplines. A Women's Studies person has an interest in a number of disciplines; she does not conceive of knowledge in a compartmentalized way. Enter the famous term 'interdisciplinary' for which many claims are made. Sometimes that term means plopping down two strangers from different disciplines in a single classroom. Or a feminist critic claims such a method because she takes social and psychological phenomena into account in the analysis of a literary work. Is this interdisciplinary? I do not think that an interdisciplinary person exists in 1980 for the very reason that the whole development of knowledge (and consequently the training of scholars) in the last forty years has been toward specialization. Academic reputations are made by working on a tiny area within the sub-field of a discipline. Perhaps one day the Renaissance man will be replaced by the interdisciplinary woman; perhaps that woman will be one of our students. But I think for the moment we should distinguish, as R.L. Meeth has, between terms such as *cross-disciplinary*, viewing one discipline from the perspective of another (art history is an example); *multidisciplinary*, presenting the way a number of different disciplines view a single problem; *interdisciplinary*, which suggests an integration of disciplinary perspectives; and *trans-disciplinary*, beyond the disciplines, which is, perhaps, where we want to go (1978, p. 10).

A few words about how it feels in 1980 to cross disciplinary barriers. All of us who are now teaching and writing in Women's Studies do have training in a single discipline. We know what it takes to be an 'expert' in one area and thus are afraid to cross this border into unknown territory. We might be caught saying something utterly wrong about a field not 'our own'! This anxiety is most vivid for me as I teach the introduction to Women's Studies, a survey course which draws upon a large number of disciplines. PhD work taught me about the layers and layers of meaning in a single discipline; teaching the introductory course, I am terrified at what feels like a superficial presentation of knowledge. It is a terror of not being The Expert. Erwin Chargaff thinks it is this very idea of the expert that has ruined scholarship. He distinguishes between the scholar and the specialist, the person writing from a broad inclusive view in order to advance knowledge and the reductionist writing to advance a career (Chargaff, 1980). In Women's Studies, our knowledge is too new for anyone to be The Expert; at the same time, we have the opportunity to avoid the mopping up work following a great discovery that leaves several scholars looking at a tiny speck. Our aim is a boundary crossing, a move away from this kind of narrow disciplinary specialization. If we fear crossing boundaries, then we should probably think harder about it. In thinking, we may realize we are not so narrow after all. Most of us changed majors at least once in college; most of us have had to do some work in at least one other discipline in order to substantiate a disciplinary perception. In my own case, the choice of comparative literature was a way to study not a single literary culture but to find relationships between traditions. After the PhD, I became a student again; much of my reading in the last four years has been in the social sciences and history. I have learned just how much I can learn if my reading is selective, if I look to colleagues in other fields for guidance. This exchange of articles sometimes even results in collaborative pieces. It has also been extremely important for me to team teach. The success of team teaching depends on two temperamentally compatible people who do not feel the need to 'one up' each other and who have a compelling interest in a particular problem area. This meeting head-on, so to speak, of scholars from different disciplines is crucial to the idea of cross-disciplinarity. In such a classroom, students and faculty alike witness the dethroning of The Expert. The experience taught me again how many forms of knowledge, how many ways of looking at the world are accessible to us; we must work hard not to cut ourselves off from these multiple perceptions — or to feel too overwhelmed by all there is to know.[11]

One final point. I used to think that despite all this work in other fields I still had a fiercely literary bias, that is a belief that we can learn most about the complexity of human beings from literature. Now I know that a 'humanistic' bias is shared by many feminist social scientists who want to avoid reductionism, who hope for a dialogue between researcher and researched in order to learn more about the inner and outer lives of all of us.

8 The mystique of the methodology

This work in more than one discipline does have its dangers. I have indicated before that one negative way to characterize the contemporary disciplines is to speak of the ways they have created secret sign systems, the way they hold fast to their own methodologies. In Women's Studies, we must guard against creating a Super Methodology, a combination of methods that will become even more impenetrable than the methodologies they are built upon. Women's Studies scholarship, at its best, is an act of translation. That is, we are trying to discover a common language, to move away from disciplinary jargon, to return to an English that we can all comprehend. In order for us to understand each other — for sociologists to talk with linguists and linguists with historians, we have to find a language that is at once sophisticated and simple.

Because of the demands of the academy, Women's Studies people could also become obsessed with method *per se*. In the best sense, method means the way you go about finding out what you want to know; it is a truism that the answer you get depends on the question you ask. Mary Daly, pursuing ideas of 'overcoming methodolatry,' says that (1973, pp. 11-12). 'One of the false Gods of theologians, philosophers and other academics is called Method. It commonly happens that the choice of a problem is determined by method, instead of method being determined by the problem.'[12] Thus, the literary critic becomes more interested in the 'how' than the 'what'; the theory is more important than the artwork. I am not saying we should not be clear about the 'how' but we can learn from the mistakes of the established disciplines.

In fact, Women's Studies scholars seem to be wary of the God Method. A new French feminist journal, *Questions féministes*, spoke in its introductory issue (1970) about women's complicated relationship to theories which serve as the basis for a method. Women are wary because theories have been used against them and because relatively few people have access to the education that will make of them theorists.[13]

Women's Studies emerged out of a political movement and very practical concerns. To pose the problem first and then devise the method has always been our way and I would not like to see these origins in experience change. For me, then, the choice of the problem is crucial. (Of course, this assumes an ability to *recognize* problems.) For me, that means, what do we need to know in order to survive? (This takes us to such 'problems' as nuclear power and ecology.) And, if we do survive, what do we have to know in order to live relatively peacefully and happily together? (This takes us to such 'problems' as the relationships between people of different sexes and races and classes.) Now these are very large questions and very political ones. They are quite unlike most of the questions the academic disciplines are asking now. Yet our concepts of Women's Studies force these questions upon us. These are the questions which are real to us, we who are both scholars and members of the women's community. Our constant reassertion of this link, a vigilance, even, will help to keep women's studies from becoming just another academic discipline, removed from the daily worlds of all of us.

Notes

1 This paper is a revised version of a presentation at the first meeting of the National Women's Studies Association in Lawrence, Kansas, May 1979. It was presented in session No. 150, 'Is Women's Studies an Academic Discipline?' chaired by the author.

2 Jo Freeman would agree. She thinks that feminist scholarship is incompatible with acedeme. See Freeman (1979).

3 Of course, feminist scholars are exposing the myth of objective pure Science. See, for example, Duelli Klein and Minden (1981).

4 For literature, for example, see Kampf and Lauter (1967).

5 Erwin Chargaff, emeritus professor of biochemistry at Columbia, wrote in 'Knowledge without Wisdom' (1980) that

> The institutionalization of all intellectual activities; a misunderstood and misapplied scientism; a crude reductionism exerted on what cannot be reduced; a galloping expertitis, degree-and-prestige-drunk; the general persuasion that anything new automatically deposes anything old — all those agents have caused scholarship nearly to vanish after having been in a slowly accelerating decline for the past 100 years (p. 41).

6 For example, see Irvin Ehrenpreis's review of *Literature Against Itself* by Gerald Graff (1979):

> Serious attention to literature tends to direct itself to an audience of specialist students and teachers . . . . Instead of appealing to persons of taste, curious about reappraisals of established works or wanting informed judgements of new ones, the critic speaks to readers with a vested interest in his professional discipline. It is against this background that one should ponder the extraordinary fascination of professors of literature — in France, Germany, Britain, and this country — with theories of criticism (p. 40).

Or Roger Shattuck in 'How to Rescue Literature' (1980):

> For many people literary *criticism* . . . continues to mean the unconfined medium of personal responses, informal and formal talk, reviews, and scholarship in which works of art circulate and finally locate themselves. For others, however, criticism has taken bold steps in the past thirty years. It now encompasses activities that have little relation to tasting or enjoying anything. [Shattuck has just compared literature with good wine.] Symbolic systems and quantified scientific analysis have become fairly common approaches to literary works. Furthermore, literary criticism has virtually abandoned a set of practices that was once considered essential to the full appreciation of literature (p. 29).

7   This is the view of Richard B. Morris, a retired Columbia University history professor. His remarks were delivered at the San Francisco meeting of the Organization of American Historians. See Morris (1980). In his own career, Morris achieved scholarly acclaim for work in American legal history and then went on to 'to bridge the two worlds' of research and popular appeal. He is the author of a number of widely read books on American history.

8   See Hochschild (1975). Arlie Hochschild's book on this subject, *The Managed Heart*, will be published in 1983 by University of California Press.

9   See Watkins (1983).

10 Truth with a capital 'T' is meant ironically, of course. In a review of *Theories of Women's Studies*, Liz Stanley understood it literally. See Stanley (1981).

11 My opportunity for team teaching came in Strawberry Creek College (the Collegiate Seminar Program) on the Berkeley campus. A course on the split between the public and private in American life taught with Lois Greenwood, a political theorist, was particularly stimulating. The seminar program was discontinued, in part because of its expense.

12 She goes on to say that,

> Under patriarchy, Method has wiped out women's questions so totally that even women have not been able to hear and formulate our own questions to meet our own experiences. Women have been unable even to experience our own experience.

13 In a charged discussion in the 'Theories of Women's Studies' Course (Fall, 1979), I was surprised at the hostility or fear women students felt toward the term 'theory.' For me, theory has come to mean 'idea,' but for these young women it indicated either something they were not a part of or *could not do*.

References

Chargaff, E. (1980), 'Knowledge without Wisdom,' *Harper's*, May, p. 41.

Daly, Mary (1973), *Beyond God the Father*, Boston, Beacon Press, pp. 11-12.

Duelli Klein, Renate and Minden, Shelley (1981), 'Feminists in Science Speak Up: Alice Through the Microscope — the Latest in a Series of Books on Women and Science,' *Women's Studies International Quarterly*, vol. 4, no. 2, pp. 241-52.

Ehrenpreis, Irvin (1979), review of *Literature Against Itself* by Gerald Graff, *New York Review of Books*, 28 June, p. 40.

Freeman, Jo (1979), 'The Feminist Scholar,' *Quest*, vol. 5, no. 1, pp. 26-36.

Haskell, Thomas (1977), *The Emergence of Professional Social Science*, Urbana, University of Illinois Press, p. vii.

Hochschild, Arlie R. (1975), 'The Sociology of Feeling and Emotion: Selected Possibilities,' in M. Millman and R. Moss Kanter (eds), *Another Voice: Femin-*

ist Perspectives on Social Life and Social Science, New York, Anchor Double-day.

Howe, Florence (1978), 'Breaking the Disciplines,' in B. Reed (ed.), *The Structure of Knowledge: A Feminist Perspective*, Proceedings of the Fourth Annual GLCA Women's Studies Conference, p. 2.

Kampf, L. and Lauter, P. (eds) (1967), *The Politics of Literature: Dissenting Essays on the Teaching of English*, New York, Beacon Press.

Meeth, Richard L. (1978), 'Interdisciplinary Studies: A Matter of Definition,' *Change*, vol. 7, p. 10.

Morris, Richard B. (1980), *The Chronicle of Higher Education*, p. 10.

Prewitt, Kenneth (1979), 'Annual Report of the President, 1978-1979,' New York, Social Science Research Council, pp. xx, xxi.

Questions féministes (1979), 'Variations sur des thèmes communs,' vol. 1, no. 1, p. 3.

Reinharz, Shulamit (1979), *On Becoming a Social Scientist*, San Francisco, Jossey-Bass.

Ross, Dorothy (1979), 'The Development of the Social Sciences,' in A. Oleson and J. Voss (eds), *The Organization of Knowledge in Modern America, 1860-1920*, Baltimore, Johns Hopkins University Press, p. 109.

Rubin, Lillian (1976), *Worlds of Pain*, New York, Basic Books, p. 13.

Scully, Malcolm G. (1980), 'Social Scientists, Unable to Explain Some Issues, Turning to Humanities,' *Chronicle of Higher Education*, p. 1.

Shattuck, Roger (1980), 'How to Rescue Literature,' *New York Review of Books*, 17 April, p. 29.

Stanley, Liz (1981), *Women's Studies International Quarterly*, vol. 4, no. 2, pp. 274-5.

Watkins, Bari (1983), 'Feminism: A Last Chance for the Humanities,' in G. Bowles and R. Duelli Klein (eds), *Theories of Women's Studies*, London, Routledge & Kegan Paul, chapter 6.

Wood, Michael, (1980), 'Taking Brecht's Measure,' *New York Review of Books*, 15 May, p. 13.

4

Women's Studies as an academic discipline: why and how to do it[1]

Sandra Coyner

In this paper I will argue that Women's Studies should abandon our fierce adherence to 'interdisciplinarity' and become more like an academic discipline. My reasons are only partly that doing so might be advantageous for our survival within universities. I also believe that a somewhat changed perspective on our work will improve its quality and help us achieve our own particular goals, including education for change.

First, however, readers of this paper must prepare to think like visionaries. By this I do not mean to abandon realism more than temporarily or to neglect the real constraints that survival in academe imposes on us. I do mean that we should regularly think about and discuss what kinds of programs, scholars and work we would most like to have if we could have anything we want. Such long-range visions are necessary if we are to make good tactical decisions day by day.

Perhaps the biggest restraints on a vision about academic disciplines are our own disciplinary backgrounds, the fact that virtually all of us have been educated within a program or department named something else. We are like fish swimming in disciplinary lakes, unable easily to perceive (much less analyze and evaluate) the transparent medium in which we live and work and through which we see everything.

Moreover, conjuring up visions is not always comfortable. Those of us who have survived and are now more or less at rest in our inter-disciplinary programs may not relish the challenge to consider scrapping the whole system. Indeed, when I invoke a future generation of scholars trained through the PhD in Women's Studies with no extraneous requirements or labels, in curricula not yet laid out, and fully qualified to teach several of the courses now divided among other departments, I meet such responses as 'but I don't *want* to have to teach Women and the Law.' Those of us who fit, however tenuously, where we are now perhaps are not the best midwives for change. But we need to think beyond what might be good for you or me as individuals, or for the teaching schedules and training we now have, or for the research we have already begun, or for the programs presently supported or tolerated by our own institutions. Consider what is best for Women's Studies, and what best serves our understanding of women's experience.

1 What is a discipline? Are we ruled out?

Before discussing why we might *want* to be an academic discipline, we must deal with various pre-emptive arguments which claim that we cannot even qualify as a discipline. These include arguments about the 'structure of knowledge,' claims that we lack unique methodologies or concepts, fusses about 'objectivity,' and insistence that the structures now established cannot be changed. In this regard it is important to consider the existing disciplines and what has been written about them, and to distinguish between the ideals and values professed within academe and what disciplines actually do and have done. I have been amazed, in discussing both the ideas in this paper and the matter of 'curriculum reform' at my own university, how easy it is to misunderstand and oversimplify what goes on in disciplines remote from our own background. From the outside, they seem more uniform, more structured, more methodical, more 'disciplined' than areas closer at hand. My brief study of the disciplines, in contrast, has been very encouraging because they don't live up to their ideals of pure disciplinarity any more than we do. We create a 'legitimacy gap' between Women's Studies and the traditional disciplines, to our own disadvantage, by comparing our practice to their ideals. At the same time, we are also too hard on the traditional disciplines. As much as we may criticize their practice, that practice alone does not condemn the underlying goals and values, some of which we may want for ourselves.

What is an academic discipline anyway? A discipline is not the same thing as a department, although on most campuses departments are assumed to represent disciplines, or at worst a combination of closely related disciplines if the number of faculty is too small for efficient administration. But a department is an administrative unit, whereas a discipline supposedly has something to do with ideas and types of knowledge.

Arguments about the nature of disciplines involve complex theories about the structure of knowledge, some of which seem spurious to me and some of which point us in directions I think we should follow. At the most basic level, a discipline is more than a subject, a way of dividing up the things that people might want to know about. Many topics are treated by more than one discipline; for example, women's employment may be analyzed by economists, sociologists, psychologists, historians, and experts in management. Nor do disciplines consist of knowledge gained through different methodologies. Most methodologies in social science and the humanities — statistical techniques, content analysis, case studies, archival research, textual criticism — are shared by many disciplines. There is no discipline built around multiple regression, for example, or around the use of questionnaires. Most people who have seriously asked the question describe disciplines as different *systems* of thought, including concepts, theories, methods and other elements.

Some philosophers, looking at the various traditional disciplines as systems of thought, have claimed that they represent distinctive ways of structuring knowledge, with distinctive concepts, systems of logic and techniques. Their conservative conclusion from their analysis was that education should be based on these several traditional disciplines (Hirst, 1965, pp. 113-38; Hirst, 1966, pp. 129-56; Schwab, 1965; Phenix, 1962, pp. 273-80).

First of all, traditional disciplines are *not* single, unified structures. Psychology, for example, embraces not only experimental and clinical approaches, but also Freudians and behaviorists. Economics includes Marxists, supply-siders, and several orientations in between. These different trends within the disciplines are not complementary; they do not 'add up' to form a consistent or somehow more complete picture. They compete with each other as alternate explanations of the same phenomena; they too are 'distinctive' systems of knowledge. Are these differences within disciplines any less than the differences between them? The same thing is true of allegedly distinctive concepts. Of course the concepts of one discipline differ from the concepts of any other. But *all* concepts are 'distinctive,' and any discipline contains many different, distinctive concepts and methods. The disciplines certainly differ; but why should the boundaries between disciplines seem to be the most important divisions of knowledge? From within any one discipline, when one has been trained thoroughly in some approaches to the neglect of those taught in other disciplines, the concepts one has learned are linked by familiarity and the other disciplines necessarily seem remote. But this is an artifact of familiarity, not an essential characteristic of the structure of knowledge. And it is a simple historical accident that some groupings of subjects are called disciplines while others are not.

Arguments about 'objectivity' may be quite naive or fairly sophisticated. It should be obvious to us all by now that the traditional disciplines are not 'objective' or apolitical, whatever some practitioners may claim. Some disciplines are or have been notably reformist, and some notably anti-reformist, but disciplines are never simply neutral. Every aspect of research, from selecting the questions to interpreting the results, is fraught with judgments that either rest on values or are narrowed by selective perception. Perhaps we can begin to take for granted that some form of non-neutrality is standard in academe and we are entitled to our own commitment to sex equality and women's perspectives. The rhetoric of objectivity came into academe in the nineteenth century, along with academic freedom and autonomy, in a process called 'professionalization' by some sociologists and historians and described for various other occupations, such as medicine and law. Professionalization promoted so-called objectivity, among other things, by limiting scholarship to experts who had survived extensive training in theory, methods, professional ethics, and the work already completed by others. Graduate training and the professional associations still active today were established; and their claim was accepted that only properly certified experts could set standards for their field and evaluate the credentials and achievements of others in that field. One restrictive result has been the exclusion of amateurs and the devaluation of work produced by amateurs outside the academy. But recent histories show that even the concepts of professionalization and academic freedom, part of the rhetoric of objectivity, have often been used in support of particular viewpoints. Mary Furner (1975), in particular, has convincingly described the professionalization of economics and a series of academic freedom cases during the founding years of the American Economic Association as primarily the triumph of conservative views over more liberal ones.[2]

Professionalization created the disciplines we know today, even if their objectivity is flawed and not a sufficient basis for excluding Women's Studies, with our commitment to improving the status of women, from their ranks. One more model of what an academic discipline is and does, however, must be considered: the sophisticated and widely known theory developed by Thomas Kuhn in *The Structure of Scientific Revolutions*, first published in 1962.

Kuhn's model has been discussed by someone in virtually every branch of learning, and his concepts are sufficiently plastic that everyone can find 'paradigms' guiding work in their field, whether that work is scholarly, creative, or activist.[3] Although Kuhn meant his model to apply only to 'science' (and certain crafts), I will follow the trend and extend its application to academic disciplines in general, to see how far the explanation goes.

Kuhn's description of what he calls 'normal science' is important here. Normal science is a relatively efficient teamwork among individual scientists working on separate projects which are nevertheless related to each other by a 'paradigm.' Although Kuhn's usage of the term 'paradigm' has been criticized and found to be both variable and vague,[4] his Postscript written in 1969 (1970) illuminates the special meaning he has assigned to the term. He does not mean simply abstracted rules, theories, and models; he also means 'exemplars' — outstanding pieces of work or 'concrete problem-solutions that students encounter from the start of their scientific education.[5] Paradigms are thus more than stated rules; they are achievements which explain many of the data important to the discipline by demonstrating solutions to problems. The paradigm points to new puzzles for the team of scientists to work out; it organizes scientific activity because it *ranks* data, problems, experiments, and techniques. Although identifying paradigms has become every discipline-watcher's favourite sport, Kuhn also notes that one should not attempt to isolate disciplines by first seeking paradigms. The paradigm is defined as what a scientific community shares. The scientific community can be identified through its behavior and group activities — and will generally be found to have gone to graduate school together, attend the same conventions, and read the same journals.

Kuhn's model of a discipline, because it is based on what scientists do rather than some idealized or categorical 'structure of knowledge,' is more flexible. It admits the possibility of change over time. And there has, of course, been a great deal of change in the disciplines over time, from the medieval trivium and quadrivium to the present day. Subjects and methods can shift dramatically. Geography in the nineteenth century was generally considered a natural science, and now it is a social science — as geographers shifted interest from physical features to human ecology. History has been moving steadily out of the humanities and into the social sciences, with less emphasis on 'great men' and more emphasis on statistics. The changes in focus, in subjects studied, in methods of study, in relationships with other disciplines, should make clear to any observer that we are not dealing with fixed categories.[6]

Kuhn also has a model to explain change, which he names a 'revolution.' I will discuss this part of his theory in more detail later in this paper, when I describe what Women's Studies might do to become an academic discipline. At this point let me say that Kuhn's great contribution in *The Structure of Scientific Revolutions* was to wound mortally the standard received model of science as openminded, objective practice which evolves gradually as it strives diligently to make theory fit well with data. Scientific revolutions are difficult passages in which 'solutions' are lost as well as gained; in which decisions about allegiance to theory may be based as much on political and personal reasoning as on data and research findings; and which may easily create new sciences or 'disciplines' as revolutions split communities.

By Kuhn's definitions, Women's Studies is clearly not an academic discipline, at least not yet. We are in a 'pre-paradigm' stage, characterized by competition among many paradigm-candidates which must each define terms and start explanations from the most basic premises, since we have so little 'core' common among Women's Studies people across the boundaries of traditional disciplines. But Kuhn's model, based on the behavior of professional communities rather than a fixed 'structure of knowledge,' allows for the possibility that we could become an academic discipline if we were to behave like one. Before continuing with the speculations, however, I want to turn to the nature of 'interdisciplinarity' and our present practice, along with a consideration of whether it would be desirable for us to become a discipline at all.

2 Interdisciplinarity and its disadvantages

Most Women's Studies programs are interdisciplinary in structure, not autonomous departments, because they coordinate courses and faculty taken from various traditional departments. These faculty and courses remain affiliated in some way with both units. The departments retain at least some of the budgetary power, scheduling authority, and power to hire, fire and promote. The negative consequences for Women's Studies in terms of program administration alone are severe and well known. We often have trouble getting our courses taught regularly; we may lose the courses if we lose the faculty member, who may not be replaced; or the department may just have other priorities. We have trouble hiring, rewarding, and even *keeping* our Women's Studies faculty. Women's Studies service — committee work or advising or working for national or regional Women's Studies associations — is very often overload. Our research sometimes lacks support, and more often is undervalued, sometimes not even 'counted' for tenure or promotion. These administrative problems inhere in the very nature of interdisciplinary programs, and we have generally tolerated them either because 'programs' have been the best we could get or because we thought such an arrangement might be advantageous for our particular teaching and research. In this paper, however, I have asked us all to conjure visions; and I am therefore most concerned with whether interdisciplinary structure is fundamentally advantageous for our work.

'Interdisciplinary' means different things to different people. As in the arguments about academic disciplines, interdisciplinary administrative structures are justified by ideas about the kind of teaching, research, program objectives, or knowledge that are served best by such a structure. The interdisciplinary model is not one we invented for ourselves and our particular needs; it was already in existence when we came along, and by adopting it we have also taken on some baggage that goes with it.

For a start, work that simultaneously addresses aspects of women's lives which are generally treated separately by the disciplines does not thereby become 'interdisciplinary.' I thus disagree with Barbara Smith (1978), for example, who claimed that black women's literature is interdisciplinary precisely because 'you find accessible black women's culture, music, politics, history, sociology — always in the work of

black women writers themselves' (p. 12).[7] Nor do we achieve interdisciplinarity when scholars trained in one field find it valuable to
learn something from another to do their work well. Both of these
phenomena are part of the normal work within traditional disciplines.

'Interdisciplinary' implies a collaboration between individuals
trained in different disciplines. As such, the concept certainly emphasizes sharing and cooperation and a final product that is better than
either could produce alone. But 'interdisciplinary,' like 'androgyny,'
implies that the parts which have collaborated retain their distinct
identities. The scholars remain 'in' their original disciplines and eventually may return to them.

The literature about interdisciplinary work, especially in the social
sciences, emphasizes a particular kind of cooperation and a particular
rationale for it. There is something of a consensus that interdisciplinary
equals 'applied' and 'problem-centered.' Interdisciplinary work is organized around a particular social or political problem which recommends
itself for some special or political reason. All available and appropriate
theories and methods are applied to the problem from whatever direction until it is resolved.[8] The distinction between this sort of interdisciplinary work and the disciplines can be clarified by reference to
Kuhn's model. In interdisciplinary collaboration, the problem, the
need, the reason to address certain questions, comes from *outside* the
scientific community − it comes from society, or perhaps from a
funding source with money to spend. In a traditional academic discipline, on the other hand, research questions come from within the
existing paradigms, theory and methods, which point to questions
worth asking and simultaneously define ways to attack them.

The attractiveness of the interdisciplinary model for Women's
Studies is obvious. We want to organize around the problem of sexism
for the purpose of changing the status of women; we want to end the
dominion of patriarchy. Letting the problem define the questions
seems superior to letting the disciplines do the defining since the disciplines have clearly failed; but I contend that this is still not good
enough.

There are two objections. First, this 'problem-centered' model does
not give the autonomy it promises. The members of the interdisciplinary
team do not have the power to say when the problem has been 'resolved' or when more work is necessary. They are dependent on forces
and whims coming from outside their own community − funding

agencies or 'society' or (for teaching programs) student demand. Linking Women's Studies to the 'problem' of sexism would allow us to fade into nonsignificance *before* we have achieved change, because our support would depend on others' *perceptions* of the importance of the problem, and thereby be subjected continually to the sexism and racism of others outside our community. Marcia Westkott (1979) has given a particularly sharp description of the process, referring to academic interest in the poor, especially blacks, during the 1960s. The vast outpouring of research studies did little to change the ghetto, but 'research on the black ghetto is now passé, although black ghettos continue to exist, and research on women is now au courant' (p. 427). We see other interdisciplinary programs fading out, especially international area studies and perhaps Black Studies, because money or 'interest' or both have faded; while new ones such as gerontology ride in on the strength of government grants and jobs for graduates. Since we have adopted the model, colleagues ask us too, what will we do when Women's Studies is no longer a 'fad'?

Even more important, the 'problem' approach *underestimates* the importance of Women's Studies. Women's Studies is not just a collaboration. It is — or can be, if we explain it right — a completely new way of viewing humanity. Interdisciplinary programs do not normally ask the parent disciplines to be revolutionized by their new insights and restructuring of theory and method. Interdisciplinary programs and projects do not normally *contribute* theory and method; they *apply* theory and method, to solve 'problems.' We may have stumbled on our treasure unaware. We started with concern about sexism. But what we have discovered in women's culture, and what we suspect about the way we will see knowledge itself when we look through our women's eyes, is certainly far bigger than what we expected and far more dramatic. Let us now consider how the model of 'interdisciplinarity' has affected our work so far, especially our research.

Perhaps it is necessary to begin with a defense of the research orientation in Women's Studies. I suspect that we have attracted to our ranks many faculty who are more interested in teaching than in research, and who may have little sympathy for scholarship, being content with any structure that permits us to teach at all. Indeed, many of the most widely accepted goals of Women's Studies, especially among people outside or peripheral to Women's Studies, concern teaching.

These range from the rather conservative goal of 'balancing' the curriculum by providing a place for feminine and/or feminist perspectives,[9] to the bigger goal of educating for social change. Nevertheless, an emphasis on research is easily justified, since we need content for our courses and we need accurate knowledge and theory to be effective at social change. I believe that research in Women's Studies is also valuable for its own sake and not subordinated to other goals. We need to support so-called 'basic research' whose ultimate application is unclear or even problematic, for the value alone of knowing more about women. And *we* need to control that research, not be controlled by the traditional disciplines for those who define 'problems.'

At present, we seem to do most of our research within disciplines. Although our interdisciplinary journals have no shortage of good material, much Women's Studies research has been published in disciplinary journals. Research conferences are frequently divided on disciplinary lines: the Berkshire Conference meetings on women's history, the Association for Women in Psychology conferences on feminist psychology, and various conferences on topics within such areas as literature. Some of the journals publishing research about women have a focus defined by a discipline, such as the *Psychology of Women Quarterly, Women and Literature*, and *Sex Roles: A Journal of Research*. Although we easily justify undergraduate concentrations in Women's Studies, research training at the graduate level must still be done within some other program, whether a traditional discipline or some other non-traditional program.

There are many reasons that our research retains such strong ties with the disciplines. Research-oriented faculty were already established within the disciplines, or were able to win establishment within them, and followed existing models to establish journals and conferences. I suspect, also, that the importance of research and publication in winning tenure and promotion from the departments that retain personnel power has also influenced many Women's Studies scholars to publish in ways that can win departmental recognition. The influence of the interdisciplinary structure, which leaves so much power in the hands of departments, is clear.

But the consequences for the nature and quality of our research are also important. One consequence is the emphasis we repeatedly place on how the disciplines should be changing because of the new scholarship about women. We want the disciplines to incorporate Women's

Studies findings into their general explanations and their introductory survey courses. We want to be acknowledged by them as legitimate and important, either as a crucial extension of work in that discipline or as a revolutionary new perspective that demands restructuring of the basic concepts in the field. Review articles frequently emphasize the impact of Women's Studies work on the disciplines, often insisting that our work should be taken more seriously by traditionalists.[10]

A different kind of review article might review and critique recent research in light of findings made about a particular aspect of women's lives by scholars in a variety of disciplines. What we neglect and what most of us cannot easily do is show how our work relates to, extends, perhaps even corrects or restructures much other work *in Women's Studies*, especially work outside the traditional discipline in which the research was conceived.[11] Beyond changing the disciplines, our central goal should be to build our own new knowledge. We need to be aware of how the disciplines can contribute to Women's Studies, not just the other way around.

Viewing ourselves as interdisciplinary tends to aggravate certain communication problems involved in keeping up with others' research. We are often unaware of work we should know about. In part, this is a matter of publication and bibliography, since so much research is published in traditional disciplinary sources and many bibliographies are also divided along disciplinary lines. The extra labor required to consult many sources to find work on an interdisciplinary topic must discourage many a scholar. As a result, we risk duplicating work. Related problems have been noted by Catharine Stimpson (1978), who, as editor of *Signs* for five years, is probably best qualified to comment on the state of 'the new scholarship about women.' She has found that, in part because of ignorance, 'even people in women's studies may not always appreciate the quantity and quality of work that has been done and that is being done.' Our still-strong disciplinary ties may affect our motivation. Stimpson notes: 'We have also been prone to overestimate our actual interest in other disciplines. As editor of *Signs*, I have met a depressing amount of resistance, among those most in favor of women's studies, to actually reading essays outside their areas of expertise.' Because disciplines tend to have their own languages which are difficult to understand without specialized training, Stimpson suggests that we now train 'translators,' who could translate the findings of one discipline to persons trained in another, and also to persons outside the academy altogether, 'without diluting ideas or patronizing that audience.' That solution seems to me, however, both too difficult and insufficient for the problem. Such 'translators' remind me of Ptolemaic circles-on-circles, and surely will be treated poorly by the universities where they should be housed. Moreover, the problems are deeper than just communication or translation. They relate to the content of our research.

Stimpson thinks we underestimated the difficulty of actually doing interdisciplinary work. She finds what she calls 'the fallacy of misplaced originality,' which results when even the most elementary findings from another discipline seem revelatory or brilliant because they are new to people not trained in that discipline. Making effusive claims about the explanatory power of concepts long familiar to other disciplines, and oversimplifying them in the process, can hardly benefit our credibility. I think such problems result because we underestimate the difficulty of interrelating findings from different disciplinary frameworks, which are incommensurable. The most basic idea in the literature on the structure of knowledge and in Kuhn is that knowledge is not simply cumulative or additive. We cannot take the research about women willy-nilly from its sources and string it together, expecting the result to be coherent. We are going to have to make choices: choices about what to include and what to leave out, and choices about how to integrate what we decide to keep. Our data will not arrange themselves.

What affects our research also affects teaching. We do not yet have a widely accepted 'core' of material which constitutes an interdisciplinary introduction. Since different faculty often feel the need to include introductions to the feminist perspective in their upper-level disciplinary courses, students taking many Women's Studies courses may find the most elementary material repeated. To the extent that our courses do not cover the gaps between the various disciplinary perspectives, our students remain confused. But most important, we do not equip students to make comparative evaluations of the various ways of addressing or explaining women in society. Surely some of the models we have 'borrowed' work better than others. But can our students make such evaluations? Can we? And have we developed a clear enough statement of 'feminist perspective' that students can criticize sexism in the traditional disciplines wherever they find it, not just in the particular examples we cite?

Since interdisciplinarity is so often defended as contributing to our survival, by keeping us out of direct competition with stronger and entrenched departments, I would like to close this section by noting some direct detriments in precisely this area. Whether we like it or not, our teaching mission will take us only so far in colleges and universities. Universities see themselves as crucibles for the production of new knowledge, and scholarly productivity is the primary basis for personnel decisions in all areas of liberal arts. For example, so long as our participating faculty are connected to Women's Studies primarily by their teaching, and remain 'in the department' for their research, and for evaluations of their research, we perpetuate the notion that Women's Studies is a teaching program only, perhaps with service added, and has no real place in the important research mission of the university. So long as research is prepared for disciplinary publication according to methods and models of disciplines, we delay and undervalue research *in Women's Studies*. The 'credit' goes to the departments, and the long-term result is that they retain the power to bestow 'credit' for research achievement on faculty. We must do research 'in Women's Studies' so that Women's Studies becomes a credible field for research achievement.

In summary, it seems to me that being 'interdisciplinary' is no longer such a valuable format for Women's Studies. At first it was attractive because it is genuinely better for our research and teaching than remaining in the disciplines. The quality and nature of Women's Studies work in the last decade, however, demonstrates that being 'interdisciplinary' is not the only possible way for us to achieve independence from the traditional disciplines; and I contend that it limits us excessively because it does not give us enough autonomy. So long as we allow disciplinary models to point out questions to us, so long as we accept disciplinary priorities about the appropriate methodologies, and so long as we see the main contribution of our work as changing those disciplinary models, so long do we delay emergence of comprehensive models in Women's Studies.

3 Disciplining ourselves

Designing Women's Studies as an academic discipline will certainly be fascinating, but cannot be easy. In this process, and despite the troubles it has given us, we should undoubtedly regard our link with the university as a two-way street. It must certainly learn from us and change itself; but we need to exercise some care in our critique that we not overlook and undervalue some aspects of academic disciplines which might strengthen Women's Studies and should be retained.

Perhaps our first step, which could be taken immediately by many, is to claim to be a discipline. Just use the words. When people ask your discipline, say 'Women's Studies.' Refer to everybody else as the 'other' disciplines. I have noted with some discomfort that when Women's Studies people meet for the first time they very often ask 'what is your discipline?' as a first order of business. If Women's Studies is our field of work, our areas of disciplinary preparation should be described as specialties. The distinction may appear to semantic, but I think it also goes deeper to a matter of identity. Are we sociologists, historians, and artists who happen to be interested in women — or are we Women's Studies people who happen to be particularly interested in social roles, history, and art? One reason we want to know each other's specialty early on is because we have discovered that historians 'think differently' from literary critics, who think differently from anthropologists, and so on. Only if we first accept that Women's Studies can be a framework for organizing knowledge, a framework with its own internal structure and approaches, can we begin to evolve a sense of what it means 'to think like a Women's Studies person.'

Structure

The administrative structure for a discipline is a department. What would this mean for Women's Studies? We would probably not have many more resources for our programs, but we would have more autonomy. Decisions about the balance and emphasis of the program would be less influenced by priorities and circumstances in other academic units. We would also have far greater responsibility, especially in the area of faculty evaluations. Departmental structure implies a unit with its own staff who need to be evaluated for their contributions to that unit. This part of disciplinary independence has seemed unattractive to many Women's Studies people: we shy away from doing to others what has been done so unfairly to many of us. Anyone who takes seriously the process of faculty evaluation knows that it is difficult at best and often more political than scholarly. Even within Women's Studies, evaluators will sometimes undervalue new or different approaches, have personal or theoretical biases, and be frustrated by apparent conflicts between judgments of quality and personal friendships. But I submit that the process, though difficult, is necessary and even has its attractions. Given the nature of the university, whose resources we wish to share, if we don't evaluate Women's Studies others will; and they will use their standards, not ours. We do not have a realistic choice of freedom and support for all minds to develop as they wish.

The advantage of controlling our own evaluations is that we can apply and develop our own standards. We must, for instance, continually agonize over controlling course content to weed out naive or biased approaches which neglect or trivialize feminist scholarship. As long as we are just an interdisciplinary collection of disciplinary courses, such efforts would be seen as violations of 'academic freedom,' which, under existing definitions, they probably are. If we are autonomous, however, we have not only the right but the obligation to demand and evaluate 'quality.' Given the importance of feminist perspectives in understanding women, I cannot imagine work 'in Women's Studies' which ignores or trivializes this approach without an enormous sacrifice in quality. All this has nothing to do with 'objectivity' and is not some sleight-of-hand. It stems from the academic tradition of departmental autonomy, which we can claim if we are ourselves a discipline. An important part of professionalization in every field has always been that only qualified experts can and must evaluate work in their fields.

The most revolutionary aspect of disciplinary structure would probably be new staffing patterns. We would expect people 'in Women's Studies' to have teaching schedules combining several courses about women, even though these courses may presently be taught in different traditional disciplines. The same person might teach, for example, 'Women in American History,' 'Psychology of Women,' 'The Family,' and a Women's Studies survey or seminar. We would thus have teachers whose different courses explore different parts of our knowledge about women, and who might be able to provide comparative evaluations of various ways of approaching this knowledge.

Such a teaching load strikes many present Women's Studies faculty as extraordinarily difficult and demanding. For those of us trained in a traditional discipline, with all the supporting fields, background knowledge, theory and methods which were required, adequately teaching even one course in 'another' discipline would seem to require preparation equivalent to at least another master's degree. Learning the terminology and secondary fields of each discipline from which Women's Studies has grown sounds like an impossible task. And it is. But I want to distinguish between Women's Studies as it exists now (disciplinary people trying to be interdisciplinary) and how Women's Studies as an academic discipline would look. What we need, simultaneously with the new staffing patterns, is graduate training to prepare teachers like these. Neither the absence of jobs nor the absence of autonomous PhD programs should prevent us from developing both.

Imagine, then, a PhD program in Women's Studies aimed, like most PhD programs, at producing scholar/teachers. A student would expect to have some basic knowledge of all the areas presently included in Women's Studies. A major field might be, perhaps, literature – with research in that field. But the PhD would also include several supporting fields, which would NOT be literature of different eras or places, but other bodies of knowledge about women. Graduates of such programs would bring to their research not only a valuable set of skills, but they would clearly be qualified to teach courses in their major specialty as well as in their subfields. This is not much different from or more difficult than the sorts of teaching combinations expected in the traditional disciplines.

Content

Discussing graduate problems leads to the issue of content. We are immediately confronted with the irreducible fact that each of us has different ideas about the balance and organization of content, reflecting among other things different disciplinary backgrounds and various styles of feminism. It should be evident that Women's Studies will probably always have different streams reflecting different priorities and approaches – as in the traditional disciplines. I would like to suggest, however, three things to keep in mind as we proceed to organize content. One is that we should avoid following the arrangement of the traditional disciplines as much as possible. It clearly will not do to imagine Women's Studies as the sum of other disciplines – psychology plus literature plus economics, for example. It is precisely the inappropriateness of the divisions this system imposes on our knowledge that brought us together into an 'interdisciplinary' program in the first place.

Secondly, it has sometimes been suggested that Women's Studies should derive its questions and its priorities from the Women's Movement, or from the general principle of developing knowledge that will benefit women.[12] This is better than the sum-of-disciplines approach, but will not produce consensus, since we have many brands of feminism. Moreover, our origin in the women's movements pushes us to downgrade basic research aimed at understanding rather than at producing immediate results. We need a larger vision.

Thirdly, the structure of a graduate curriculum will not come about by force, legislation, foundation-funded programs in curriculum development, or any conscious specification. We do not have to worry about, or devote any attention to, trying to push a consensus or eliminating our differences of opinion and approach. What will happen is that several key works will emerge from the literature we are now producing; they will attract supporters because of their compelling intellectual power, their ability to organize data and make women's experience comprehensible, and their illumination of new research questions and usable methods.[13] If we pay attention to each other, we ought to be able to see this happening even now.[14]

Perhaps even more difficult than the issue of paradigms, and even more important for the development of graduate programs, is methodology, which is another aspect of the content of Women's Studies. Paradoxically, we have seemed sometimes to scorn methodology, and at other times to revere it from a distance, fearing that Women's Studies lacks a 'unique' methodology and therefore cannot be a 'discipline.' As noted above, however, it is incorrect to conceptualize disciplines as enthronements of methodologies. Certainly all the methods we now use are borrowed from traditional disciplines — but virtually all of the methods anybody uses in social science or the humanities are adaptations of logic, statistics, examination of texts, and observation. What individual disciplines do is choose methods that are appropriate and adapt them to the particular subject or theory at hand. Women's Studies can do the same. With methods, as with concepts, we need to identify which ones are useful for a wide range of questions and begin to teach our methodologies systematically — rather than sending students to other disciplines to learn that discipline's particular array of methods. Our goal here is not to teach every student all the methods, not even statistics courses do that. Our goal is to teach our particular combination, so that our graduates can understand most of the work we are publishing, expecting that those pursuing research projects will learn (or invent!) the advanced methods they need as they go along. Women's Studies doesn't *lack* methodology; on the contrary, we have too many methodologies. We need to rank them and teach them systematically.

The search for a distinctive methodology, and a related effort to purify Women's Studies of 'male' methods, could be quite unfruitful. While it is undoubtedly true that many abuses have been committed in the name of a 'rationality' that does not include women's experiences, we should not run too far in the opposite direction. If traditional academic scholarship has emphasized observation (implying a separation of the observer and the observed) and logic, we are not thereby limited to subjectivism, spiritualism, revealed knowledge, and intuition. It is undoubtedly true that a central development of 'Women's Studies method' has been to incorporate our own experiences and perceptions as women into both teaching and research. We have frequently contrasted the abstractions of social science with a woman's own story told in her own words, finding that the latter is a better explanation than the former. Our classrooms are distinguished by the sharing of experience and the conscientious attempt to make Women's Studies information relate to women's lives, especially students' lives. But to substitute experience for theory and summed observations, including statistics, is either to believe that all women's experiences are inherently similar, denying race, class, cultural and other differences, or to abandon hope of being able to generalize about women. What we need to do in reacting to the limitations of previous scholarship is not emphasize its direct opposite, but create a new spectrum of methods which is more inclusive. We may include our own experiences and perceptions, comparing them with others' perceptions and results from other methods; and we should also apply traditional methods to new problems. Sometimes their limitations are not in the method but in the application. Quoting Stimpson (1978) again: 'Now that Women's Studies has a bit of a tradition, we need to find a judicious balance between the claims of personal authority and the waste of re-inventing the wheel that occurs when non-personal authority is rejected.' (p. 17).

Behavior

Imagining a structure and a content for Women's Studies as an academic discipline is a speculative enterprise, of grand design. Some rather more subtle steps intervene between here and there, changes in focus and direction which facilitate the emergence of the discipline.

Generally, we could now pay more attention to each other and correspondingly less to our colleagues in the traditional disciplines. We need to read more widely in other areas of Women's Studies, write for Women's Studies journals, attend Women's Studies conferences. We need to design courses that focus on Women's Studies subjects, concepts and methods, and choose research problems that elaborate existing key approaches in Women's Studies. We need to spend more time communicating with each other, learning each other's different dialects so that we can develop through usage our own common professional language.

Much of this work could be accomplished through the National Women's Studies Association, if we were to add certain kinds of research content to our annual meetings and perhaps in publications. We must expect and invite the outstanding researchers about women in every field to participate in our one unifying conference. For example, we might cut down on reviews of work in individual disciplines, or panels on 'new work in women's history — or art — or whatever,' in favor of reviews and panels focused on single subjects with participants specifically charged to compare approaches and see integration, rather than cumulation, of insights. I see two central questions we need to ask:

1 What are key generalizing concepts that explain large amounts and disparate kinds of information about women? and
2 How do these key Women's Studies concepts relate to each other?

Many of us were drawn to Women's Studies by the possibility of community, both personal and professional, with other feminist scholars. A well-integrated community is also highly efficient. A shared language, a shared knowledge of basic texts, permits researchers to develop comparatively narrow subjects and write up only their particular findings, with confidence about significance and acceptability. In contrast, many projects in Women's Studies must justify the subject and approach from the foundation, adding to the number of competing explanations rather than strengthening or deepening a clearly fruitful approach. Our conflicts with each other are often over priorities, not validity; and I suspect that some of these conflicts arise because so many of us keep one foot in a traditional discipline.

This discussion should make clear, however, that I am talking about more than just 'better communication;' I am also talking about more conscious standards. I see the task not as increasing our approaches to knowledge or adding new data, but *organizing* more effectively the wealth we already have. If we begin to knit parts of our work into a more coherent picture, other parts are going to be left out. If we rank methods, conceptualizations, or paradigms, some will be low as others are high. This process carries risks as well as benefits.

Criticism

One of the major criticisms of traditional disciplines, and arguments for retaining the looseness of a non-standardized 'interdisciplinary' approach, is that we might become as rigid as they are. We might be hostile to valuable new ideas with merit; we might develop our own esoteric language and standards which exclude outsiders. All these behaviors are abuses, even in the disciplines which practice them. Resistance to theory, method, and standards in Women's Studies probably arises because these things were used against us in the disciplines, whose theories and priorities sometimes declared women and Women's Studies trivial or unresearchable. Hence, some of us have come to see theory, method and standards as inherently constricting and have attempted to be as eclectic as possible. But we are wrong to blame the tools when the real problem is mainly that they have been used by people not focused on women. They use the tools towards different ends. We need to imagine boldly a discipline organized solely around our own priorities. Is it then necessary that we become narrow? We need not abandon our well-developed concerns to use everyday language comprehensible outside the academy, to honor common sense, and to make sure our work relates well to real women.

Another important criticism is based on the fear of 'ghettoization.' As Elsa Greene put it:

'How do we gain the visibility and influence of a strong association without becoming a token ghetto of feminists surrounded by an unaltered patriarchal monolith? Too much associating exclusively with each other and — as Florence Howe has warned — we could go the way of the home economics profession which has many students, moderate status and no power to affect the general curriculum' (1976, p. 3).

Another negative example frequently cited is Black Studies, which has much autonomy but inadequate respect. Ghettoization is a real danger and a real temptation. The constant struggle for recognition is sufficiently painful that separatism, giving freedom to do our work without harassment, often seems attractive.

But I think we often misinterpret the reasons for the weak influence of the programs we cite. Especially with Black Studies and Home Economics, the problem is not just separation but continuing racism and sexism. These scholars do not fail to communicate with their colleagues, but the rest of academia often refuses to listen. There are other interdisciplinary programs which have separated themselves, in many institutions into separate departments, without losing credibility: my favorite examples are biochemistry and linguistics. Fearing 'ghettoization,' we may fail to observe that even the interdisciplinary structure is not working especially well in changing our colleagues. Merely retaining ties is not sufficient to achieve any power to change the general curriculum, and these ties may not be necessary.

I suspect that another motivation behind the fear of ghettoization is a strong need for approval from the traditional disciplines. Excluded for so long from disciplinary recognition, we don't want to jeopardize the foothold we have. Since this seems a professional extension of women seeking approval from men and male institutions, I am immediately and perhaps excessively suspicious.

In fairness, many people in Women's Studies enjoy their contacts with their colleagues in a traditional discipline. What seem to me frustrating split loyalties are to them a double circle of valued colleagues and friends. Many women place high priority on making contributions to a traditional discipline, and genuinely value the work of others in the discipline. More autonomy for Women's Studies seems to suggest that they abandon or be cut off from those contacts.

It is therefore essential to emphasize that we cannot establish

Women's Studies as an academic discipline overnight, and we must be prepared for a period of mixed models — perhaps a long period, given economic conditions. We cannot and should not eliminate or devalue work done within disciplinary frameworks, or relent in our efforts to change the traditional disciplines. We need all the help we can get. Even autonomous Women's Studies departments will need the contributions of faculty within the departments. What I am suggesting, at this point in our history, is a new option, the specialist in 'pure' Women's Studies who can work with our existing staffs, and a new orientation, the disciplines contributing to Women's Studies, not just the other way around.

Having completed my argument for why and how we should become an academic discipline, I would like to close by returning to Kuhn's model of scientific revolutions to explain why autonomy seems to me our only real alternative. Kuhn noted that sciences go through periods of anomaly and crisis when their data do not seem to fit the theories and the experiments do not seem to be working out. These crises are generally resolved by a 'revolution' in which the science shifts its assumptions dramatically. There must be a revolution, rather than gradual change, because 'normal science' does not aim at, cannot tolerate, and generally cannot even see novelty; particular investigations are designed specifically to advance accepted theory, and when researchers do not work out as expected, the scientist usually questions the technique and goes back to try again. Because the assumptions of a discipline — and its paradigms, its exemplars, its models — shape the scholar's very perceptions, anomalies are visible only in a crisis period. Crises are rather agonizing times in which scientists begin for the first time to specify and codify the rules and boundaries of their enterprise. Crises are resolved when a new paradigm, embodying an idea which may have been around already for a while, gains adherents who then return to their laboratories.

Different paradigms cannot be blended together in the Kuhn model. Indeed, a shift from one to another involves loss as well as gain, since a revolution changes definitions, destroys the validity of some previously accepted 'solutions,' and re-orders the hierarchy of work still to be done. This process of revolution is principally one of politics or persuasion, not of simple truth. The older generations must die off, be converted, or lose influence. Scientific revolutions are not simple matters of accumulating or improving the quality of explanation.

This part of Kuhn's model helps to explain why it seems so absurdly difficult to get the traditional disciplines to 'expand' their vision to admit the new perspectives of Women's Studies. We generally propose, for each discipline, what amounts to scientific revolution. Our findings do not fit the established paradigms.[15] We rank priorities quite differently: we study different literature, we put family and reproductive relationships near the top of the list, not the bottom; we want to know about women's relationships with women, and a women's culture previously ignored; we see qualities of sensitivity and nurturance as achievements, not leftovers.

What this means is that we cannot expect our colleagues in the traditional disciplines to say simply, 'Yes, what a good idea! I'll put this in my new textbook right away.' They may take some of our findings — their choices will perplex us — but they will probably not take our perspective. The best we can get from them is an admission that we have another, separate body of knowledge and literature of which we are the guardians. We can convince them of this more easily if we adopt a parallel structure than if we depend on the traditional disciplines to give us separate seals of approval.

In one of my visions, Women's Studies is an established, autonomous discipline occupying a central position in every university and college, because our research and teaching are so valuable in explaining and understanding human experience. We are notoriously successful in preparing people, especially women, to actualize their own visions and promote equality. Then everyone who sees a special 'problem' needing a new interdisciplinary examination will call Women's Studies to be one of the key contributing autonomous disciplines, because no human problem can be understood without us as full and equal participants.

Notes

1 An earlier version of this paper was presented at the National Women's Studies Association convention in Lawrence, Kansas, in June 1979. I am indebted to Gloria Bowles and Renate Duelli Klein, Nick Burbules, Women's Studies faculty at Kansas State University and Wichita State University, and students in my Senior Seminar for critiques and comments.
2 See also Haskell (1977), Kuklick (1976), and Veysey (1965).
3 See, for example, Perry (1977) who examines the ways in which different

analysts have applied Kuhn's model to political science, sociology, religion and fine art. Dozens of articles in various journals evaluate Kuhnian models of particular disciplines, and the *Social Science Citation Index* lists over 300 references to Kuhn each year.

4 See Lakatos and Musgrave (1970), especially Margaret Masterman, 'The Nature of a Paradigm.'

5 Examples used repeatedly by Kuhn (1970) are Newton's *Principia*, Darwin's *Origin of Species* and Einstein's theory of relativity.

6 Book-length 'histories' have been written for most disciplines. Some are rather abstract 'histories of ideas' while other give more attention to the development of social institutions (professionalization) and the social-political context in which change took place. A useful collection of articles is Bonjean, Schneider and Lineberry (1976).

7 See Barbara Smith, *The Structure of Knowledge: A Feminist Perspective* (1978).

8 See Sinaceur (1977) and Sherif and Sherif (1969).

9 See Okerlund (1979).

10 See, for example, Parlee's review of 'Psychology of Women' (1979), Carroll's review of 'Political Science' (1979) and Norton's review of 'American History' (1979) — all in *Signs*. Similar reviews are in earlier issues of *Signs* and, of course, in disciplinary journals.

11 In fairness, *Signs* also contains reviews which might be described in this way, since the author reviews literature about a certain topic and often very consciously considers several disciplinary sources. See, for example, Brown's review of 'Women and Business Management,' and Hayler's review of 'Abortion' (1979). Such reviews often include a brief consideration of whether the literature so far covers the important questions about the topic, but almost never consider how knowledge about this topic fits into our overall understanding of women.

12 See Stimpson (1978).

13 I have obviously derived this model from Kuhn, but with adaptations spelled out by Mulkay (1975). Mulkay finds that, in addition to the process of revolution *within* scientific communities, which Kuhn describes and which is more a political than an intellectual process, a 'branching' process occurs when new problem areas are created and 'scientific migrants' join together to create new social networks. The Mulkay model seems to fit Women's Studies better than the Kuhn model, although I think Kuhn's description of revolution does explain what we would expect the traditional disciplines to do if we were to stay in them, as noted below.

14 For example, we have a consensus so old it is almost invisible that, in the 'nature vs. nurture' debate, Women's Studies emphasizes social and cultural factors over biological ones. Another old theme is that relations between the sexes are political, and men have both dominion and privilege; this assumption is a profound challenge to past assumptions that environment or culture is basically compatible with individuals, since we see culture as often hostile to women (Westkott, 1979, pp. 423-4). Much recent Women's Studies work focuses on women's culture as a separate system, providing

a challenge to the oppression model; this research approach has sparked lively debate about the extent to which women have 'power' within a separate culture or are still dominated by men (Rosaldo, 1974; Rich, 1976; Cott, 1977; Miller, 1976; Bernard, 1981; Smith-Rosenberg, 1975). We are also beginning to realize that profound differences exist among women of different races, classes, and cultures — which may confound the further development of large-scale explanatory models in Women's Studies.

15 For example, consider the psychology of sex differences, in which even the smallest instance of sex difference has been published (and over-generalized), but the vast areas of sex similarities have not. Studies which find no differences have been considered failures, especially when done by graduate students.

References

Bernard, Jessie (1981), *The Female World*, New York, Free Press/Macmillan.

C. Bonjean, L. Schneider and R. Lineberry (eds) (1976), *Social Sciences in America: The First Two Hundred Years*, special issue of the *Social Science Quarterly*, vol. 57.

Brown, Linda K. (1979), review of 'Women and Business Management,' *Signs*, vol. 5, no. 2.

Carroll, Bernice (1979), review of 'Political Science, Part I,' *Signs*, vol. 5, no. 2.

Cott, Nancy (1977), *The Bonds of Womanhood*, New Haven, Yale University Press.

Furner, Mary (1975), *Advocacy and Objectivity: A Crisis in the Professionalization of American Social Science, 1865-1905*, Urbana, University of Illinois Press.

Greene, Elsa (1976), 'The Case for a National Women's Studies Association,' *Women's Studies Newsletter*, vol. 4, no. 1, p. 3.

Haskell, Thomas L. (1977), *The Emergence of Professional Social Science*, Urbana, University of Illinois Press.

Hayler, Barbara (1979), review of 'Abortion,' *Signs*, vol. 5, no. 2.

Hirst, Paul H. (1965), 'Liberal Education and the Nature of Knowledge,' in R.D. Archemboult (ed.), *Philosophical Analysis and Education*, London, Routledge & Kegan Paul, pp. 113-38.

Hirst, Paul H. (1966), 'The Roles of Philosophy and Other Disciplines in Educational Theory,' in J.W. Tibble (ed.), *The Study of Education*, London, Routledge & Kegan Paul, pp. 29-56.

Kuhn, Thomas (1970), *The Structure of Scientific Revolutions*, 2nd, enlarged edn, University of Chicago Press.

Kuklick, Henrika (1976), 'The Organization of Social Science in the United States,' *American Quarterly*, vol. 28, pp. 124-41.

Lakatos, Imre and Musgrave, Alan (eds) (1970), *Criticism and the Growth of Knowledge*, Cambridge University Press.

Miller, Jean B. (1976), *Toward a New Psychology of Women*, Boston, Beacon.

Mulkay, M.J. (1975), 'Three Models of Scientific Development,' *Sociological Review*, vol. 23, pp. 509-26.

Norton, Mary Beth (1979), review of 'American History,' *Signs*, vol. 5, no. 2.

Okerlund, Arlene N. (1979), 'Will Women's Studies Survive?' *Chronicle of Higher Education*, 16 April, p. 80.

Parlee, Mary B. (1979), review of 'Psychology and Women,' *Signs*, vol. 5, no. 1.

Perry, Nick (1977), 'Comparative Analysis of Paradigm Proliferation,' *British Journal of Sociology*, vol. 28, pp. 38-50.

Phenix, P.H. (1962), 'The Use of the Disciplines as Curriculum Content,' *Educational Forum*, vol. 26, pp. 273-80.

Rich, Adrienne (1976), *Of Woman Born*, New York, Bantam.

Rosaldo, Michelle (1974), 'Theoretical Overview,' in M. Rosaldo and L. Lamphere (eds), *Women, Culture and Society*, Stanford University Press.

Schwab, J.J. (1965), 'Structure of the Disciplines: Meanings and Significances,' in G.W. Ford and L. Pugno (eds), *The Structure of Knowledge and the Curriculum*, Chicago, Rand McNally.

Sherif, M. and Sherif, C.W. (eds) (1969), *Interdisciplinary Relationships in the Social Sciences*, Chicago, Aldine.

Sinaceur, Mohammed A. (1977), 'What is Interdisciplinarity?,' *International Social Science Journal*, vol. 29, no. 4, pp. 571-9.

Smith, Barbara (1978), *The Structure of Knowledge: A Feminist Perspective*, Proceedings of the Fourth Annual GLCA Women's Studies Conference, November, p. 12.

Smith-Rosenberg, Carol (1975), 'The Female World of Love and Ritual: Relations Between Women in Nineteenth-Century America,' *Signs*, vol. 1, no. 1.

Stimpson, Catharine (1978), 'Women's Studies: An Overview,' *University of Michigan Papers in Women's Studies*, Special issue, May, pp. 12, 22-3.

Veysey, Lawrence (1965), *The Emergence of the American University, 1865-1910*, University of Chicago Press.

Westkott, Marcia (1979), 'Feminist Criticism of the Social Sciences,' *Harvard Educational Review*, vol. 49, p. 427.

5

Learning Women's Studies

Taly Rutenberg

We are all familiar with the cliché of the professor, pointer in hand, stoically drilling information into the heads of students who appear as bored as he does. In this scenario, the three components of education — the student, the teacher and the material — are not interacting. The result is an alien and alienating educational experience. One of the unique and inspiring features of Women's Studies is that it is a discipline which inherently appreciates and encourages the interrelationship between these components of learning. Because Women's Studies course material addresses the experience of women in our society, women students have to strain *not* to identify. Instructors are often enthusiastic about the material because Women's Studies is a new and personally relevant discipline. Women's Studies is not an isolated study; it is intimately connected with the women's movement which is a dynamic and politically volatile social force. Appropriately, the principles of the movement are evident in the content and method of teaching Women's Studies. Feminist process (e.g., politicizing the personal, interacting cooperatively), manifested academically as Women's Studies, creates the potential for what I call a fulfilling learning experience.

In the minds of students, the university is no longer merely a sanctuary of knowledge. Academicians should not develop or disseminate their theories in an intellectual vacuum nor should the application of those theories be restricted to the academic setting..We expect a college education to be intellectually stimulating as well as practical. In order for students to have a meaningful learning experience, we must be educated in ways which not only stimulate our creative conceptual faculties but which facilitate the application of creative thought to circumstances in the outside world.

We know that no theory or critique has a purely intellectual foundation: we are emotional as well as intellectual beings. To be wholly effective, education must be approached with an appreciation of the totality of our natures.

Finally, we should be trained and encouraged to think beyond our fore-scholars. We should not be indoctrinated with their Truths; rather, we should be invited to criticize or alter theories and methods with respect to our present cultural disposition and social circumstances. I believe that a 'fulfilling learning experience' develops a student's creative intellectual faculties and encourages her to see the relationship between her intellect, her personal life and her politics.

The traditional disciplines

Merriam-Webster defines 'discipline' as (1) control gained by enforcing obedience or order, (2) orderly or prescribed conduct or pattern of behavior, and (3) a field of study. I suggest that the 'traditional' academic disciplines currently approach education on the basis of all three definitions. Most disciplines are committed both to their discipline-specific perspectives and to traditional assumptions about the purpose and method of 'academia.'[1] By discipline-specific, I am referring to the sets of assumptions around which the disciplines ask questions and form conclusions. Each discipline perceives the world through a different colored lens and is committed to that hue. Schools of thought within these disciplines whose approach to knowledge and education parallels that of 'traditional academia' further distort their inherently narrow spectrum. Responding to this phenomenon, Gloria Bowles describes a traditional discipline as 'a particular body of knowledge which has its own ways of finding out what it wants to know.' In order for a student to excel in a traditional discipline, she must temporarily perceive the world through the lens of the particular discipline. She must familiarize herself with its theoretical foundation, its jargon and its maxims in order to squeeze facts and phenomena into theoretical molds. The better the fit, the higher the grade. While this method 'disciplines' our minds and secures 'A's,' it ultimately stunts our intellectual growth. The present goal of education is not to challenge the basic assumptions of the disciplines but to use one's mechanical ingenuity to reach the same basic conclusions. While this method may exercise a student's faculties for linear analysis, it does not necessarily develop the faculties which potentially create new assumptions or perspectives.

The traditional disciplines do not incorporate into their methodology or material the knowledge which is derived from a student's personal or emotional experiences. For the traditional disciplines, legitimacy is achieved through 'objective' methodology; because personal experience and emotion cannot be empirically derived, they have no place in traditional academia. An emotional reaction or personal experience is, however, often the foundation of critical thought and more astute theory. The assumption that women derive ultimate satisfaction from their roles as mother and wife, for example, was not challenged by academia until the actual experiences of women were finally considered and 'legitimated.' Through an analysis of diaries, journals, interviews and other 'subjective' resources, this assumption was refuted and exposed as a mechanism for social control. Women's 'diseases' as well as their level of satisfaction can be interpreted as effects of patriarchal control. Feminists have explained that 'hysteria,' for example, was a rebellion and outlet for the frustration felt by nineteenth-century housewives who were forced to repress their creativity or intellect. Theories developed by traditional academicians and physicians of the day held that 'hysteria' was the disease which stemmed from a woman's inability to accept her God-given, biologically mandated role as wife and mother. Had these theoreticians listened to the feelings of women about their lives as wives and mothers, had they not been exclusively academic in their approach to 'hysteria,' and were they without a vested interest in the subjugation of women, their theories would have been based on fact rather than on objective fantasies. We should learn from these lessons: if students are not taught to use personal experience and emotions as viable tools of criticism, we will leave the university with a superficial sense of the methods of critical thinking. An educational experience which ignores sentience cannot be a fulfilling learning experience.

The quest for objectivity and the tendency towards isolation inherent in the traditional disciplines also explain why students feel that the relevance of course material is limited to a particular class, rather than applicable to their education in general, or more significantly, to their lives outside the academy. Not only is the material presented to students often obscure, but it is presented in a manner which reflects the strict rules of 'academia.' Narrow and rigid in scope, these rules are not appropriate in our personal lives and cannot be applied to a multi-faceted and dynamic society. At this point, academia becomes 'useless.' I believe that what we learn is not as important as how well we apply a thoughtful method. A 'thoughtful method' does not overemphasize the intellectual approach; rather it is the combination of intellect and emotion and is concerned with practical and personal as well as academic application.

The learning experience in Women's Studies

How does Women's Studies, in contrast, offer students a fulfilling learning experience? The most significant difference between Women's Studies and the traditional disciplines is that Women's Studies emerged from a political and social movement outside the walls of the university. As a result, its concerns are not strictly academic and its legitimacy is dependent on its acceptance by the feminist community as well as by the standards of the academy. Women's Studies is responsible to the goals of the women's movement, goals which include a critique of these traditional 'standards of academia.'

Political and economic trends as well as standards for behavior often have their roots in theories developed in academia. Consequently, it is important that a feminist perspective be actively represented in the university. As the feminist force, Women's Studies translates and communicates the ideas of the movement through the channels of the university. The priorities of Women's Studies often conflict with those of the traditional disciplines and cannot be transmitted through traditional methods.

I am not arguing that all 'non-traditional' disciplines, by virtue of their deviation from traditional content, offer students a more rewarding learning experience. Rather, I will attempt to show that Women's Studies, by virtue of its connection to the ideals of the women's movement, has features which increase the potential for a fulfilling learning experience.

As I said earlier, Women's Studies arose partly as a critique of the traditional disciplines because they do not accommodate the experiences of women in their theories or methods. Women's Studies is concerned with the patriarchal biases inherent in the traditional disciplines and attempts to deconstruct them. Part of learning Women's Studies, therefore, is learning how to criticize basic assumptions underlying traditionally accepted theories. Women's Studies teaches us to identify and critique different perspectives, not to feed them back to our instructors 'in our own words.' Along with the deconstruction of patriarchal myths, Women's Studies is concerned with the reconstruction and construction of new, more viable theories which are drawn from the experiences of women and other oppressed groups. Creativity and imagination are inherent in this process. Because the struggle against hierarchical stratification is embedded in the ideals of the women's movement, students themselves are encouraged to use their creative resources to reconstruct and construct new theories.

The movement's emphasis on cooperation instead of competition is embodied in Women's Studies and serves to enrich a student's learning experience. The goal of feminist scholarship is not to form conclusions about all women; rather, feminist theory attempts to reflect the diversity of women's lives. To do this effectively, we must talk to each other while we conceive, develop and rework our theories. Feminist scholarship is collective in both form and content. As such, Women's Studies students are encouraged to learn from each other; our individual and collective insights and stories become our scholarship.

Women's Studies is relevant to those who are concerned with political and social reform because it prepares us to recognize and confront the tensions we will encounter in our feminist struggles outside the university. The relationship between Women's Studies and the university at large can be used as an example. As Women's Studies represents the interests of the women's movement, the university represents the interests of segments of a more traditional society. Clearly, these two sets of interests may conflict. The very survival of Women's Studies is often threatened because the university does not consider it a 'legitimate' study. As a result, the Women's Studies program has difficulties securing a permanent budget — the guarantee for its survival. Such marginality is an instant lesson in politics. By virtue of her connection to a vulnerable discipline, a Women's Studies student is forced to confront tensions similar to those she will encounter in the struggle against oppression outside the university.

Women's Studies is relevant to students because it validates personal experience within the context of academia. Throughout history, women have been relegated the familial and 'expressive' role. The personal nature of this sphere has been devalued by society at large and ignored in traditional scholarship. Women's Studies, on the other hand, clearly values personal experience and tries to integrate it into classroom experience. Although some lecture courses are held within Women's Studies, usually as introductory classes, most Women's Studies courses are conducted in the small discussion-group format. This format creates an intimate setting where students can feel comfortable reacting personally as well as intellectually to the ideas being discussed. The deconstruction of sexist myths which women often internalize on a deep personal level can only occur in a setting which facilitates the expression of both the intellectual and emotional realms. The Women's Studies classroom is a place to identify feelings of oppression, ventilate these feelings and constructively redirect them towards change. Although Women's Studies delves intellectually into conflicts once they are identified, the identification process is inherently linked to a visceral experience. Contrary to the traditional disciplines, Women's Studies has a firm commitment to subjective knowledge and learning.

Careers and the disciplines

Because students expect their education to be career-oriented, it is important to examine how the traditional disciplines and Women's Studies approach this aspect of education. It is important to note that few disciplines actually 'prepare' one for later work. We are all too familiar with the decreasing practical worth of the BA degree. But if people want to succeed in the traditional career world, the traditional disciplines do have an advantage over the non-traditional disciplines; the qualities one must have to 'succeed' in the traditional disciplines are similar to those required to 'succeed' in the career world. That is, an understanding of the mechanisms of the academic system or discipline will often engender high marks. Furthermore, the traditional disciplines characteristically stress competition, specialization and a myopic devotion to their specific field. In our society, professional and financial success is rewarded to those with exactly these characteristics.

Women's Studies provides us with a perspective on the traditional academic world and its corollary in the 'real' world so that we may consciously decide whether to accept, reject or attempt to modify those worlds. And it helps us to see alternatives: an education which encourages students to think beyond tradition and to incorporate their emotions into this process benefits students who wish to create or engage in feminist work. 'Feminist work' cannot be described in terms of a specific occupation or career because it is an approach to working. That is, in choosing work, one must consider individual needs and talents as well as the needs of the larger community. One must also consider how to structure one's work so that it does not contradict or undermine its primary function. This approach to work parallels the Women's Studies approach to education in that it appreciates the relationship between the individual, the community and her work. Feminist work, like a feminist education, cannot thrive in a competitive and hierarchical climate. Women's Studies, then, in terms both of ideology and structure, can help a student formulate and engage in work which is innovative and personally relevant as well as useful to the community.

Students who seek a discipline which encourages creativity and values personal experience and a social conscience do not have many options in the university today. I feel it is vital that society's institutions evolve to meet the needs of its members. In order for the university to be useful it should reproach stale academic methodology and encourage creative education. The priorities of the traditional disciplines parallel those of our present society and thus perpetuate the status quo; the university, because it is ruled by the traditional disciplines, is not fulfilling its responsibility to progress. And with the exception of programs such as Women's Studies, it is becoming less useful to students dedicated to social change.

Notes

1 For a definition of 'academia,' see Gloria Bowles, 'Is Women's Studies an academic discipline?' in this volume, chapter 3.

6

Feminism: a last chance for the humanities?[1]

Bari Watkins

It has become a commonplace that the humanities are in serious trouble in American universities. Everywhere we look, there are warnings that liberal arts education is dying, that students are interested only in future careers, that professors care only for research, and that the evil technocrats have taken over all aspects of the educational process. Scholarly journals and highbrow magazines abound in essays calling for a return to commitment to the humanities, 'back-to-basics' curricular reforms are justified as last-gasp efforts to save the television-generation from illiteracy, and individual faculty members confess to feelings of malaise and purposelessness.

These concerns, of course, pervade the whole of the university world. Jobs are scarce in virtually every field, money for research and innovative programs is rapidly drying up, and in every field one hears the same complaints about career-oriented students and frightened faculty. But the traditional fields of the humanities — literature, languages, philosophy, history, the classics — seem hardest hit. Declining enrollments, a dearth of jobs for the remaining majors, and a general perception of helplessness, often coupled with gallows humor, make university life especially unhappy. Finally, and I think crucially, scholars in these fields have little experience with the large funded research projects which are the last remaining financial salvation of colleagues in policy-oriented fields. No research projects employing graduate assistants and supporting large percentages of faculty salaries are to be found in, for example, the average classics department. At my own

79

university, political scientists easily raised a million dollars to learn if people like being victims of crimes. A faculty member in the English department could not find $176 to fly to New York for research essential to her promising new book.

But all is not so gloomy. At my own school, Northwestern, and at other universities, anecdotes and reports or evaluations suggest that faculty and students involved in Women's Studies have created and maintained a sense of excitement about teaching and learning. Expressions of despair about the future of the university do not occupy the Women's Studies faculty, even when we bemoan budget cuts and a shortage of time for research and teaching. They display enthusiasm about teaching and research, create new courses, join new organizations, and write for the new journals of Women's Studies. Undergraduates in Women's Studies also seem different. I'm sure your own experience has shown them singularly excited about learning and convinced the university has something to offer them beyond grades or admission to law school. In all our experience, we find Women's Studies students preparing elaborate research projects, reading 'recommended' books, and urging their friends to join them in Women's Studies courses. Among all of these women, from distinguished senior professors to the most inexperienced freshman, liberal arts education holds a promise and a sense of purpose sadly lacking in much of the university. And all this is true even in the fields hardest hit by financial and emotional depression.

Although this situation clearly calls for self-congratulation, in which I cheerfully indulge, it also offers an interesting opportunity for analysis. Let us presume that universities can be thought of in two ways. First, they are social institutions (non-profit corporations, to be exact) in which people get paid to teach and do research and in and through which they make careers and create and recreate professional ideologies. Second, we can think about the things that get thought in universities. That is, we must consider the models for research, modes of understanding, social theories, critical theories, and so forth forming the overarching parameters of work within the various disciplines. To be sure, my distinction between institution and ideology is almost entirely false. We must always think dialectically about their relationship, for the social institution in which one gets paid to think and the things one does in fact think are inextricably intertwined as base and superstructure. Yet I will separate the two for a time, heuristically, for it seems to me that feminist scholarship differs from everyday or garden variety scholarship in both respects, that those differences can be examined separately, and the conclusions we reach in putting them back together are very useful. They offer, in fact, a model of intellectual revolution which may well prove to be most effective for all of the humanities. I mean quite seriously that the feminist model for teaching and learning can provide a solution to the dilemma faced by the liberal arts.

To begin with, what distinguishes feminists from other scholars is their commitment to a movement for social change, and their conviction that women have been excluded, devalued, and injured by many aspects of human society, including the traditional academic disciplines. They therefore pose two separate but related challenges to the ordinary business of the university. As scholars, they want to see women and issues of concern to women included in the canons of academic research and thinking. But in order to change the work that scholars do, feminists have also found that they must challenge the institutional arrangements of the university. Both efforts provide useful lessons for non-feminist humanists. I will begin at the intellectual level.

As our presence here and the issues we discuss clearly testify, Women's Studies as an academic discipline has undergone a remarkable evolution in the past decade. Ten years ago, its goal was simple: to add women to academic fields where they had been ignored, and to correct inaccurate or biased presentations of women. So historians, for example, began to demand that women's lives and women's accomplishments be added to the professional canon. Or in sociology, researchers found that many studies and experiments had been performed using only male subjects, often without even noting that limitation, so they did new studies to correct the omission of women. Women scholars in many fields produced what we now, following Catharine Stimpson, call 'compensatory' scholarship, adding women to make up for neglect or bad treatment.

Such studies were surely revealing, but what happened next was far more exciting. Feminist scholars found that you could not simply add women to fields where they had previously been ignored. The models and paradigms of existing scholarship did not simply leave women out; they did not permit satisfactory explanations of women's experiences. They painted a picture of the world which was basically wrong or mis-

guided because women's lives did not fit into its outlines. It was therefore necessary to transform and reconstruct traditional ideas and
methods in order to include women.

In history, for example, Renaissance scholars like Joan Kelly-Gadol
reconstructed theories of social progress by noting the human costs
paid by women (loss of social autonomy and cultural regard) in a
period previously thought of as 'progressive.' Studies of Europe and
America in the nineteenth century by women like Nancy Cott similarly
reconstructed our ideas of capitalist culture by presenting new information and theories about the importance of the male/female cultural
dialectic of Victorianism. In these two cases, and in dozens like them,
scholars gained new understanding of social processes and periods by
beginning to look at the victims of progress.

In this respect, I would include feminist anthropologists as a humanistic discipline. And they have similarly changed the basic assumptions
of their field. They have, for example, challenged existing ideas of what
is truly 'natural' in human behavior by pointing out cultural patterns
which have disguised women's inferior social position as a result of
biological differences. Well known work by Louise Lamphere questions
received notions of gender differences, finding the assignment of
women's and men's roles far more dependent on culture than previously assumed. Further, they began to posit the truly revolutionary
notion of a separate female culture, determined by historical domination by men and marked by a separate women's consciousness, in
dialectical opposition to patriarchy.

That idea — female consciousness — is, of course, at the heart of the
recent exciting innovations in literary theory. The pioneering work of
French critics on a female voice and their discovery of lost women's
literature in non-canonical forms has been eagerly greeted by American
scholars. Those women have challenged, through their new work, the
male-dominated canonization of what is 'literature' — and, more
important, what constitutes culture itself. For a humanist, what could
be more revolutionary?

Even philosophers, seemingly above such social battles, have had to
change their way of thinking once they began to consider women.
Kathryn Pyne Parsons, for example, challenged the bastion of analytic
philosophy, long dominant in the field, by studying the ethical decisions women face over abortions. She found that the analytic method
simply could not deal with those problems — so she suggested necessary

and important revisions. Another feminist philosopher in political philosophy refashioned traditional ideas by considering feminism as a political movement. Because it could not be fitted into the existing categories, she sensibly concluded that the categories themselves did not account for all of human experience. In both cases, the way philosophers thought 'people' understood their world did not include half the human race.

Examples from various fields could be multiplied endlessly. If one cares to add to a definition of the liberal arts or humanities the non-quantified social sciences, the list gets even longer. Sociology, economics, and political science have also been challenged by new questions and new information about women. But the lesson is the same for all of these fields: the humanities can be revivified by the expansion and deepening achieved through new discoveries, new ideas, and new perspectives. Efforts to 'preserve' the humanities by maintaining their restricted focus on Western culture, a white male elite, or particular 'great' thinkers are only defensive holding actions against change.

Most important at this level of change is the challenge explicit in feminist scholarship that our earlier notions of human culture were in fact ideological justifications of a particular distribution of power within society. And that, of course, is a political challenge to definitions of life which *exclude* experience, *deny* expression, and *negate* the work of the non-powerful, the non-white, the non-Western, the non-male. Traditional humanists, especially those trained in the prestigious graduate institutions, are very fond of two claims: first, that their work is essential and global because it concerns 'humanity,' all of human experience. Second, that their work, unlike that of the morally suspect social scientists and social technocrats, is morally pure because it is *not* 'political,' not influenced by immediate social concerns. Feminist scholarship has revealed both claims as lies, ideological mystifications of the role cultural, artistic, and literary notions and conventions have in creating, patterning, and shaping everyday life. In the end, the unmasking of that lie is salutary for two purposes. For women and all the other excluded groups, avenues are opened for the expression and study of our feelings, our experience, our lives. But for all humanists, the results are even more startling. In exposing the power of cultural prescriptions and mystifications in everyday life, revolutionary scholarship paradoxically rescues the humanities from their current obscurity.

Let me elaborate. In our own educational experiences, we are all too familiar with odd mixtures of embarrassment and pride with which traditional humanists describe their own 'uselessness.' The straw person classicist, reveling in the arcane delights of Greek participles, the stereotypical critic, monomaniacally dedicated to Renaissance metrics, or the medieval historian, cheerfully claiming the Council of Trent as 'only current events,' have victimized themselves and denied the importance of humanistic studies through their denials of relevance. They have dug their own cultural grave by denying the immediate, political importance of their work. They have almost — if not entirely — achieved the ultimate in false consciousness by devoting their lives to work which denies its own importance. By so doing, they have guaranteed its absolute hegemony. Who, after all, could attack or even perceive the cultural injury and patriarchal domination perpetrated by such innocent and harmless bumblers?

It seems to me that their game is up. Feminist scholars, along with other groups of the powerless, have revealed the humanists' mystified domination of our lives and experience by revealing its limitations. If the humanities, as we now see, exclude, they must do so for a reason. And once we see that they exclude, it is not hard to understand why and on what basis.

In the end, the humanities win. Their past corruption exposed, their power is revealed. And no one can see their work as irrelevant, quaint, or arcane anymore. We can only conclude that our classicist, Renaissance scholar, or medievalist should thank feminists for exposing their importance and social power, if negatively. I rather suspect they will not. But future research and teaching in the humanities, even if not explicitly feminist, can never be the same again.

But that intellectual revolution does not take place in isolation. In doing their research and writing, feminist scholars have also come to some important conclusions about the universities in which they work — and have mounted new models of behavior and organization which attempt to change them. Based on a sense that the structure of society has worked to exclude women, feminists have looked at all social institutions with an eye to their failures and weaknesses. In the case of the university, their discoveries tend to buttress their intellectual demand that life be rehumanized and reconstructed for the benefit of all.

Modern American universities have come, since the Second World War, to aspire to the standard of the elite research institution. As

Patricia Graham (1978), among others, recently observed, such schools are designed to further the research and careers of the senior faculty, to produce mountains of data, articles, and scholarly books, and to fulfill what they perceive as a responsibility to provide services to government, corporations, and other large social institutions. They are, in certain important respects, entirely indistinguishable from the capitalist enterprises which support and surround them. Unlike the colleges which preceded them, modern research universities are not primarily oriented toward undergraduate education, nor do they tolerate personal eccentricity or primary devotion to teaching among faculty members. They are hierarchical, competitive, and individualistic, and they discourage institutional loyalty among faculty in favor of loyalty to professional disciplines. And, most important, they perceive and describe themselves as being socially 'neutral' and 'objective,' meaning that the university does not take sides in social battles and that scholarship is seen as existing outside of politics.

Feminist scholars, devoted to teaching as a part of their politics and to research oriented toward a particular social movement, do not fit very well into such a university. Women's culture is as incompatible with the organizational style, discourse, and interactional patterns of, say, Harvard, as it is of Exxon. (This is a blunt truth we all surely recognize in our own lives.) Feminist work within the university, whether it is research about women or the necessary collection of information for new and innovative courses, is therefore perceived by the university as somehow trivial or unserious, the words used to discredit and destroy threats to professional hegemony. The feminist political goal of creating a more just society for women and other powerless groups is similarly seen as a direct challenge to the stance of the university as neutral and 'above' politics.

This situation is especially true within the humanities for the ideological reasons I discussed earlier. For the keepers of culture, in fact the most hegemonic and powerful of university researchers, it is most important to appear harmless, 'above' politics, and disconnected from everyday life. So a woman with explicit political goals in, say, philosophy, literature, or the classics, is more quickly labelled an outsider and 'unprofessional' than her counterpart in the *less* culturally powerful (and hence less mystified) fields of policy-oriented social science. Personal idiosyncrasy ('she's a crazy radical'), doctrinal deviance ('this work is political, not historical'), are more quickly labelled and punished.

There are two possible responses to such a situation, and women scholars have experimented with both. The first can be called accommodationist. It consists of trying to make research on women look as much like 'real' research as possible, emphasizing its scholarly complexity and distance from everyday life, of trying to make women scholars behave as much as possible like their male colleagues, imitating the individualism, devotion to hierarchical relations, and dispassionate style of the research institution's superstars, and of de-emphasizing the teaching of undergraduates, concluding that classes and students are to feminist scholars what they are to traditional men: an impediment to the real work of research. It would be a lie to say that there are no women scholars who have adopted this model, and it would be equally untrue to argue that it holds no rewards for those who master its precepts. But it is not feminist. The accommodationist style, like the early compensatory studies of women, does nothing to change the rules of the game, nothing to make scholarly work more open to diversity and human liberation, and certainly nothing to make the humanities more humanistic.

Most feminist scholars early rejected the reconstruction of their professional lives to fit the male-dominated model, refusing to make themselves over in a male image. From their position at the bottom of the social hierarchy, they had seen too clearly what such a society does to its victims, and from their socialization outside the male models of individualism and competiveness, they brought to their work in the university a counter-example of cooperativeness, collective effort, and sisterhood. Most important, they correctly perceived the 'neutral' ideology of the university for what it is, a disguise for active support of the social status quo.

In the past decade, therefore, feminist scholars have mounted an open institutional challenge to ordinary life within the university, demanding changes making it a better place for everyone. They see undergraduate education as a central part of their duties, share research efforts and results, resist authoritarianism in their own classrooms and programs, and generally try to resist the bureaucratization of intellectual life. Because they are outsiders, they feel strongly that the university should be open to a diversity of personal styles and priorities. And, most important, they understand that committed scholarship, research and teaching which tries to make an active difference in the world, is truly humanistic.

In the long run, the intellectual and institutional challenges of feminism to the ideals and structures of the university are two sides of the same coin. In each case, feminists discovered a world where women could not simply be added, like so many new recruits, to a game with permanent rules. The rules specifically excluded their particular experiences, accomplishments, and desires, so the rules had to be changed. Women must become a legitimate subject of scholarly inquiry, but their inclusion into the humanities must broaden the base for other inclusions and expansions of its interests. Women insist on bringing their social commitments to teaching and other activities within the university, but that change must be part of a general reconceptualization of the university's role in society. And the competitive and hierarchical bureaucracy of the university, supportive only of personal ambition rather than cooperative work and communal goals, must make way for a new way of living and working in an academic community. In each of these cases, feminist scholarship may represent the beginning of a flowering of the humanities and a rehumanization of humanistic study. But to be truly revolutionary, those new ideas must permeate the whole life of the university. Women's freedom must be won, but so also must human freedom.

Notes

1   This paper was presented at the National Women's Studies Association Conference in Lawrence, Kansas, 1 June 1979.

References

Graham, Patricia A. (1978), 'Expansion and Exclusion: A History of Women in Higher Education,' *Signs*, vol. 3, no. 4, pp. 759-73.

7

How to do what we want to do: thoughts about feminist methodology[1]

Renate Duelli Klein

1 The case for feminist methodology

This paper is concerned with the fact that until very recently feminist methodology as a topic of its own had not been given much consideration. Books and articles on the development of feminist scholarship focus on its new content rather than on its methodology and although the need for feminist *theory* has been widely recognized feminist *methodology* does not as yet get nearly as much attention.[2]

No one doing research from a feminist perspective would deny that indeed the choice of the research topic — the 'what' to investigate — must come prior to the decision of 'how' to go about doing one's research. In fact, as Mary Daly has said, the male 'God Method' has contributed to women's oppression and we need to break his tyranny: 'Under patriarchy, Method has wiped out women's questions so totally that even women have not been able to hear and formulate our own questions to meet our own experiences' (1973, pp. 11-12). However, while I certainly would not want to invent an equally tyrannical 'Goddess Method' I think feminists need to be very clear about how we want our research to differ from patriarchal scholarship and to that end we have to think about how we are going to do what we want to do.

In other words, after the initial excitement of how absolutely marvellous and ingenious our ideas for a research project are, whether we like it or not, the moment of the down-to-earth task of the conception of our research — including the choice of a feminist methodology — will inevitably come. 'Feminist' for me implies assuming a perspective in which women's experiences, ideas and needs (different and differing as they may be) are valid in their own right, and androcentricity — man-as-the-norm — stops being the only recognized frame of reference for human beings. And by 'methodology' I mean both the overall conception of the research project — the doing of feminist research — as well as the choice of appropriate techniques for this process, including forms of presenting the research results. I use the word 'methodology' (as well as 'theory') in the singular, but by no means do I wish to suggest we work towards the one and only 'correct' feminist methodology: clearly feminist methods can and must differ according to the specific circumstances of our research projects.

It is my contention that to think about what a feminist methodology is, or could be, is imperative for the doing of feminist research if we want to put our feminist theories into practice. For me, theory and methodology are closely interrelated in a dialectical relationship: a feminist methodology can help us to validate emerging feminist theory and indicate the need for modifications. The new theories then in turn are likely to pose demands that stimulate the generation of new methods. In this way both the theory and methodology of feminist scholarship might avoid the fate of becoming static, rigid and dogmatic — and might help preventing Women's Studies from becoming 'just another academic discipline.'[3] If indeed feminist scholars want to be 'agents for change' (Westkott, 1979a) rather than simply investigating women as a new topic, if we indeed want to work towards a future that, as Marcia Westkott (1979b) says 'is not merely an extension of the present but more significantly a qualitative transformation of the present' then I think we need to consider which methods are best suited to our quest for feminist knowledge in which women's concerns are central and inspire our questions.[4]

The wish to delve into an exploration of feminist methodology came during my research in 1979 on the attitudes of young women towards feminism, the women's movement and Women's Studies (Duelli Klein, 1980, 1982) in which I struggled with the problem of finding an appropriate methodology to investigate my topic. This paper is the beginning of a theoretical discussion of what feminist methodology might be, rather than a detailed analysis of existing methods in the social and natural sciences and the humanities, and the reader should not expect detailed 'how-to-recipes' for feminist methodology. On principle I do not separate disciplines because for me, the implementation of feminist methodology is by definition a pursuit 'beyond the disciplines' and will, at its best, produce research that is 'transdisciplinary.'

2 Research 'on' women and the role of methodology

I want to start with the provocative statement that I think a considerable amount of the so-called feminist scholarship of previous years has not contributed to women's visibility in a feminist frame of reference but instead continued to perpetuate the dominant androcentric one. Thus it is research 'on' women rather than research 'for' women. I define research for women as research that tries to take women's needs, interests and experiences into account and aims at being instrumental in improving women's lives in one way or another. Research 'on' women, in my view, often is conducted without careful examination of the suitability of the methods used for feminist scholarship and the researchers do not state why they chose a particular method and what problems occurred during the research project. In other cases, even if the theoretical section of a research project reflects feminist views, the practical part may use methods ranging from uncritical to blatantly sexist. To say this is not necessarily to blame the researcher, as I will discuss later in this paper.

Thus, although in the last decade women scholars have produced an enormous body of knowledge on women in sociology, psychology, history, etc., much of this research consists of duplicating traditional research: knowledge about women was *added* to the knowledge about men. However, we should be aware that by choosing the 'adding-on' approach we assume that our environment emits the same signals for women and men, has the same bearing on women's and men's lives and that the answers it elicits in women are comparable to the answers it elicits in men. Such thinking represents an 'equal-rights-philosophy' which completely ignores the fact that not only was our past man-made, but that our present still is. Answers from and about women are evaluated against *male* standards. Such research perpetuates a view of women from an androcentric perspective. It also ignores the historical perspective, the fact that over millenia women and men have internalized 'feminine' and 'masculine' molds (changing through periods and cultures) in which *he* is the norm and *she* is 'the other'. Such research does not investigate women as people in our own right: it perpetuates 'Men's Studies' (Spender, 1981). If we substitute *male* research objects with *female* research objects we have changed the 'object' of the research, but not necessarily the philosophy of the researcher who might still believe in her position as the distant 'expert' who investigates a certain trait/disposition/variable out of 'objective' interest. Often this kind of research uses what has been called 'context-stripping' methods. As Mary Brown Parlee describes them: 'Concepts, environments social interactions are all simplified by methods which lift them out of their context, stripping them of the very complexity that characterizes them in the real world' (1979, p. 131).

This kind of knowledge is produced for the sake of knowledge rather than with the desire to put the knowledge into practice to induce changes. But, if what we want is research that will contribute to women's liberation, we have to scrutinize our methods more carefully to see if they are in fact congruent with our feminist principles. Thus, the claim that research on women is conducted with a feminist perspective can be made only when the methods applied take women's experiences into account. These experiences, of course, vary depending on cultural identification, ethnicity, social status, age, sexual preference, period of the research, etc.

For example, an important factor that has been ignored so far in most research on women (and men) is the phenomenon of 'faking.' As Carole Beere describes it, faking is 'to give socially desirable responses rather than honest attributes,' and does happen consciously and unconsciously (1979, p. 385). It may well be that faking is necessary for the psychological survival of many women because, without faking, reality would seem unbearable. And indeed, who among us has never faked anything, either to ourselves or to others? Thus, whereas traditional research tries to eliminate faking by using 'tricks' when asking questions, feminists should consider acknowledging and *incorporating* faking into our research methods. The significance of faking may become very important for the concept of feminist research: by accepting and taking it seriously, we accept and take ourselves seriously.[5]

Another problem that so far has not been given sufficient attention by feminist scholars is the need to become conscious about the inherent sexist (and of course racist, heterosexist, classist, ageist . . .) *biases* in the methods we use. It is interesting and encouraging to see that the myth of value-free objective science has started to crumble away, even in non-feminist circles. That is, among 'progressive' thinkers it has become almost fashionable to state one's biases in the introduction to one's research, to acknowledge the truism that the questions we ask determine the answers we get. However, equal consideration has not yet been given to inherent biases in the research methodology scholars use. For example, when measuring the attitudes of women in a selected research population with one of the various scales available, we must ask how valuable the results can be. Margrit Eichler (1980) argues against the use of these masculinity/femininity scales because they 'scientifically reinforce *man-made* sex role stereotypes about what appropriate "feminine" and "masculine" behavior is.' In my view, Eichler speaks precisely to the point when she says: 'The stereotype takes on a life of its own, becomes normative, and empirical reality is measured and evaluated against this norm. Reality has been stood on its head' (Ibid., p. 64).[6]

This idea that 'reality has been stood on its head' applies to much of the research that has been done on women adhering to the use of androcentric methods. The conceptualization of research along the lines of *differences* is the 'normal' way for us to look at a problem: Western culture has socialized us to perceive the world in terms of incompatible differences. However, formulating research along the lines of differences, thinking in dichotomies − either/or, black/white, male/female − and 'proving' in what ways the average man differs from the average woman by emphasizing differences makes us overlook important similarities and does not account for the constant interactions that go on in reality. Such research again takes as the norm the androcentric view of the world in which the circumstances of women's (and other oppressed groups') lives are seen as aberrations from this norm: 'deviant,' 'other,' the exception. Furthermore, such research cannot tell us anything about the problems of individual persons investigated in the research project. However, to recognize an individual woman's 'personal' problem as similar to many women's 'personal' problems − which renders the personal political − is one of the fundamental feminist principles.

To repeat that I believe an important goal of all feminist scholarship should be to contribute to ending the oppression of women, I think that methods which are 'context-stripping', unconscious of inherent masculinist biases, and which rely on sexist 'feminine/masculine' gender stereotypes are *not* suited for research on how women (and men!) in today's society come into being, come into holding the views they hold. Clearly, such a *process* cannot be recognized, understood and worded by 'simply' compiling data and analyzing them. New methods have to be developed that go *beyond* the traditional 'scientific' methods where hypotheses are tested by isolating variables and investigating them separately in an additive, linear fashion. We should recognize that to keep variables artificially constant, or to choose which one is the dependent and which the independent variable, reflects our needs to categorize rather than trying to convey a holistic picture of the problem researched. Not surprisingly, the research results may not be satisfactory because as they (often unconsciously) perpetuate androcentric norms, they may not reflect women's realities and thus will not be applicable to strategies for social change. They remain research 'on' women.

In the following I will briefly discuss a research project from Germany which I think is research 'for' women. As both its theory and methodology are feminist it offers strategies for change through the research process itself as well as through the 'results' and I would like to point to some criteria which in my opinion we should consider when embarking on doing feminist research.

3 An example of research 'for' women

Maria Mies, a German social scientist, reports a research project of what she calls 'action research as it was originally designed' (1978).[7] The newly emerging 'Frauenforschung' in Germany — not yet organized as separate Women's Studies programs and research institutes at universities but rather existing within traditional departments or outside academia — has rediscovered action research and adapted it to women's needs. In Cologne in 1976 women active in the women's movement, among them a group of sociologists, fought for a shelter for battered women and, together with the women who came for help, started a research project. Its aim was not only to document the women's life-histories as individuals, but also to record a collective experience of women in our society which would lead to theories and strategies for change.[8] By sharing their life-histories with each other, it was hoped that the women would be relieved from guilt and a sense of personal failure (a classic example of a consciousness-raising process) and be motivated to work for change. The project seems to have been successful: not only did the women start finding the courage to change their own situation, but they also began to recognize connections between their life and the lives of the researchers. These researchers may not have been battered in the same way, but, by living as *women* in this society, they had experienced comparable forms of humiliation.

Research methods included taping interviews, conversations and discussions between the participants, listening to them in groups of various sizes, having all of the participants (researchers and researched) describe their impressions of the ongoing process; translating life experiences into role-playing; and developing strategies for the months to come. These strategies ranged from projects for their personal lives, to the history of the whole research project and political actions including the publications of their life-histories to help other battered women and to alert the public. Thus the outcome of this investigation of a group of battered women went beyond a mere 'academic' report on the 'conditions of battered women' to be shelved and put aside but came up with suggestions for *changes* in the lives of these and other battered women.

The methods demanded *conscious subjectivity* (not to be confused with uncritical acceptance of a person's statements), which replaced the 'value-free objectivity' of traditional research. The subjective experience of each of the participating women was validated and acknowledged. Thus, the battered women were not looked upon as research 'objects' but as sisters, as mirrors of selves, as 'subjects'.[9] They in turn, as Mies states, lost their initial skepticism and fear that the 'scientists' might exploit them and their histories. This growing feeling of confidence established a fruitful sense of interrelatedness among all participants and was a learning experience for all of them. It was this method of the collective perception of their situation that lead to the formulation of theories and to action.

Marcia Westkott (1979a) defines such a dialectical relationship between the subject and object of research as *intersubjectivity*. Whenever possible, feminist methodology should allow for such intersubjectivity; this will permit the researcher constantly to compare her work with her own experiences as a woman and a scientist and to share it with the researched, who then will add their opinions to the research, which in turn might again change it.[10]

A methodology that allows for women studying women in an inter-active process without the artificial object/subject split between re-searcher and researched (which is by definition inherent in any approach to knowledge that praises its 'neutrality' and 'objectivity') will end the exploitation of women as research objects. It thus transforms a *psychology/sociology/biology OF women to a psychology/sociology/biology FOR women*. Women are at the *center* of the study and they are neither compared to nor measured against normative (male) standards. What counts are our own experiences. The theory and practice of a woman's experience is not split.

Another important aspect of feminist research is the obligation to *try* to maintain honesty between researcher and researched.[11] In the German project, it was precisely this commitment to honesty which led at first to problems, but then resulted in a new understanding of methodology. In some instances, the battered women obviously were *not* telling the truth about their past; such 'errors' were discovered when children made statements differing from those of their mothers. After the initial confusion and frustration over this discovery, the researchers realized that they should not dismiss their method of openness and honesty, but, on the contrary, that they should acknowl-edge the obvious need of these women to 'fake' as an important part of their strategy to survive. As Mies comments 'we then realized that the truth of a person cannot be asked for, is not static, but grows and develops during the course of a life time' (1978, p. 61).

It seems to me that this 'complication' — having to deal with 'rela-tive' truths rather than with Truths with a capital 'T' — illustrates perfectly how exciting and far-reaching a new methodology is that dares to open up questions where the answers might have to be recorded in an interactive rather than a linear way. What we have to do, then, in order to perceive what is happening, is to open ourselves up to using such resources as intuition, emotions and feelings both in ourselves and in those we want to investigate. In combination with our intellectual capacities for analyzing and interpreting our observations, this open ad-mission of the interaction of facts and feelings might produce a kind of scholarship that encompasses the complexity of reality better than the usual fragmented approach to knowledge. Hopefully such an approach will help us free ourselves from paralyzing stereotypes, which freedom is imperative if the move towards a liberated future is to be successful.

However, although I consider feminist action research to be a very useful method, it is evident that in many instances it clearly will not be applicable. Not every research topic is suited to action research methods. And even if we opt for it in theory, circumstances in the lives of those involved in a research project can make it impossible to work closely with each other. Thus, feminists must be flexible enough to adapt their methods to the needs of each individual research situation. I think that this ability to be flexible should be seen as one of our powers to bring about change: feminist research is not (and hopefully never will be) trapped in a set of rigidly fixed rules the way much of traditional research is. We should be free to combine whatever parts of whatever methods we think are promising for our research goals.

But unfortunately, as we know, research which admits to working for change (and thus to being 'political'), which demands conscious subjectivity and which acknowledges (women's) feelings, emotions and intuition is not taken seriously in academic circles and many a feminist scholar has her tale to tell about her research being labelled 'journalistic' and 'popular' rather than 'scholarly.'

Not being taken seriously may range from being ridiculed to being denied funds and tenure. In all cases, however, it does not provide us with the support necessary to do our work. The pressures to produce academically 'sound' work lead committed feminists into a schizoid situation: on the one hand, we develop our 'revolutionary' theories, but when it comes to doing our research, we have to use traditional 'scientific' methods to make our work acceptable. Our discontent with the final 'product' (which might then even be accused by the feminist community of being non-feminist) may be responsible for our decision to leave academia — or to conform to the existing demands and 'do' our feminism in our spare time. Put differently, I believe that the pressure to use recognized methods is one of the reasons a lot of feminist research remains research 'on' women and also accounts for the fact that up to now little work has been done on the topic of feminist methodology *per se*.

To be realistic, we must admit that today's feminist scholarship, other than within the circles of the convinced, has no considerable impact on academia at large. Mary Brown Parlee, a feminist psychologist, says in a review essay on psychology and women:

Nowhere is it possible to find evidence suggesting that the scientific importance of a feminist perspective is recognized by those in the mainstream . . . . Women psychologists work creatively to adapt existing developmental theories to accommodate reality, while male psychologists continue to study men in the usual way . . . The evidence is fairly compelling that the feminist perspective is actively excluded from the mainstream: feminist research continues to be seen as falling between the cracks of topic areas covered by major journals, departments do not perceive the need to include the psychology of women in their graduate programs, research on women and publications in journals that will publish it do not 'count' in tenure evaluations (1979, p. 129).

And Gloria Bowles (this volume) confirms this bleak picture of the ongoing exclusion of feminist scholarship for the domain of 'main-stream' — which is of course 'malestream' — Literary Criticism.

The refusal to acknowledge feminist research is not surprising for it confirms precisely what feminists are up against: androcentrism in its purest form. However, if feminists want to have our say in the generation and distribution of knowledge, what strategies should we use to be able to do what we want to do? Put differently: how do we get in power inside academia?

4 Towards paradigms for feminist research in theory and practice

In search of strategies that will bring feminists into positions of power[12] inside academia, Thomas Kuhn comes to mind. Kuhn (1962) has become world famous with his model for change and his theory might shed some light on why feminist scholars have *not yet* become power-ful and strong in academia so far.[13] He disputes the notion of *gradual* change and posits that established paradigms will be overthrown only with the triumph of new paradigms, which profoundly alter the nature of the scientific process. If we find Kuhn's theory convincing we might argue that in order to gain power and be taken seriously, Women's Studies needs to claim that we have paradigms and make them visible! But what is a paradigm? Margaret Masterman (1970) has pointed out that Kuhn himself used paradigm in at least twenty-one different ways of which 'a source of tools', 'a new way of seeing' and 'something which defines a broad sweep of reality' might come closest to our own definitions of feminist scholarship because they affirm one of the principles of feminism: to remain flexible and open for change.

Possibly, then, in describing how we are doing what we are doing, we might discover that in many instances we are already in a paradigm state — or at least close to entering it. After all, is not feminism in itself a crucial paradigm shift? Naming our paradigms could be empowering: both for ourselves and in order to gain legitimacy. Looking 'forward' and inventing, creating, changing, adapting and improving existing research methodologies will make us far more visible than working 'backwards': justifying our work to those who do not want to hear what we are doing, why we are doing it and how it differs from their approaches. Since our time and energy are limited why not use our feminist intellect[14] to work towards *our own* paradigms instead of changing theirs? Which elements of patriarchal scholarship can we use to build feminist paradigms — and thus Women's Studies as an academic discipline — in our endeavour to practise feminism within the doing of our research? How can we change and enlarge them in order to suit our need not only to collect 'facts and figures' but also to research what Mary Brown Parlee calls the 'unmeasurable': 'phenomena which cannot readily be abstracted, even conceptually, from the complex rich, and varied world of human experience — phenomena which clearly cannot be simulated in laboratory experiments' (1979, p. 128)? How do we go about researching the process: the interaction, the mutual and inseparable dependency of facts *and* feelings, figures *and* intuition, the obvious *and* the hidden, doing *and* talking, behaviors *and* attitudes? What approaches satisfy our need for 'intersubjectivity' and are flexible enough to be adapted to varying research circumstances? Which are not 'context-stripping'? Which allow for the disclosure of the self-perpetuating influences of an androcentric world, and can be translated into the range of women's varying perceptions of people's experiences?

Thinking about how to put the further development of feminist methodology into practice I see various groups of women working together. One includes feminist scholars who have been trained in traditional disciplines but are working towards the new discipline Women's Studies. They get acquainted with each other's methods, discover similarities, understand differences; in short they further a critical dialogue which might narrow the gap between them that was artificially created by our 'disciplinary' education. Certainly, our individual preferences will still vary, but the feminist working with battered women and the one working on poetry might move closer to each other. Jointly, they start developing concepts for 'transdisciplinary' research that suit their particular needs and interest. And in line with feminist thinking, the development of feminist paradigms should not be undertaken by individuals isolated within the ivory-tower system. Rather, new concepts should be created by closely interacting groups of women both inside and outside academia and – whenever possible – they should be tested in action-oriented research projects in order to translate our theories into practice.

Another group working on methodology development could consist of faculty and students who explore the topic in *courses* on feminist methodology in Women's Studies.[15] As today (in the US at least) it is possible, though difficult, to become a 'genuine' Women's Studies person by entering college in this field and leaving the university with a PhD in Women's Studies, these students need access to a methodological training which in line with the very nature of feminist research goes beyond the limits of one traditional discipline. The critical inspection of methods from the traditional disciplines and the translation of their useful parts into feminist methodology – including their application in a practical research project – would not only provide the students with highly useful skills but would help them to develop their identity as 'Women's Studies Persons.'

I believe that working for the advancement of our paradigms instead of trying to adjust our visions for doing research in order to make them acceptable to those whose paradigms still triumph today, will ultimately be more successful both in the outside world and within our own circles. Striving towards our own aims will make it possible for us to take ourselves and each other seriously: in developing 'tools' to do our work, we simultaneously provide ourselves with *and* create 'woman-powered' energy – we empower and (maybe) will get in power!

However, while pursuing such methodology development, we have to be particularly careful about the following aspects of our work. First, we have to avoid what Gloria Bowles has called the danger of creating a 'supermethodology.' I think her point is well taken when she warns feminists to be wary of methods that will become even more 'impenetrable' than the methodologies they are built upon (p. 41, this volume). Feminist methodology should not consist of piling the methodology of five or six disciplines upon one another. Not only would we make our task harder than any one else is, we might even risk paralyzing our work because our methodology could become too complex to be applicable in practice. Also, we have to write and speak in plain and comprehensible language and avoid excesses of feminist esoteric jargon which would certainly be counter-productive to our aim of making our research accessible (and useful) to as many women as possible.[16]

Second, I think we have to be patient and not expect too much too soon. We should allow ourselves time to experiment with our new approaches and we must accept failure as a constructive learning experience. Only by working with our new paradigms will we see their strengths and weaknesses. We should not be discouraged and frustrated if our emerging methodology does not work as well as we imagined it would. And because, ideally, our work is undertaken in groups, we should not underestimate the barriers that keep women from working with each other. It seems to me that we sometimes ask too much of each other, and our disappointment is enormous if our high expectations are not met. Most importantly we should be very clear about the fact that most of us who have gone through all those years of traditional education have a hard time shedding the layers of 'indoctrination' of what is declared 'good' research and 'up to standards'. Experimenting with creative thinking and innovative methods is risky. And yet it seems to me we have to try. The way we build our future will influence its outcome.

As Maria Mies points out (1978, p. 45), as feminist researchers we face the challenge that as women all of us have experienced male supremacy to some degree. But as members of a privileged group with access to education, we are in a position to work for change within academia. I agree with her that we should perceive this 'double-consciousness' of female academics as a methodological and political opportunity which gives us an edge over male scholars. In a time of financial cuts and threats to feminists inside and outside academia we must make ourselves visible and known to each other which in the context of this paper includes publishing 'how' we did our research and what problems we faced while doing it.

All of us who work in Women's Studies are excited about the new 'what's' and the new 'why's' of our field. I suggest we get equally excited about the new 'how's'. Since without appropriate methodologies we cannot do what we want to do, we should acknowledge their importance and concentrate on their development. They are here, partly distorted by past method-makers, partly hidden from us because we don't know our own heritage, and partly suppressed within ourselves. But they are starting to emerge — not as easily as Athene emerged from Zeus' head, because it is *we* who have to do the work and it is not only our heads that are involved but our whole beings.

Notes

1 Many people read the earlier draft of this paper and gave valuable suggestions and comments. I would particularly like to thank Gloria Bowles, Sandy Coyner, Maresi Nerad, Nina Nordgren, Sharon Garnica, Dorothy Brown, and Kristen Wenzel. And my special thanks go to Susan Chisholm who tried hard to translate my Swiss English into American English.

2 Some exceptions are Marcia Westkott (1979a), Margrit Eichler (1980) and Shulamit Reinharz (1979), and of course the contributions by Du Bois, Mies, Epstein Jayaratne, Reinharz and Stanley and Wise in this volume.

3 For a definition of 'academic' from a feminist perspective, see Gloria Bowles's and Sandy Coyner's articles in this volume.

4 Feminists are not the only group that proposes to work for change. Male thinkers, e.g., the members of the Frankfurt Schule and philosopher Paul Feyerabend, have been claiming to do this too. However, theirs is a wish to transform the society of 'man' without changing the paradigm that 'man-is-the-norm.' A feminist approach to knowledge, however, defines as an indispensable prerequisite women's right to a place among those who create and transmit knowledge on *our* terms and meeting *our* needs. Such an approach, I think, makes feminist research distinctly different from research undertaken by so-called progressive male thinkers who continue to operate from within an androcentric frame of reference.

5 I agree with Gloria Bowles who has criticized the term 'faking,' noting that it clearly blames the victim and that we should exchange it for a less accusing word.

6 Margrit Eichler extends her critique to the concept of androgeny because 'the androgeny score is derived from the masculinity and femininity scores' (1980, p. 69) and continues, 'In other words, the concept of androgeny itself reinforces the notion that sex-linked traits do, in fact, exist' (Ibid., p. 70).

7 Action research (*Aktionsforschung*) as defined by one of its founders (Kurt Lewin, 1978) consists of

comparatively investigating the conditions and the effects of various forms of social action and is research that will lead to action. At least for a certain period of time the researcher has to give up the distance to his or her research object and must assume a consciously interactive position with the research object [translation mine].

According to Maria Mies, during recent years male-dominated German scholarship has redirected action research and shifted its focus from social outreach in the community back to the university. She states that: 'Action research thus has become acceptable to traditional scholarship but in its self-confinement to "value-free" dialogue without working for change, and its renunciation of supporting dialectical processes of change, it has almost totally lost its liberating impulse' (1978, p. 43; translation mine).

8   The English version of Maria Mies's paper is included in this volume; in the original publication of *Theories of Women's Studies*, it appeared in volume II (1981), Women's Studies Program, University of California, Berkeley.

9   Sandy Coyner has pointed out to me that kings (and psychologists!), too, talk about 'subjects.' It should be clear from the rest of this paper that I use 'subject' in the grammatical sense of the term, i.e., putting researcher and researched on the same level as actors (whereas an 'object' would constitute something one acts upon). However, as 'sub-ject' has a dominant/domineering connotation, we should look for a more egalitarian term and possibly might want to borrow the term 'member' from ethnomethodology.

10 Again, others — men — have already worked with a perspective that credits the researched with their own experience. Paulo Freire's (1970) approach, for instance, is based on people's experiences and interactions with their environment. However, *vis-à-vis* women, the same critique holds as it does against other nonconformist male thinkers: Freire does not depart from taking androcentricity as the norm and consequently, feminists need to do the work for women that he did for men.

11 This avowal to be frank and honest with each other contradicts the practice of traditional social science where, under the pretext of eliciting 'objective, unbiased' answers, it is still acceptable to name false reasons to the participants of a survey.

12 Since I mention 'power' so frequently, I should make it clear that I do not wish feminists to have power to dominate others, but to use it collectively for ending the oppression of women. This is Florence Howe's definition of power (1975). Whether to have power within academia is at all desirable would be the topic of another paper. Feminist academics, it is argued, cannot but become co-opted and/or lose our energy for social change and/or be for sure kicked out in those rare cases where we *do* stay radical: we simply cannot, it is said, remain revolutionaries within the confines of present academia (see, for example, Freeman, 1979). I obviously haven't given up hope (yet) that some of us can . . . moreover, I think that academia's impact on society is far too important (and too dangerous) to be left to those perpetuating Men's Studies from their androcentric perspective.

13   For an in-depth discussion of Kuhn and the implications of his theory for Women's Studies, see Sandy Coyner's article, this volume, whose demand for autonomous Women's Studies reflects my own ideas.

14   I am indebted to Karen Davis for this term which I heard for the first time from her in our class, 'Theories of Women's Studies,' UC Berkeley, Fall 1979. I think it is a very special and promising one for feminist scholars.

15   The Women's Studies Program at UC Berkeley offers a course on feminist methodology in the humanities and a course on feminist social science methods. Together with a class on 'Theories of Women's Studies,' such methodology courses should form the core of 'discipline-structuring' courses in Women's Studies. I think they should be mandatory for anyone who aspires to be a feminist scholar.

16   Many thanks to Dale Spender and Jane Cholmeley for stimulating and challenging discussions on this subject.

References

Beere, Carole (1979), *Women and Women's Issues: A Handbook of Tests and Measures*, San Francisco, Jossey-Bass.

Daly, Mary (1973), *Beyond God The Father*, Boston, Beacon Press.

Duelli Klein, Renate (1980), *Between Progress and Backlash: Exploring the Attitudes of Undergraduate Women at UC Berkeley Towards Feminism, the Women's Movement and Women's Studies*, Women's Studies Program, Berkeley.

Duelli Klein, Renate (1982), 'Women College Students and Feminism,' *The Radical Teacher*, vol. 21, pp. 12-13.

Eichler, Margrit (1980), *The Double Standard: A Feminist Critique of Feminist Social Science*, New York, St Martin's Press.

Freeman, Jo (1979), 'The Feminist Scholar,' *Quest*, vol. 5, no. 1, pp. 26-36.

Freire, Paulo (1970), *Pedagogy of the Oppressed*, New York, Seabury Press.

Howe, Florence (1975), *Women and the Power to Change*, New York, McGraw-Hill.

Kuhn, Thomas (1962), *The Structure of Scientific Revolutions*, University of Chicago Press.

Lewin, Kurt (1948), *Die Lösung Sozialer Konflikte (Resolving Social Conflicts)*, New York, Harper & Row.

Masterman, Margaret (1970), 'The Nature of Paradigms,' in Imre Lakatos and Alan Musgrave (eds), *Criticism and the Growth of Knowledge*, Cambridge University Press, pp. 59-91.

Mies, Maria (1978), 'Methodische Postulate zur Frauenforschung — dargestellt am Beispiel der Gewalt gegen Frauen' ('Methodological Postulates for Women's Studies — exemplified through a project dealing with violence against women'), *Beiträge zur Feministischen Theorie und Praxis*, vol. 1, no. 1, pp. 41-63.

Parlee, Mary Brown (1979), 'Psychology and Women,' *Signs*, vol. 5, no. 1, Autumn pp. 121-33.

Reinharz, Shulamit (1979), *On Becoming a Social Scientist*, San Francisco, Jossey-Bass.

Spender, Dale (ed.) (1981), *Men's Studies Modified: The Impact of Feminism on the Academic Disciplines*, Oxford and New York, Pergamon Press.

Westkott, Marcia (1979a), 'Feminist Criticism in the Social Sciences,' *Harvard Educational Review*, vol. 49, no. 4, November, pp. 422-30.

Westkott, Marcia (1979b), 'Feminist Criticism of the Social Sciences,' presentation given at the First National Women's Studies Association Conference, Lawrence, Kansas.

8

Passionate scholarship: notes on values, knowing and method in feminist social science[1]

Barbara Du Bois

I

Science is *not* 'value-free'; it cannot be. Science is made by scientists, and both we and our science-making are shaped by our culture. Science moves within culture, and only slowly expands the limits of its own vision. Social scientists are certainly no more able than others to pursue inquiry free of the assumptions and values of their own societies. In fact, the closer our subject matter to our own life and experience, the more we can probably expect our own beliefs about the world to enter into and shape our work — to influence the very questions we pose, our conception of how to approach those questions, and the interpretations we generate from our findings.

Our models of inquiry, of science-making, are also models of reality: they reflect how we conceptualize what is, what is to be known, and how it is to be known. The beliefs we hold about the nature of reality and of human beings are ways in which we organize and make meaning out of experience and information; beliefs, too, are ways of knowing. This history of science is a long history of organizing information, observation and experience. And that history contains many instances of so-called 'scientific' fact or knowledge being proven later to have been little more than the dominant beliefs of the culture itself.[2]

Science and the science-making tend to serve and reinforce dominant social values and conceptions of reality — as much as and often more than they serve to challenge them; the history of social science theory on women is a history of this phenomenon. And the science-making that is in fact based on different values than those prevailing in the culture at a given time, and thus attempts to discover, explore and explain different realities, tends to be ignored — or attacked as 'unscientific.' This judgment can frequently be understood for what it really is: not in fact a judgment about science, but a charge of heresy.

II

The 'power' of an equation, formula or theory lies in its ability to explain, to account fully for the phenomenon being studied. In this sense, the power of social science theory about women has been and is still very low indeed. As psychologist Naomi Weisstein (1971) bluntly put it several years ago, psychology has very little to tell us about what women are really like. And that's many years after Freud said his last words on the subject — which were, essentially, that femininity was still a 'riddle', and that we'd probably do best to turn to the poets for the answers![3] (And I don't think he meant *women* poets — although they undoubtedly do have more to tell us about women than traditional psychology and social science have had.)

We have yet no psychology of women, no sociology of women, no anthropology of women, no real history of women, no thorough and coherent social science theory about women. Through feminist scholarship we are now beginning to learn about women and women's lives in all these areas.[4] But in all these fields of social science — and in at least some of the humanities — art history is a striking example — what we have had up to now is theory that purports to speak of human beings, of people — but theory that is in fact grounded in, derived from, based on and reinforcing of the experience, perceptions and beliefs of men. The male perspective throughout all our modern disciplines is overriding, and, until very recently, with the beginnings of feminist scholarship, unquestioned, axiomatic. Even when it has been women who have been studied (and in psychology, at least, unlike some of the social sciences, women have been very much studied!), the perspective and the modes of study have remained masculine, those of the dominant culture — with all its myths and beliefs and prescriptions about who women are, who and what women should be; and with all its apparent inability or unwillingness to listen to women say what we really experience, what we really see, who we really are.

The androcentric or phallocentric fallacy about women in virtually all of social science has been this: The 'person' has been considered to be *male*, and the female, the woman, has been defined in terms, not of what she *is*, but of what she is not. Woman has been defined as '*not-a-man*.' And things female have tended to be seen — in sociology, anthropology, history, as well as in psychology — as anomalies, deviations from the male norm and ideal of the 'person' (viz. our language, with all of humanity subsumed under the pronoun 'he').

The questions a science poses, though they strive toward the unknown, must always refer to, be based in, the known. When distorted conceptions of reality are the ground of science, distorted perceptions of reality will be the fruits of science. The androcentric perspective in social science has rendered women not only unknown, but virtually *unknowable*.

III

I emphasize that this has to do not only with the substance of particular theories, but with the very conventions of science-making. It has to do with what is considered worthy of study, worth knowing, and what is not, and with how it is studied, how it is known.

For all that we may talk about 'a' scientific method (and by this is most often meant the experimental method that obtains in some of the physical sciences), there are in fact a number of methods and several different phases of science-making — and methods differ, or should, according to the question at issue, the development of knowledge in that area, and the phase of science-making involved.

The different phases of science-making involve the posing of the problem or question, then observation, naming, description, explanation, and eventually, in some fields, prediction and control of the phenomena under study (though I am convinced that we leave the domain of science altogether when we start talking about 'control' of human beings). These 'phases' are of course not strictly linear in relationship, but rather circular, interactive, and reflexive. They constitute a *process*. To some extent (especially in qualitative research) they can and do proceed together.[5] The values and epistemology of the researcher inform each phase of the process, and, contrary to general ideas of strict scientific neutrality, the process of science-making in fact involves interpretation, theory-making, and thus values, in each of its phases. 'Naming' is probably the first order of interpretation in science — the naming of the question, the naming of one's observations, and so on — and naming, the capacity to name what we see, is, as a matter of language, inherently expressive of culture.

In science as in society, the power of naming is at least two-fold: naming defines the quality and value of that which is named — and it also denies reality and value to that which is never named, never uttered. That which has no name, that for which we have no words or concepts, is rendered mute and invisible: powerless to inform or transform our consciousness of our experience, our understanding, our vision; powerless to claim its own existence.

This has been the situation of women in our world. And this silence, this invisibility, has been confirmed and perpetuated by the ways in which social science has looked at — and not seen — women. But in this silence and invisibility is to be found the reality of women, of our lives, our experience, our vision — and the potential for new understandings and constructions of ourselves and our world. To address women's lives and experience *in their own terms*, to create theory grounded in the actual experience and language of women, is the central agenda for feminist social science and scholarship.

For this endeavor we need, we require, woman-centered scholarship. The goal, of course, in all the fields of science, is ultimately to be able to see, describe and understand the world and human experience in universal terms. But what has so far been called 'universal' in vision and knowledge has in fact been male science and scholarship — and the knowledge it has produced is seriously, fundamentally flawed for that very reason.[6] Any 'universal' understanding of human beings and human society that leaves women out and, when it brings us in, renders us unknowable even to ourselves, is not only inaccurate but mystifying, damaging. Science and scholarship that make visible the experience of women, and that 'reinterpret knowledge in terms of that experience,' is, as Adrienne Rich says, 'the most important task of thinking' (1977a, p. xxiii).

Yet, even changing the focus of inquiry and study to women is not likely to reveal us to ourselves any more clearly if we are using the same old lenses to look through.[7] The agenda and the conventions of our science-making are as important a focus for our scrutiny and creativity as is the actual substance of our inquiry.[8]

IV

What I'd like to be able to do now, of course, would be to propose some radical new method for feminist social science. But I do not in fact hold that there is or ought to be *a* distinctively feminist scientific method. I do believe that feminism empowers and requires us to think very differently about the purposes and methods of social science than we have been able to do within the confines of hegemony of androcentric science and worldview. What is generally considered scientific in social science inquiry reflects, expresses and therefore perpetuates patriarchal conceptions and values about the world in both purposes and methods. Thus feminist social science and scholarship offer the possibility of necessary, vital and vitalizing departures from the norms and functions, both scientific and political, of traditional social science.

The persistent debate over the scientific value of qualitative versus quantitative methods in social science actually obscures some basic questions that need to be raised in conjunction with all inquiry. If the starting point in science-making is the posing of a meaningful problem or question, then what is scientific in method is to address that question in the manner and terms most consonant with its substance, and most likely to lead to relevant 'answers.' The first criterion involves philosophical and epistemological issues, the second primarily methodological considerations. Further, at different stages in the development of knowledge in a given area, the purposes of inquiry — and therefore its methods — will properly differ. At one point it will be necessary and appropriate to identify and describe phenomena; then to generate concepts, propositions, hypotheses; at another stage, to refine these, test them, relate them to findings in different areas, and so on. What is scientific at one stage will not necessarily be so at another.

I see feminist social science and scholarship as being at the earliest stages of its science-making in all areas, and particularly about women. Across all the disciplines of social science and many of the humanities, feminist scholars are engaged in almost an archaeological endeavor — that of discovering and uncovering the actual facts of women's lives and experience, facts that have been hidden, inaccessible, suppressed, distorted, misunderstood, ignored. This is the early work of observation, naming and description that prepares the ground for theory-making. And in this early work we must first, quite literally, learn to *see*. To see what is *there*; not what we've been taught is there, not even what we might wish to find, but what is. We literally *cannot see women* through traditional science and theory.[9] Learning to do so is no simple task; it is not simple even for feminists. The distorting perceptual and conceptual lenses of patriarchy are the lenses we have all been taught to look through; removing them is slow, sometimes painful and frightening as it opens our eyes to reality-without-explanation; and it is often startling. It is also a *communal*, not an individual, task.[10] As each one of us removes those lenses and is able to say what she sees, the world opens up for all of us: things can begin to make sense. And our *description* of what we see needs to be careful, detailed, rigorous. It is here that we make visible the realities of our experience, here that we begin to elucidate the inherent patterns of significance that can lead to the making of truly grounded theory about women.[11]

We are also at the stage where our work needs to be *conceptually oriented*, directed to the *generation* of concepts. The languages and theories we have to work with still lack the very concepts by which the experience and reality of women's lives can be named, described and understood. Our work needs to generate words, concepts, that refer to, that spring from, that are firmly and richly grounded in the actual experiencing of women. And this demands *methods* of inquiry that open up our seeing and our thinking, our conceptual frameworks, to new perceptions that actually derive from women's experience.

We must also make our *processes* accessible to each other — our work processes, our decision-making processes, our analytic processes — so we can learn from and with each other; so *we* don't mystify _ d thus rigidify *our* science-making; and so we can provide each other continually with validation and encouragement and support for exploring the different cosmos of value and reality which our individual and shared intuitions and cognitions suggest.

In learning to see, name and describe the experience and realities of women, we learn to see and conceptualize *complexly*, *contextually*. We must become not only accepting of but eager for the increasing complexity that we discover as we look at ourselves and our world.[12] To be open to this complexity and to see things in context means to move out of the realms of discourse and logic that rely on linear and hierarchical conceptions of reality, on dualistic models of human nature and intercourse, on dichotomous modes of thought, discourse and analysis.

Dichotomy, duality, linearity, fixity: these are not the properties of nature nor of human life and experiencing. They are the properties of a learned mode of thought, a way of seeing and knowing that casts reality into rigid, oppositional and hierarchical categories. This model of reality has shaped our conceptions of the world and of science. Scientific method is *not* exclusively or even primarily the method of the erector set or the method of taking things apart and putting them back together in order to understand them.[13] Our scientific methods, as women, as feminists, require seeing things *as they are*: whole, entire, complex. Our work requires that we see things in context, that we understand and explain our eventful, complex reality within and as a part of its matrix. It is only within its matrix that experience, reality, can be known.

And this matrix *includes the knower*.

V

Traditional Western science states that the observer and the observed, the knower and the known, are separate, that the one must not 'contaminate' the other if true objectivity is to be attained. Feminist scholarship reveals a different animating assumption: that the knower and the known are of the same universe, that they are *not* separable.[14]

In its conceptions of science and knowing, our society has embraced and reified the values of objective knowledge, expertise, neutrality, separateness, and *opposed* them to the values of subjective knowledge, understanding, art, communion, craft and experience. The science that works on the basis of these dichotomies supports oppositional and hierarchical notions of the 'natural order' and at the same time makes the statement that it is value-free science. To polarize the subjective and the objective falsifies experience and reality, *and* the possibility of knowing them. Objectivity and subjectivity are modes of knowing, analysis, interpretation, understanding. They are not independent of each other, and should not be.

As women, we inhabit our world with a 'double consciousness.'[15] We are in and of our society but in important ways also not 'of' it. We see and think in the terms of our culture; we have been trained in these terms, shaped to them; they have determined not only the ways in which we have been able to perceive and understand large events, but even the ways in which we have been able to perceive, structure and understand our most intimate experiencing. Yet we have always another consciousness, another potential language within us, available to us. We are aware, however inchoately, of the reality of our own perceptions and experience; we are aware that this reality has often been not only unnamed but unnameable; we understand that our invisibility and silence hold the germs of both madness and power, of both dissolution and creation . . . .

We are observer and observed, subject and object, knower and known. When we take away the lenses of androcentrism and patriarchy, what we have left is our own eyes, ourselves, and each other. *We* are the instruments of observation and understanding; *we* are the namers, the interpreters of our lives. To try to work without this instrument and this language is to do nothing other than what most of science has tried to do: pretend to leave the self[16] and the valuing process out of science-making, and thus perpetuate the image of science as the objective observer of fixed reality, the neutral seeker after an external and objectifiable truth.

Traditional science reacts to and builds on a consensual construction of reality; that construction of reality is seen as given, real, graspable. It is to be known, from the outside, objectively, neutrally, impersonally. Feminism withdraws consent from the patriarchal construction of reality. We do not accept it as given, inevitable, or real. Thus feminist science-making withdraws consent from given constructions of what is to be known and how. We reject the dichotomies between science and the maker of science, between observation and experience; we reject the idea that the task of science is to examine a given, fixed reality of which we are observers, not participants.[17] The challenge for feminist science will be to see, name, describe and explain without recreating these dichotomies, without falling into the old pattern of objectifying experience, processual reality, by withdrawing from it and ourselves to a position of assumed neutrality.[18] Our science-making, rooted in, animated by and expressive of our values, empowered by community, is *passionate scholarship*: necessary heresy.

There is no question that feminist scientists and scholars will continue to be charged with bias, advocacy, subjectivity, ideologizing, and so on. We can expect this; we can even welcome it. If our work is not in some way threatening to the established order, we're on the wrong track.[19]

But it is harder when we question ourselves about our own honesty, responsibility and sanity in our work. I'd be surprised if there is anyone who is doing feminist scholarship who hasn't at some point wondered whether she were being honest and 'objective' in her work, whether she weren't perhaps 'making it all up,' whether she were being manipulative or biased in her design, her reporting, her interpretations. I know my own work and thinking have been fraught with these questions, and will continue to be. They are natural; they express the fertile conflict between the ways we've been taught to see, know and judge reality, and the beginnings of a different cosmos of values about what reality is and how it can be known. Our doubts and uncertainties are not only natural, they are even desirable. They keep us honest, for one thing — by obliging us continually to question our purposes, our motives, our values, our integrity, our scholarship. And they make for better science, in fact — for what I call the 'fertile conflict' our uncertainties express holds the beginnings of the *synthesis* of subjectivity and objectivity that is the source of intellectual power and responsibility — and truth.

Those who have most vividly illumined our vision of the world, whether in the natural sciences, the social sciences, the humanities or the arts, understand the meaning of what Michael Polanyi (1958) calls 'personal knowledge,' the relationship of the knower to the known, the 'passionate participation of the knower in the act of knowing.' Passionate scholarship in no way means mushiness or a focus on our own navels; it demands rigor, precision and responsibility in the highest degree. And it makes possible a common endeavor of science-making that can actually engage the conjunctions among values, purposes, methods and modes of knowing — that can begin to integrate subjectivity with objectivity, substance with process, passion with responsibility, and the knower with the known.

May 1979

Notes

1 This paper was presented at the First National Convention of the National Women's Studies Association, in the panel on 'Feminist Research and Traditional Methodology,' 1 June 1979, Lawrence, Kansas. An earlier version was presented at the Annual Meeting of the American Association for the Advancement of Science, January 1979.

2 See, for example, Williams (1977) who describes some of the myths by

which men have characterized women.

3 See Freud (1933), especially pp. 116 and 135.

4 Among many others: in psychology, Miller (1973, 1976) and Williams (1977); in sociology, Millman and Kanter (1975) and Safalios-Rothschild (1972); in anthropology, Reiter (1975); in history, Lerner (1971, 1972, 1977a); in art and art history, Harris and Nochlin (1976), Chicago (1977) and Lippard (1976); in literature Moers (1977) and Donovan (1975).

5 See Glaser and Strauss (1970).

6 The need for woman-centered science is noted by a number of feminist scholars. See Lerner (1977b), Miller (1973) and Reiter (1975).

7 See Carlson (1972).

8 For further thoughts on 'Feminist method' in the social sciences, see Du Bois (1976), especially Chapters II and V in which I propose 'educative' method as an approach to research with and about women, and as a way of developing grounded theory about women.

9 I thank Leigh Star for helping me 'see' this point.

10 Adrienne Rich (1977a), speaks of the importance of community in feminist work and scholarship;

> if, in trying to join the common world of men, the professions molded by a primarily masculine consciousness, we split ourselves off from the common life of women and deny our female heritage and identity in our work, we lose touch with our real powers and with the essential condition for all truly realized work: community (p. xviii).

And Miller (1973) notes that the

> community of women . . . advances and fosters both attempts at knowledge and a personal conviction about the content and methods of getting at knowledge. It creates a new sense of connection between knowledge, work and personal life (p. 136).

11 For more on grounded theory, see Glaser and Strauss in Filstead (1970).

12 'There is no "the truth," "a truth" — truth is not one thing, or even a system. It is an increasing complexity', Rich (1977b).

13 For further discussion of 'agentic' and 'phallocentric' styles in the conceptions of research, see Carlson (1972) and Helson (1972).

14 This understanding animates advanced experimental and theoretical work in contemporary physics, too, of course — as it has, for thousands of years, the thought and experience of the mystics, eastern and western. See, for example, Zukav (1979) and Capra (1975).

15 For discussion of Du Bois's concept of 'double consciousness' in relation to women scholars and their work, see Rohrlich-Leavitt, Sykes and Weatherford (1975).

16 Warren's comments on the self of the research in the research process are worth noting. See Warren (1977).

17 Refer to note 10.
18 I thank Heather Wishik and Campbell Harvey for our lively and productive discussion of these aspects of feminist science.
19 Ruth Bleier (1978) notes:

> No doubt, as feminist scholars reconstruct prehistory and history, as they offer their theories about biology and social behavior, they will continue to be accused of promoting their own bias. It is a pity that the sensitivity to bias comes so late (p. 162).

And Howard Becker (1970) observes that it is in fact not possible to do research that is 'uncontaminated by personal and political sympathies,' and that in research with political implications 'the accusation of bias in a fellow-researcher arises, in one important class of cases, when the research gives credence, in any serious way, to the perspective of the subordinate group in some hierarchical relationship' (pp. 15-17). Becker emphasizes that, 'Our problem is to make sure that, whatever point of view we take, our research meets the standards of good scientific work, that our unavoidable sympathies do not render our results invalid' (p. 23).

References

Becker, Howard (1970), 'Whose Side Are We On?,' in W.J. Filstead (ed.), *Qualitative Methodology; Firsthand Involvement with the Social World*, Chicago, Markham.

Bleier, Ruth (1978), 'Bias in Biological and Human Sciences: Some Comments,' *Signs*, vol. 4, no. 1, p. 162.

Capra, Fritjof (1975), *The Tao of Physics*, Boulder, Shambala.

Carlson, Rae (1972), 'Understanding Women: Implications for Personality Theory and Research,' *Journal of Social Issues*, vol. 28, no. 2, pp. 17-32.

Chicago, Judy (1977), *Through the Flower*, New York, Doubleday.

Donovan, Josephine (ed.) (1975), *Feminist Literary Criticism: Explorations in Theory*, University of Kentucky Press.

Du Bois, Barbara (1976), 'Feminist Perspectives of Psychotherapy and the Psychology of Women: An Exploratory Study in the Development of Clinical Theory,' doctoral dissertation, Cambridge, Massachusetts, Harvard University.

Freud, Sigmund (1933), 'Femininity,' *New Introductory Lectures on Psychoanalysis*, transl. by James Strachey, New York, W.W. Norton.

Glaser, B. and Strauss, A. (1970), 'Discovery of Substantive Theory: A Basic Strategy Underlying Qualitative Research,' in W. Filstead (ed.), *Qualitative Methodology: Firsthand Involvement with the Social World*, Chicago, Markham, pp. 289-90.

Harris, Ann S. and Nochlin, Linda (1976), *Women Artists: 1550-1950*, New York, Knopf.

Helson, Ravenna (1972), 'The Changing Image of the Career Woman,' *Journal of*

Social Issues, vol. 28, no. 2, pp. 33-46.

Lerner, Gerda (1971), *The Woman in American History*, Reading, Addison-Wesley.

Lerner, Gerda (1972), *Black Women in White America*, New York, Pantheon.

Lerner, Gerda (1977a), *The Female Experience: An American Documentary*, Indianapolis, Bobbs-Merrill.

Lerner, Gerda (1977b), 'The Challenge of Women's History,' lecture delivered at the Aspen Institute for Humanistic Studies.

Lippard, Lucy (ed.) (1976), *From the Center: Feminist Essays on Women's Art*, New York, Dutton.

Miller, Jean B. (1973), *Psychoanalysis and Women*, New York, Penguin.

Miller, Jean B. (1976), *Toward a New Psychology of Women*, Boston, Beacon Press.

Millman, Marcia and Kanter, Rosabeth M. (1975), *Another Voice: Feminist Perspectives on Social Life and Social Science*, New York, Anchor/Doubleday.

Moers, Ellen (1977), *Literary Women: The Great Writers*, New York, Anchor/Doubleday.

Polanyi, Michael (1958), *Personal Knowledge: Towards a Post-Critical Philosophy*, University of Chicago Press.

Reiter, Rayna (ed.) (1975), *Toward an Anthropology of Women*, London, New York, Monthly Review Press.

Rich, Adrienne (1977a), 'Forward: Conditions for Work: The Common World of Women,' in S. Ruddick and P. Daniels (eds), *Working it Out*, New York, Pantheon, p. xxiii.

Rich, Adrienne (1977b), 'Women and Honor: Some Notes on Lying,' Pittsburgh, Motheroot/Pittsburgh Women Writers.

Rohrlich-Leavitt, Ruby, Sykes, Barbara and Weatherford, Elizabeth (1975), 'Aboriginal Women: Male and Female Anthropological Perspectives,' in Rayna Reiter (ed.), *Toward an Anthropology of Women*, London, New York, Monthly Review Press.

Safalios-Rothschild, Constantina (1972), *Toward a Sociology of Women*, Massachusetts, Xerox College.

Warren, Carol A.B. (1977), 'Fieldwork in the Gay World: Issues in Phenomentological Research,' *Journal of Social Issues*, vol. 33, no. 4, pp. 93-107.

Weisstein, Naomi (1971), 'Psychology Constructs the Female,' in V. Gornick and B. Moran (eds), *Women in Sexist Society: Studies in Power and Powerlessness*, New York, Basic Books, p. 135.

Williams, Juanita (1977), *Psychology of Women: Behavior in a Biosocial Context*, New York, W.W. Norton.

Zukav, Gary (1979), *The Dancing Wu Li Masters*, New York, Morrow.

9
Towards a methodology for feminist research

Maria Mies

New wine must not be poured into old bottles.

I Introduction

After more than a decade centered on mobilization, consciousness-raising and struggles on issues such as equal rights, abortion laws, rape and violence against women, the women's movement is still gaining momentum, drawing more and more women into its vortex. This quantitative expansion, particularly in the rich capitalist countries, however, has also given rise to specific problems. There seems to be an ever-rising wave of rebellion against patriarchy and sexism, accompanied by expectations of women's solidarity and emancipation. But this rebellion, these expectations, have not yet led to a clear understanding of the relationship between women's exploitation and oppression (sexism), on the one hand, and the overall class exploitation and oppression of workers and peasants. Many women who have been in the movement since its beginnings feel increasingly worried about this lack of analysis and direction. One of the outcomes of this uneasiness is the recent emphasis on feminist research and theoretical work. In many universities in Europe and the USA feminist women have been able to set up centers for Women's Studies. In a number of disciplines women have formed feminist groups or associations. In West Germany, for example, feminist social scientists formed an association for 'Feminist Theory and Practice in Social Sciences'. Similar associations were started on other disciplines as well as on an inter-disciplinary base. During the summer vacations, so-called Women's Summer Universities in Berlin are being organized which attract thousands of women. This keen interest in the study of sexism and in women's history, women's anthropology, etc., and the endeavors to establish a feminist theory of society, has led to a spate of literature, books, journals, pamphlets on women's issues. Not only are there many feminist publishing houses and bookshops exclusively run by women, but the general bookshops have discovered women as a new market and invariably reserve some shelves for women's literature. This new theoretical interest, in itself an encouraging sign of the deepening of the movement, has thrown up a number of theoretical questions for which no ready-made answer is available in the existing system of academic work. The main problem that Women's Studies face on all fronts is the male bias or androcentrism that prevails in practically all disciplines, in most theoretical work done through centuries of scientific quest. This androcentrism is manifested not only in the fact that universities and research institutions are still largely male domains, but more subtly in the choice of areas of research, in research policies, theoretical concepts and particularly in research methodology. The inadequacy of predominant research methods was first painfully felt by feminist historians, who tried to reconstruct women's history. Women's contribution to history is hardly recorded in the history books. Within a framework of science that is based on written records only, this means that their contribution does not exist for as far as historical science goes. It is this experience which has given rise to the expression: the 'hidden women'. The virtual exclusion of women, of their lives, work and struggles from the bulk of research can be adequately epitomized in Bertolt Brecht's phrase: 'One does not see those who are in the dark.' When women now try to bring light into this darkness, they encounter specific methodological problems, because the prominent social science research methodology, i.e., mainly the quantitative survey method, is itself not free from androcentric bias. The present paper, therefore, tries to address itself to the methodological problems of feminist social scientists who want to study women's issues. Its aim is to lay down some methodological guidelines, which may be further discussed and developed into a new methodological approach consistent with the political aims of the women's movement.[1]

It is the outcome of my experience as a social scientist and a participant in the women's movement.

Criticism of the dominant quantitative social science research methodology started earlier than the women's movement. My first doubts about the scientific relevance and ethical justification of this methodology were raised when I was working as a teacher and researcher in a Third World country. Here I realized that the research situation as such, due to colonialism and neo-colonialism, was a situation of clear dominance between research subject and research object, which tended to lead to distorted data.[2] In the USA, however, criticism of the established social science research methodology came up in connection with the protest movement against American involvement in Latin America and Southeast Asia. Scholars like Horowitz (1976), Wolf and Jorgenson (1970), and Huizer (1973) raised their voices against this kind of research as a tactical tool in the 'Counter-insurgency-and-containment-of-Communism' strategy of the USA. The emphasis of their criticism was on political and ethical questions.

In West Germany, at about the same time (1967-72), the positivist and functionalist theory of society, propagated throughout the Anglo-Saxon world, and the quantitative analytical research methodology were being attacked by the theoreticians of the Frankfurt school: Horkheimer, Adorno, Fromm, Habermas, *et al.*, who evolved the critical theory of society from a dialectical and historical point of view. The focus of their criticism was the claim of value neutrality and the structural separation between theory and practice of positivism. They attacked the scientific irrelevance, the elitism and inherent class bias of this approach and tried to revive the emancipatory potential which social theory had had in the eighteenth century, the beginning of the bourgeois epoch. The criticism of 'Critical Theory,' however, remained confined to the magic circle of academic institutions. It did not reach the working masses and thus reproduced the structural separation between theory and practice, characteristic of the capitalist mode of production. In the mid-1970s an effort was made to bridge this gap by the proponents of action research, first evolved by Lewin (1948).

The thoughts which follow on a methodology for feminist research grew out of the debates on these three waves of criticism against positivism as the dominant social science theory and its accompanying methodology. Therefore, they will repeat many points which are already known. However, they are the outcome of my involvement in the women's movement and of my experience in action research projects. They are not to be understood as prescriptions to be followed dogmatically, but as an invitation for methodological experiment and innovation. The assumption underlying these guidelines is the following: *there is a contradiction between the prevalent theories of social science and methodology and the political aims of the women's movement*. If Women's Studies is to be made into an instrument of women's liberation, we cannot uncritically use the positivist, quantitative research methodology. If Women's Studies uses these old methodologies, they will again be turned into an instrument of repression. New wine should not be poured into old bottles.

> THESIS: When women begin to change their situation of exploitation and oppression, then this change will have consequences for the research areas, theories, concepts and methodology of studies that focus on women's issues.

'Women's Studies' means more than the fact that women have now been discovered as a 'target group' for research, or that an increasing number of women scholars and students are taking up women's issues. If Women's Studies is to contribute to the cause of women's emancipation, then women in the academic field have to use their scholarship and knowledge towards this end. If they consciously do so they will realize that their own existence as *women* and *scholars* is a contradictory one. As women, they are affected by sexist oppression together with other women, and as scholars they share the privileges of the (male) academic elite.

Out of this split existence grows a double consciousness which must be taken into account when we think about a new methodology. Women scholars have been told to look at their contradictory existence, i.e., at their subjective being as women as an obstacle and a handicap to 'pure' and 'objective' research. Even while studying women's questions they were advised to suppress their emotions, their subjective feelings of involvement and identification with other women in order to produce 'objective' data.

The methodological principle of a value-free, neutral, uninvolved approach, of an hierarchical, non-reciprocal relationship between research subject and research object — certainly the decisive methodological postulate of positivist social science research — drives women

scholars into a schizophrenic situation. If they try to follow this postulate, they have constantly to repress, negate or ignore their own experience of sexist oppression and have to strive to live up to the so-called
'rational' standards of a highly competitive, male-dominated academic
world.

Moreover, this methodological principle does not help us to explore
those areas which, due to this androcentric bias, have so far remained
'invisible'. These include: women's social history, women's perception
of their own situation, their own subordination and their own resistance. Women in the universities have also shown a tendency to ignore
these areas out of motives of self-preservation.

The contradictory existential and ideological condition of women
scholars must become the starting point for a new methodological
approach. The postulate of truth itself makes it necessary that those
areas of the female existence which so far were repressed and socially
'invisible' be brought into the full daylight of scientific analysis. In
order to make this possible, feminist women must deliberately and
courageously integrate their repressed, unconscious female subjectivity,
i.e., their own experience of oppression and discrimination into the
research process. This means that committed women social scientists
must learn to understand their own 'double consciousness' as a methodological and political opportunity and not as an obstacle. Leavitt
et al., wrote about this double consciousness which women have in
c⊝mmon with other groups who have suffered from oppression: 'Members of subordinated groups must, if they are to survive, develop to
those who control them, at the same time as they are fully aware of
the everyday reality of their oppression, a quality the superordinate
groups lack' (Leavitt, Sykes and Weatherford, 1975, p. 112).

This extra quality consists mainly in the fact that women and
other oppressed groups, out of their subjective experience, are better
sensitized toward psychological mechanisms of dominance. As objects
of oppression they are forced out of self-preservation to know the
motives of their oppressors. At the same time they have experienced
in their own psyche and bodies how oppression and exploitation feel
to the victims, who must constantly respond to demands made on
them. Due to this 'inner view of the oppressed' (Nash, 1974), women
social scientists are better equipped than their male counterparts to
make a comprehensive study of the exploited groups. Men often do not
have this experiential knowledge, and therefore lack empathy, the

ability for identification and because of this they also lack social and sociological imagination. If women social scientists take their own subjective experience of sexist discrimination and their rebellion against it as a starting point and guiding principle for their research, they first become critically aware of a number of weaknesses of established research which, according to Gerrit Huizer, is characterized by a lot of ego-tripping, slander, power intrigues and lack of equal participation (1973). Moreover, they discover the theoretical and methodological shortcomings of androcentric concepts of science. Thus Leavitt, Sykes and Weatherford criticize the Aristotelian dichotomization that is characteristic of structuralist and functionalist theories. Another instance of a pervasive and androcentric scientific manipulation is the 'Man the Hunter' paradigm, propagated by behaviorists and neo-evolutionists. According to this paradigm all human social development began with the (male) hunter and his invention of arms. Although a mass of evidence shows that the human race could not have survived had it not been fed by 'Woman the Gatherer', this paradigm has been accepted by most social scientists, including most Marxists, as an established truth (cf. Martin and Voorhies, 1975).

Women scholars who are committed to women's liberation, however, cannot stop at criticizing and exposing these androcentric manipulations. It is necessary to develop a new methodological approach and new research tools to prevent such manipulations.

In the following I shall try to lay down some methodological guidelines for feminist research. These will be followed by an account of an attempt to put these guidelines into practice in an action research project.

II Methodological guidelines for feminist research

(1) The postulate of *value free research*, of neutrality and indifference towards the research objects, has to be replaced by *conscious partiality*, which is achieved through partial identification with the research objects. For women who deliberately and actively integrate their double-consciousness into the research process, this partial identification will not be difficult. It is the opposite of the so-called 'Spectator-Knowledge' (Maslow, 1966:50) which is achieved by showing an indifferent, disinterested, alienated attitude towards the 'research objects'.

Conscious partiality, however, not only conceives of the research objects as parts of a bigger social whole but also of the research subjects, i.e., the researchers themselves. Conscious partiality is different from mere subjectivism or simple empathy. On the basis of a limited identification it creates a critical and dialectical distance between the researcher and his 'objects'. It enables the correction of distortions of perception on both sides and widens the consciousness of both, the researcher and the 'researched'.

(2) The vertical relationship between researcher and 'research objects', the *view from above*, must be replaced by the *view from below*. This is the necessary consequence of the demands of conscious partiality and reciprocity. Research, which so far has been largely an instrument of dominance and legitimation of power elites, must be brought to serve the interests of dominated, exploited and oppressed groups, particularly women. Women scholars, committed to the cause of women's liberation, cannot have an objective interest in a 'view from above'. This would mean that they would consent to their own oppression as women, because the man-woman relationship represents one of the oldest examples of the view from above and may be the paradigm of all vertical hierarchical relationships.

The demand for a systematic 'view from below' has both a scientific and an ethical-political dimension. The scientific significance is related to the fact that despite the sophistication of the quantitative research tools, many data gathered by these methods are irrelevant or even invalid because the hierarchical research situation as such defeats the very purpose of research: it creates an acute distrust in the 'research objects' who feel that they are being interrogated. This distrust can be found when women and other under-privileged groups are being interviewed by members of a socially higher stratum. It has been observed that the data thus gathered often reflect 'expected behavior' rather than real behavior (Berger, 1974).

Women, who are committed to the cause of women's liberation, cannot stop at this result. They cannot be satisfied with giving the social sciences better, more authentic and more relevant data. The ethical-political significance of the view from below cannot be separated from the scientific one: this separation would again transform all methodological innovations in Women's Studies into instruments of dominance. Only if Women's Studies is deliberately made part of the struggle against women's oppression and exploitation, can women prevent the misuse of their theoretical and methodological innovations for the stabilization of the status quo and for crisis management. This implies that committed women scholars must fight, not only for the integration of women's issues into the academic establishment and research policies but also for a new orientation regarding areas and objectives of research. The needs and interests of the majority of women must become the yardstick for the research policy of Women's Studies. This presupposes that women in the academic world know these needs and interests. The 'view from below', therefore, leads to another postulate.

(3)   The contemplative, uninvolved 'spectator knowledge' must be replaced by *active participation in actions, movements and struggles* for women's emancipation. Research must become an integral part of such struggles. Because Women's Studies grew out of the women's movement, it would be a betrayal of the aims of the movement if academic women, who were never involved in any struggle or were never concerned about women's oppression and exploitation, should try to reduce Women's Studies to a purely academic concern, restricted to the ivory tower of research institutes and universities, thus blunting the edge of all this discontent.[3] To avert this danger, Women's Studies must remain closely linked to the struggles and actions of the movement.

The concept of integrating praxis and research was concretely formulated by Mao Tse-Tung in his essays on contradiction and praxis. It must be emphasized that this concept goes beyond the prevalent understanding of action research. Action research has not been able so far to solve the dilemma of trying to establish a materialist praxis and theory which integrate the understanding of science and knowledge within a paradigm in which the separation from praxis is one of the most important structural prerequisites. But the demand to link praxis and research consistently follows an historical, dialectical and materialist theory of knowledge. According to this concept, the 'truth' of a theory is not dependent on the application of certain methodological principles and rules, but on its potential to orient the processes of praxis towards progressive emancipation and humanization. This potential, however, is not acquired in the sheltered world of academic institutions but in participation in social processes and in reflection about them.

Max Weber's famous principle of separating science and politics (praxis) is not in the interests of women's liberation. Women scholars who want to do more than a mere paternalistic 'something for their poorer sisters' (because they feel that, as a privileged group, they are already liberated) but who struggle against patriarchy as a system, must take their studies into the streets and take part in the social actions and struggles of the movement.

If they do so, their contribution will not be to give abstract analyses and prescriptions but to help those involved in these struggles to discover and develop their own theoretical and methodological potentials. The elitist attitude of women social scientists will be overcome if they are able to look at all those who participate in a social action or struggle as 'sister-or-brother-sociologists' (adapting Gouldner). The integration of research into social and political action for the emancipation of women, the dialectics of doing and knowing, will lead not only to better and more realistic theories. According to this approach, the object of research is not something static and homogeneous but an historical, dynamic and contradictory entity. Research, therefore, will have to follow closely the dynamics of this process.

(4) Participation in social actions and struggles, and the integration of research into these processes, further implies that the *change of the status quo* becomes the starting point for a scientific quest. The motto for this approach could be: 'If you want to know a thing, you must change it.' ('If you want to know the taste of a pear, you must change it, i.e., you must chew it in your mouth', Mao Tse-Tung, 1968). If we apply this principle to the study of women, it means that we have to start fighting against women's exploitation and oppression in order to be able to understand the extent, the dimensions, the forms and causes of this patriarchal system. Most empirical research on women has concentrated so far on the study of superficial or surface phenomena such as women's attitudes towards housework, career, part-time work, etc. Such attitudes or opinion surveys give very little information about women's true consciousness. Only when there is a rupture in the 'normal' life of a woman, i.e., a crisis such as divorce, the end of a relationship, etc., is there a chance for her to become conscious of her true condition. In the 'experience of crises' (Kramert, 1977) and rupture with normalcy, women are confronted with the real social relationships in which they had unconsciously been submerged as objects without being able to distance themselves from them. As long as normalcy is not disrupted they are not able to admit even to themselves that these relationships are oppressive or exploitive.

This is the reason why in attitude surveys women so often are found to subscribe to the dominant sexist ideology of the submissive, self-sacrificing woman. When a rupture with this normalcy occurs, however, the mystification surrounding the natural and harmonious character of these patriarchal relations cannot be maintained.

The motto of changing a situation in order to be able to understand it applies not only to the individual woman and her life crises, but also to collective processes. The very fact that today we are talking about a methodology for doing research in Women's Studies is the result of a change in the status quo that was brought about by the women's movement and not by intellectual endeavors in universities.

If women scholars begin to understand their studies as an integral part of an emancipatory struggle and if they focus their research on the processes of individual and social change, then they cannot but change themselves also in this process, both as human beings and as scholars. They will have to give up the elitist narrow-mindedness, abstract thinking, political and ethical impotence and arrogance of the established academician. They must learn that scientific work and a scientific outlook is not the privilege of professional scientists, but that the creativity of science depends on its being rooted in living social processes. Methodologically, this implies the search for techniques with which to document and analyze historical processes of change.

(5) *The research process must become a process of 'conscientization'*, both for the so-called 'research subjects' (social scientists) and for the 'research objects' (women as target groups). The methodology of 'conscientização' was first developed and applied by Paulo Freire in his problem-formulating method.* The decisive characteristic of the approach is that the study of an oppressive reality is not carried out by experts but by the objects of the oppression. People who before were objects of research become subjects of their own research and action. This implies that scientists who participate in this study of the conditions of oppression must give their research tools to the people. They must inspire them to formulate the problems with which they struggle in order that they may plan their action. The women's movement so

---

*Editors' note: By 'conscientização,' Freire means 'learning to perceive social, political and economic contradictions and to take action against the oppressive elements of reality.' In the following we will use the English version, 'conscientization' (Freire, 1970).

far has understood the process of conscientization largely as that of becoming conscious of one's individual suffering as a woman. The emphasis in consciousness-raising groups was on group dynamics, role-specific behavior and relationship problems rather than on the social relations that govern the capitalist patriarchal societies.

The problem-formulating method, however, sees individual problems as an expression and manifestation of oppressive social relations. Whereas consciousness-raising groups often tend to psychologize all relations of dominance, the problem-formulating method considers conscientization as the subjective precondition for liberating action. If processes of conscientization do not lead subsequently to processes of change and action, they may lead to dangerous illusions and even to regression.

(6) I would like to go a step further than Paulo Freire, however. The collective conscientization of women through a problem-formulating methodology *must be accompanied by the study of women's individual and social history*. Women have so far not been able to appropriate, i.e., make their own, the social changes to which they have been subjected passively in the course of history. Women do make history, but in the past they have not *appropriated* (made it their own) their history as subjects. Such a subjective appropriation of their history, their past struggles, sufferings and dreams would lead to something like a collective women's consciousness (in analogy to class consciousness) without which no struggle for emancipation can be successful.

The appropriation of women's history can be promoted by feminist scholars who can inspire and help other women to document their campaigns and struggles. They can help them to analyze these struggles, so that they can learn from past mistakes and successes and, in the long run, may become able to move from mere spontaneous activism to long-term strategies. This presupposes, however, that women engaged in Women's Studies remain in close contact with the movement and maintain a continuous dialogue with other women. This in turn implies that they can no longer treat their research results as their private property, but that they must learn to collectivize and share them. This leads to the next postulate.

(7) Women cannot appropriate their own history unless they *begin to collectivize their own experiences*. Women's Studies, therefore, must strive to overcome the individualism, the competitiveness, the careerism, prevalent among male scholars. This has relevance both for the individual

woman scholar engaged in research and for her methodology. If she is committed to the cause of women's liberation, she cannot choose her area of research purely from a career point of view but must try to use her relative power to take up issues that are central to the movement. Therefore, she needs dialogues on methodology with other feminists. The emphasis on interviews of individuals at a given time must be shifted towards group discussions, if possible at repeated intervals. This collectivization of women's experiences is not only a means of getting more and more diversified information, but it also helps women to overcome their structural isolation in their families and to understand that their individual sufferings have social causes.

III An attempt to apply these postulates by the action group: 'women help women', Cologne 1976-77

These methodological guidelines were not evolved merely through the study of social science literature but also through my participation in several field projects and the discussion of these experiences with women students and other colleagues. I had a first chance to try out some of these guidelines in an action research project which grew out of an initiative responding to violence against women in the family. This initiative was started by the women students of Social Pedagogy in Cologne in Spring 1976. They founded an association called 'Women Help Women' and started a campaign to get a house where women who had been beaten by their husbands or friends could find shelter.

Although this initiative did not start with an explicit interest in research, the need for documentation and analysis became urgently felt in the course of its development. The following description of our attempt to link social research to the requirements of this field project will give an idea of how some of the guidelines mentioned above can be put into practice. It should be kept in mind that it was not a systematic attempt to apply a certain methodology of social research, but that the main motive was to further the objectives of the action group. The following should, therefore, be understood as a sharing of our experience rather than as a systematic study. The aim is to invite others to experiment along similar lines.

1 A problem must be 'created' (Postulate 4: in order to understand a thing, one has to change it.)

After an action group of fifteen women had been constituted, a position paper was drafted on its objectives, methods and organizational principles. The group then approached the Social Welfare Department of the Municipal Administration and asked for a house for battered women. There had been reports in the press about increasing wife-beating in German families and about houses for battered women in England and Holland. The reply of the Social Welfare authorities, however, was that there was no need for such a house in Cologne; there were various homes for destitute and poor women to which battered women could go. The fact that there were hardly any battered women in these homes was sufficient proof for the authorities that the problem did not exist on any large scale. The group was advised first to make a survey and to give the authorities exact figures about the extent of wife-beating in Cologne in order to prove the need for a special house for this target group.

Such surveys are usually made by commercial research institutes with the help of professional social scientists, using the techniques of questionnaires and interviews. They not only cost a lot of money (which the group did not have) but they also have the political effect that no action is taken before the results of the studies are available. In this way, a problem is often swept under the rug.

The action group therefore chose another method of proving the need for a house for battered women. It organized a street action with posters, photos of battered wives, newspaper-clippings and signatures collected from passers-by, about the need for a Women's House for battered women. At the same time, people who came to their stand were interviewed about their experiences with and their views on wife beating. These interviews were recorded and provided first-hand data about the existence of this problem in Cologne.

These interviews also gave the group initial feedback about people's reactions to private violence in the family, about the class position of men who beat women, about people's opinion as to the causes of this private violence and about police indifference towards the problem.

This information helped the group to plan their next steps, but it was also a bit of social research which could immediately be used to further the action. The whole action was reported in the press, including some of the statements made by the people. This publication of a problem which so far had been considered a purely private affair mobilized many people to discuss the question of a Women's House.

The municipal authorities found it difficult to maintain their indifference and finally had to mobilize their own research cell to investigate the problem of wife beating. This was the first time that any attempt had been made to obtain statistics about cases of wife beating in the city. Neither the police nor the various social welfare homes had kept statistics about women who approached them for help. The Social Welfare Department carried out this inquiry only in the homes under their control, not in private homes. The results of the study showed that an average 100 women per month approached these homes because they had been beated by their husbands. The homes have no means by which to help such women quickly and unbureaucratically, however, and therefore sent them back to their husbands.

With the aid of systematic publicity work in the press, on the radio and TV, the organization grew and became known in the city. Many women who had been mistreated by their husbands rang the number given in the press. Three months after the start of the project, women began to ask the group for help. At that time the group did not yet have a house and its members thus began to give shelter in their own homes to the women who asked for help.

This made the need for a Women's House all the more urgent. When the Social Welfare Department published the results of its own investigation, the action group stated that they had given shelter to about 30 women between June and September 1976. It could no longer be said that the problem of private violence against women did not exist in Cologne. Eventually the members raised enough money to pay the rent of a suitable house, and later the municipality provided a subsidy.

2 Partiality and egalitarian involvement in a social action (Postulates 1 and 3)

Members of the action group clearly stated in their position paper that they did not want to allow new hierarchies to grow or experts to dominate the organization. Therefore, they made it a precondition for membership that women who wanted to join 'Women Help Women' had to do any type of work that came up. In the long run this proved to be a correct decision. The women social scientists who joined the organization had to give up their status of uninvolved, neutral, scientific observers or experts; they not only had to take sides with and for the mistreated women, but also to participate actively and on an equal footing with non-academic women in all the work. Some pressure was exercised by the public to elect some eminent women as members of the Board of the Association. Officers of the Social Welfare Department would have felt more at ease negotiating with academics than with unknown and inexperienced young women. The action group did not yield to such pressure, however, and stuck to its egalitarian principle of organization. This had the effect that all members had to feel actively responsible for the progress of the movement. There was no bureaucratic center of authority to which responsibility could be delegated.

The result for the academic women was that their horizon in day-to-day struggles was immensely broadened. In their discussions with women who sought shelter in the Women's House they learned more about the true social conditions of German families than from any number of quantitative surveys. For the women who had started the action group, the decision that there should be no hierarchy or bureaucracy meant that they had to learn many things that women usually do not know: from dealing with officials, lawyers, policemen, to speaking at press conferences, studying Social Welfare Laws, to whitewashing and painting, driving alone at night to unknown places to meet women who sought their help, etc. The principle of action and egalitarian participation was also applied to the women who sought the help of 'Women Help Women'. After a time of rest and recovery in the Women's House, they were encouraged to participate in all the activities of the organization. This was not always easy because the women who sought shelter had run away from an acute crisis situation. They expected help and looked upon the organization as an ordinary social welfare institution. It was difficult to get them to understand gradually that women's liberation rather than social welfare and charity was the aim of the action group. This understanding was furthered by the principle of active and egalitarian participation of all, including the academic women.

The difficulties that arose from this struggle towards inner democracy and integration of praxis and theory were caused by the contacts with the outer world, i.e., mainly the municipal authorities, with their highly hierarchized and bureaucratized organizations. Constant friction was caused by the fact that these bureaucracies have no latitude for egalitarian initiative.

3 Discussion and 'socialization' of life-histories as therapy, as a basis for collective women's consciousness and as a starting point for emancipatory action (Postulates 5, 6, and 7)

In the first phase of the action, intensive individual and group discussions took place with women who had run away from their homes because their husbands or fiancés had beaten them black and blue. These intensive talks were institutionalized after the group had rented a house in November 1976 and many more women rang up. (Only the telephone number was known, not the address, in case the men should follow their wives and harass them and the children.)

At first these informal yet intensive talks were mainly about the forms, duration, extent and repercussions of male violence in the family. They necessarily emphasized the psychological dimension of a woman's individual history. Since no amount of psychological counselling could solve the practical and material problems that these women faced after leaving their husbands (no job, no flat, insecurity of income, no training), it became evident that psychological introspection alone could not lead to a deeper understanding of the social forces which had put women into such a state of dependency.

It became necessary to help women understand that their own experience of male violence was not just their individual bad luck or even their fault, but that there is an objective social basis for this private violence by men against women and children. This meant that they had to understand the sociological and historical dimensions of male violence if they were to get out of the masochistic tendency to attribute the failure of their marriage to their own failure as women.

The best method by which to make women in this crisis situation aware of the sociological and historical roots of their suffering appears to be the documentation and analysis of their life histories; by making their stories public, women acknowledge that their experiences have social origins. This method, evolved as a technique of action research (Osterland, 1973), is not only an effective way by which to integrate the time dimension into social research; it is also an excellent method of conscientization. The methodology of a small-action research project which grew out of these informal talks in the Women's House is described below.

It was our objective to document, analyze and discuss the life histories of a number of women who came to the Women's House. We wanted to publish these life histories because it was our aim to conscientize and mobilize the public at large about the problem. To achieve this, much more information was needed on this hidden side of our society, which professes to be democratic and peaceful. It is the task of social researchers to provide this information.

Methodologically, the small group of women who started this project (myself and six students) tried to follow the postulates laid down above.

3.1 The starting point for the documentation of a life history is the break in the woman's so-called normal life. The façade of normalcy which these women have desperately maintained for perhaps 10-30 years of married life — in the face of brutal violence and humiliation — breaks down as soon as they come to the Women's House. The structural violence, which is the basis of the bourgeois, patriarchal family, has become manifested in open violence, and the women are able to admit it. This rupture with oppressive continuity usually does not occur until women see a realistic alternative. Before they see such an alternative, no amount of persuasion will convince them that they are oppressed. In fact, they cannot allow their own oppression and humiliation to come to the surface of their consciousness if they want to preserve a minimum of self-respect. Therefore, they try to find any conceivable rationalization for the fact that they have tolerated masculine brutality for so long. As soon as the rupture has taken place, however, their whole life of repression and humiliation gushes forth like a stream whose sluices have been opened. As soon as they realize that there are other women who will listen to them with sympathy and understanding, they begin to talk about their life, their husbands, their marriage; spontaneously they try to understand why this has all happened to them. We realized that the need of these women to talk and to communicate their experiences to us and to their fellow sufferers was boundless. For most of them it was the first time that there had been anyone who was willing to listen to them.

3.2 This first stage of sharing experiences and of spontaneous solidarity, however, does not lead automatically to an analysis of the social causes of private violence or to a new consciousness. We interviewed individual women and asked them to tell us their whole life history from their childhood up to the time when they had come to the Women's House. Most of them were very eager to do so. We first taped their stories individually, then we wrote them down. After a number of such biographies were written down, we organized a group meeting. We gave those written life-stories to the women, asked them to read them and to see whether they wanted to alter or to add anything. After a cursory analysis of the biographies, we wanted to have a group discussion with all the women on some of the salient points that came up in many of the cases. As we wanted to avoid a discussion in which only a few people would participate, we suggested that we should make a role play based on problems and incidents that were most common to their histories. The women themselves suggested what should be included in the play and some also volunteered to stage it. We invited all women to see the play and then to discuss it, and made a video-film while it was being staged. After it was all over, the women talked about the play and this discussion was also filmed.

When we planned this small action research project, we had the following objectives in mind, which cover not only our research interests but are closely linked to the individual interests of the women concerned, as well as to the broader aims and perspectives of the women's movement.

(a) For the women concerned, the systematic documentation of their life histories has the effect that their own subjective biography assumes an objective character. It becomes something at which they can look from a certain distance. They are not only prisoners of their own past and present sufferings and mistakes, but they can, if they want to, draw lessons for the future from their own past history.

(b) Writing down their biographies also serves a very practical purpose. These women need documentation and hard data in order to re-organize their lives. They need such documents for their lawyers, for example, if they want to have a divorce. On the other hand, the action group also needs documentation of women's histories if it is to avoid endless Sisyphian charity work.

(c) From the point of view of research, these biographies contain data not only on the individual destinies of the women but also on objective social relations such as class, and the women's

reactions towards these. The biographical method also links
the individual history to the overall social history of an epoch.
The individual's life manifests the contradictions and stresses
of an epoch. Many of the women have experienced the war and
post-war years; some are refugees from East Germany. Many of
the men are workers; many are unemployed and have started
drinking. The question of when the man started to beat his wife
often gives insight into the interplay between crises: increased
phenomena of alienation (work stress, alcoholism, job insecurity,
competition) and private violence and aggression. Reflection and
appropriation of individual women's histories, therefore, cannot
be separated from the reflection and appropriation for feminist
use of the overall social history of an epoch.

(d) Apart from the individual, practical and theoretical dimensions,
the writing-down and discussion of life histories also has political
and action-oriented dimensions, aiming at creating a new collective consciousness among women and mobilizing them for further
social action. For this it was necessary to generalize the individual
life histories, which we tried by staging the play and by the ensu-
ing discussion of the video film.

In the collectivization and discussion of their individual experiences, the women transcend their narrow isolated horizon and
begin to understand that women in general have a common
social destiny. In fact, most of the women, when they listened
to the stories of others, were struck by the similarity of their
experiences, i.e., the commonness and monotony of the everyday
violence. There was hardly anything individual or extraordinary
in their narrations.

(e) Mere scientific documentation and analysis, and even a group
discussion on the common destiny of women, does not lead by
itself to an active collective consciousness 'for themselves'.

Only when women can use their own documented, analyzed, understood and *published* history as a weapon in the struggle for themselves
and for all women will they become subjects of their own history.
This implies that the documentation of their life histories — the video
film, the book, the discussions — have to be integrated into the overall
strategy of the women's movement. This mobilization of all women
who so far had been passive victims of patriarchal structural and direct

violence may transcend the scope of a small action-research project. But the fact that the women who took part in the research showed keen interest in starting a public campaign against private violence is an indicator that they are moving away from their status as mere objects of charity and social welfare and are on the way to becoming subjects of their own history.[4]

Postscript

I have often been asked whether the guidelines or postulates spelled out above could also be applied to research on women in Third World countries. In 1978-9 I carried out an ILO-sponsored research project on rural women in India, where I tried to implement some of these methodological principles. A full account of my experience is given in my reports on this subject.[5] Here I wish only to highlight a few necessary points in order to counter certain illusions which may arise regarding the scope of this approach to further social change.

We (the Indian women who assisted me and I) applied this approach in three rural areas, where we carried out fieldwork among women in the subsistence sector. In one area a social movement for the organization of landless laborers and their social betterment had been in progress for several years. The landless female laborers had already formed their own autonomous organizations, which had carried out a number of successful actions for better wages, work contracts and nightschools for women. It was not difficult to use the methodological principles spelled out above and the women participated enthusiastically in our research. They first started doing research *on us*, however, asking all sorts of personal questions regarding our husbands, children, our bodies, clothes; what we did during menstruation, whether we used cotton or cloth; and above all, why we were interested in them. In other words, they did not uncritically accept the hierarchical research situation but turned it into a dialogue. This was facilitated because we lived among them and needed to be helped in many ways. In their songs, dances, dramas, role plays, group discussions, the recording of their life histories, in mass meetings, it became evident that not only were they quite capable of analyzing and understanding their own situation, but also of drawing practical conclusions from this analysis. The project provided a forum for discussions and meetings and, as such, not only helped to conscientize these women, but created a wider net-work of communications for women from different villages, thus giving them a new sense of power.[6]

It would have been impossible for us, however, to mobilize and organize the scattered women through the research project *alone*. Even if it is action-oriented, Women's Studies cannot *on its own* do such work. Perhaps this should not even be attempted: the researchers usually will leave the area after a certain period of time and the women who are left behind will have to face the political consequences of their mobilization. If a research project is carefully linked to an ongoing movement, however, the separation between research and action, theory and practice can be overcome — at least we can move in that direction. The degree to which the resources and services of a research project can be used to further the aims of the movement will depend on the movement itself.

Similar autonomous organizations did not exist in the other two areas, and we thus found ourselves in the typical research situation of outsiders who had come to snoop around. In one area the situation was complicated further by the fact that for approximately the last hundred years the local women had become accustomed to being the objects of charity for the Christian church and Western business inter-ests. It was difficult to explain to them that we had no such charity to offer, and at first they did not see any point in talking to us. They were completely atomized as workers and housewives, and although we were able to organize group discussions in which they talked about their problems, the initiative was clearly in our hands. These women belonged to a better class and caste than the women in the first area, but their consciousness and self-confidence were much lower.

We realized that a research project that does not link up with some local group which will constitute a permanent base for conscientization, mobilization and action, will remain at best a pleasant episode in the lives of the women, and will be unable to develop its emancipatory potential. In any case, women's research projects as such should not be expected to *start* a conscientization movement. This would presuppose greater commitment and involvement of the research team in a parti-cular area than is possible for most urban-based women in Third World countries.

Even in areas where no movement was yet in progress, however, we realized that it was impossible *not* to become involved. Given the general sex-segregation and oppression of women in India, the women very soon came to tell us about their private problems with their husbands, their mothers-in-law, the quarrels in the village, etc. This 'women's gossip' was obviously encouraged by the fact that we were women, belonging to the same social category, *and* were also outsiders and researchers who were ready to listen to their stories. This general feeling of 'being on the same side' helped to overcome the usual barrier between people from different classes and cultures. The establishment of an open and friendly rapport between us and the women was mainly due to the commitment and enthusiasm of the Indian women on the research team, who were not only capable of partial identification with the problems of the rural women, but who also enjoyed being with them and temporarily sharing their lives.

Notes

1 This paper was first read at an interdisciplinary feminist seminar in Holland and it is published in German in *Heksenkollege: de feeks viool* (Nijmegen, Holland, 1978, out of print); and in *Beiträge zur Feministischen Theorie und Praxis*, 1978.
2 Mahmood Mamdani (1973) describes the functioning of this kind of research.
3 The present world-wide interest in Women's Studies may also be attributed to certain efforts to neutralize the protest potential of the movement. In many countries there is already a gap between Women's Studies and the Women's Movement.
4 The results of this project were published under the title: *Nachrichten aus dem Ghetto Liebe* (1980).
5 The research report on my work in India is entitled 'Housewives Produce for the Worldmarket: The Lace Makers of Narsapur' (1982).
6 An account of this experience is given in my paper 'Peasant Women get Organised' (1981).

References

Berger, Hartwig (1974), *Untersuchungsmethode und soziale Wirklichkeit* (*Research Methods and Social Reality*), Frankfurt.
Frauenhaus Köln (1980), *Nachrichten aus dem Ghetto Liebe*, Frankfurt, Verlag Jugend and Politik.
Freire, Paulo (1970), *Pedagogy of the Oppressed*, New York, Seabury Press.

Horowitz, Irving L. (1976), *The Rise and Fall of the Project Camelot: Studies in the Relationship between Science and Practical Politics*, Harvard, MIT Press.

Huizer, Gerrit (1973), 'The A-Social Role of Social Scientists in Underdeveloped Countries: Some Ethical Considerations,' *Sociologus*, vol. 23, no. 2, pp. 165-77.

Kramert, Helgard (1977), 'Wann wird die Selbstverständlichkeit der geschlechtlichen Abeitsteilung in Frage gestellt?' ('When Will the Assumed Sexual Division of Labor Be Questioned?'), paper delivered in Frankfurt.

Leavitt, R., Sykes, B. and Weatherford, E. (1975), 'Aboriginal Women: Male and Female Perspectives,' in R. Reiter (ed.), *Toward an Anthropology of Women*, New York, Monthly Review Press, pp. 110-26.

Lewin, Kurt (1951), *Feldtheorie in den Sozialwissenschaften (Field Theory in Social Science)*, New York, Harper & Row.

Lewin, Kurt (1948), *Die Lösung Sozialer Konflikte (Resolving Social Conflicts)*, New York, Harper & Row.

Mamdani, Mahmood (1973), *The Myth of Population Control: Family, Caste and Class in an Indian Village*, New York, Monthly Review Press.

Mao Tse-Tung (1968), *Über die Praxis, Über den Widerspruch (On Practice. On Contradiction)*, Calcutta, National Book Agency.

Martin, K.M., and Voorhies, B. (1975), *Female of the Species*, New York, Columbia University Press.

Maslow, Abraham H. (1966), *The Psychology of Science: A Renaissance*, New York, Harper & Row.

Mies, Maria (1978), 'Methodische Postulate zur Frauenforschung — dargestellt am Beispiel der Gewalt gegen Frauen,' *Beiträge zur Feministischen Theorie und Praxis*, vol. 1, no. 1, pp. 41-63.

Mies, Maria (1980), 'Housewives Produce for the Worldmarket: The Lacemakers of Narsapur', Geneva, ILO Working Paper WEP 1OWP 14.

Mies, Maria (1981), 'Peasant Women get Organised' (mimeo), The Hague, Holland, Institute of Social Studies.

Mies, Maria (1982), *The Lacemakers of Narsapur: Indian Housewives in the World Market*, London, ZED-Press.

Nash, June (1974), Report on the Conference on Feminine Perspectives in Social Science Research, Buenos Aires, March.

Osterland, Martin (1973), 'Lebensgeschichtliche Erfahrung und gesellschaftliches Bewusstsein. Anmerkungen zur soziobiographischen Methode' ('Life History Experience and Social Consciousness: Notes on a Social-Biographical Method'), *Soziale Welt*, vol. 24, no. 4, pp. 409-17.

Wolf, E. and Jorgenson, J.G. (1970), 'Anthropology on the Warpath in Thailand,' *New York Review of Books*, vol. 15, no. 9, pp. 26-34.

10

The value of quantitative methodology for feminist research[1]

Toby Epstein Jayaratne

In the past several years the feminist community has increasingly debated the merits of traditional research in the social sciences and specifically the quantitative methodologies used in that research. Many feminists, both those in the social sciences and in other disciplines as well, argue that traditional research in the social sciences is used as a tool for promoting sexist ideology and ignores issues of concern to women and feminists (Stasz Stoll, 1974; Frieze, Parsons, Johnson, Ruble and Zellman, 1978; Fox Keller, 1980). As a result of this and other criticisms of traditional research and quantitative methods, some feminists have suggested the increased use of qualitative research in order better to reflect the nature of human experience (Reinharz, 1979; Fox Keller, 1980; Depner, 1981). Furthermore, there has been some discussion of the need to reduce or eliminate the use of quantitative research as a valid methodology for social scientists (Reinharz, 1979). This debate between quantitative and qualitative researchers is not new. In fact, Glaser and Strauss (1967) indicate that this dialogue has been ongoing for several decades.

The primary purposes of this paper are (1) to explore briefly some of the issues surrounding this controversy from a feminist perspective and (2) to suggest some changes in the traditional quantitative research process and in traditional research environments which would make quantitative research useful for testing feminist theory.

I also advocate the use of qualitative data, in conjunction with quantitative data, to develop, support and explicate theory. My approach to this issue is political; that is, I believe the appropriate use of *both* quantitative methods and qualitative methods in the social sciences can help the feminist community in achieving its goals more effectively than the use of either qualitative or quantitative methods alone. Both quantitative and qualitative research can be and have been effectively used by feminist researchers to promote feminist theory and goals and to document individual and institutional sexism (for example, see Weisstein, 1970; Chesler, 1972; Levitin, Quinn and Staines, 1973; Reinharz, 1979). While this paper only summarily touches on some of the major issues in this debate, a more thorough discussion and analysis of this topic is needed not only in the feminist community, but in the scientific community as well.

Before examining these issues more closely, it is important to outline what is meant by the traditional or quantitative research *process*, quantitative and qualitative *methods* and other terms relevant to this discussion. I will provide illustrations and examples from the field of survey research because I am most familiar with that research methodology. However, the general points made in this paper should pertain to a broad range of research methodology in the social sciences.

The quantitative research process

The traditional research process is often termed 'quantitative' because the data are analyzed as numerical values. However, there are other procedures not directly associated with quantification which typically characterize this kind of research. It is important to distinguish between methods of quantification, involving data collection and analysis, and the more general research process, including theory formulation, interpretation and dissemination. It is the entire quantitative research process which is described and explored below, and not just quantitative methods of data collection and analysis.

Theory formulation

Most quantitative survey research is initiated from a theoretical base. Theory, as it is used in the social sciences, is simply an explanation of some phenomena which specifies relations among elements (Kerlinger,

1979). The purpose of the research process is to gather and examine evidence (data) in order to test the validity of such an explanation. The process of theory validation is continuous, since new evidence often suggests revisions to existing theory. Therefore no theory is ever 'proven' correct.

To develop, test and validate feminist theory is critical if feminist goals are to be enacted (see Depner, 1981). Jaggar and Struhl (1978) argue this point and offer several reasons why it is important. First, when we condemn prevailing sexist theories, we need to propose alternatives. Second, theory helps to generate consistency between our feminist ideology and our beliefs about human nature and human fulfillment. Third, if we are going to combat sexism we need to understand how it operates. We can direct our energies where they will be most effective if we can identify vulnerable points in the social structure. Feminist theory can thus describe and explain women's oppression and offer us guidelines for combatting it.

Although some would argue that social scientists are notorious for finding evidence to support their own theories and thus all theories are equally valid, Jaggar and Struhl (1978) argue differently. They believe that

> one framework [theory] is *not* as good as another [and] that all descriptions of social reality are not equally valid . . . we may then evaluate feminist frameworks according to their success in identifying the conditions which prevent women from freely choosing which of our potentialities we wish to fulfill (pp. xi, xii).

In other words, we can judge feminist theories according to their ability to improve the lives of women.

There is more subjective input in theory generation than in other aspects of the research process, since theories are 'typically the end of observation and interpretation, looking and thinking' (Babbie, 1979, p. 23). While this may seem problematic since research aims to be an objective process, it is the goal of scientific inquiry to make an objective judgment about a theory whose development was more or less subjective. It is the theory's ability to reflect aspects of social 'reality' that allows us to accept or reject it. Furthermore, much theory generation is really theory revision, which is based on a systematic evaluation of relevant research — a less subjective process than starting from scratch. If existing theory seems inadequate for describing our own realities, we may need to rely on our own experiences as part of theory development. This has been the case with much of feminist theory formulation.

Theory testing

Theory forms the basis of the quantitative research process and generates specific hypotheses which are then tested by means of research methodologies. In the field of survey research this involves numerous procedures. A questionnaire or interview is constructed to measure various aspects or components of the model or theory being tested. A pre-test or pilot study is usually done to test the validity of the questions being asked and items are revised as necessary. A sample of respondents is selected so that it represents the population (group of people) to which findings are generalized. The data are collected by administering the interview or questionnaire to respondents in that sample. Before analysis, responses to questions are usually quantified, that is, they are converted to numbers to facilitate analysis. It is this 'quantification' of responses which, in essence, characterizes traditional research. Although these data are analyzed as numerical values, it is still the *meaning* of the numbers which determines how analysis proceeds and is the basis for interpretation of results. Most analyses are statistical 'judgments' on the data which specifically test hypotheses generated from the theory. The data indicate varying degrees of support or lack of support for these hypotheses. Conclusions are drawn which evaluate the merit of the theory and then generalizations are made to the larger population from which the sample was drawn. Rarely are complex theories conclusively supported or rejected in this process. Instead, smaller parts of theories are evaluated and related to the larger body of evidence for the theory. A comprehensive evaluation of theory usually involves the consideration of a large research literature. The final product of most survey research is a report or publication which presents descriptive and/or predictive quantitative results and their interpretation and theoretical implications.

The above account of the traditional quantitative research process is, of course, an idealized version. Not all research proceeds in such an orderly fashion. Problems can arise at many points. For example, there may be difficulties with the interview (misinterpreted questions, unanswered questions), the sample (low response rate, poor representativeness), the data (coding errors, keypunching errors), analysis (incorrect statistical techniques, incorrect use of variables) and interpretation (ignoring important results), to name just a few. However, use of established guidelines for conducting survey research can result in a high quality research project. These guidelines for implementation of social science methodology are well established and fairly specific, although by no means static. They were developed, and are appropriately updated, to offer the most valid methods of theory testing.

Qualitative research

The above account of the traditional research process describes the collection of quantitative data. In contrast, qualitative data is rarely seen in traditional research and is almost entirely absent in the research of some social science disciplines. While most quantitative researchers can agree fairly closely on what the quantitative research process is, qualitative research is not that easy to define. A review of suggested research techniques in several qualitative research texts indicated considerably more variety of methodology than in quantitative research (see Glaser and Strauss, 1967; Schatzman and Strauss, 1973; McCall and Simmons, 1969; Bogdan and Taylor, 1975).

While most quantitative data result from questions which allow only a limited number of answers, questions resulting in qualitative data usually do not have this constraint. For example, in a quantitative study the kind of question which asks about job satisfaction might only be answered on a scale of '1' to '7'. A similar question in a qualitative study is 'open-ended' and might instead be answered by a long description of the respondent's feelings about her job in her own words. However, the distinction between qualitative and quantitative research is not always a function of the kind of data collected, since many quantitative studies ask open-ended questions. In the latter case, responses to these open-ended questions are usually quantified for analysis but remain as is for qualitative analysis. Thus another distinction between these methods is that quantitative data are analyzed as numerical values and qualitative data are analyzed using the language of the respondent. Bogdan and Taylor (1975) describe qualitative methods as referring to research procedures which produce descriptive data: people's own written or spoken words and observable behavior. This approach . . . directs itself at settings and the individuals within those settings holistically; that is, the subject of the study, be it an organization or an individual, is not reduced to an isolated variable or to an hypothesis, but is viewed instead as part of a whole (p. 4).

Examples of qualitative methods are oral history, experiential analysis (Reinharz, 1979), participant observation, and case history.

Qualitative data — whatever method is used — do convey a deeper feeling for or more emotional closeness to the persons studied. A detailed account of an individual's struggle against oppression is more emotionally touching than a research report giving statistical evidence of the struggle of a group of individuals. For example, ethnographic accounts of representatives of oppressed groups are very effective in instilling empathy for those individuals (see Lewis, 1961; Kroeber, 1969; Liebow, 1967). Case histories and other accounts in similar style have always been interesting and appealing to many readers. None the less, the interpretation of qualitative data is subjective and therefore open to all of the biases inherent in subjective assessments.[2]

While some sanction has been given to the collection of qualitative data (or at least some level of subjective judgments) for use in theory formulation (Babbie, 1979), there is an open and strong opposition against the use of qualitative data in many social science disciplines (Reinharz, 1979). Some feminists view this opposition as a reflection of the relationship between gender and science (Fox Keller, 1978). Their point is that most social scientists are men and that the masculine values of autonomy, separation and distance are embodied in 'objective,' quantitative research. Thus, the more qualitative aspects are rejected as being too subjective, too 'female.'

Feminist criticism of the quantitative research process and quantitative analysis

Feminist criticism of research in the social sciences is directed toward both the general quantitative research process and quantitative data and data analysis in particular. The primary criticisms arise because so much of traditional quantitative research seems inconsistent with feminist values. First, much social research has been used to support sexist and elitist values. Little effort has been made to explore issues of importance to women. Second, the socially relevant research which has been generated often is not utilized 'appropriately,' that is, it has no real impact on social problems. Too many final reports or journal articles get dusty on the bookshelves of academicians or government bureaucrats. Third, there exist exploitive relationships among the research staff and between the staff and the respondents in the study. Too many needs or concerns of the research staff are secondary to the more immediate needs of meeting deadlines, seeking scarce funding or getting out a final report. And respondents are often seen as 'objects' of study, deceived and manipulated for the benefit of the research product. Fourth, the high standards of methodological rigor are often simply overlooked when expedient. To learn and then employ all the quality controls of a research project is not a simple task and too often the standards for appropriate use of quantitative methodology are set aside when it is convenient. Fifth, quantitative data cannot convey an in-depth understanding of or feeling for the persons under study. This final criticism of the quantitative research process concerns the objective *appearance* of the quantitative research. There is an 'objective' aura about traditional research which makes it convincing and influential. Thus, findings which are often products of poor methodology and sexist bias are interpreted by the public as fact.

While most of these claims do have merit, the conclusion by some feminists that we must reject traditional research outright is debatable. A closer examination of each of the criticisms and a discussion of possible alternative procedures will clarify other options which are available to us.

Exploration of sexist and elitist issues

Anyone who glances through the indices of social science journals for the past thirty or forty years cannot deny that the great majority of research addresses issues of importance to white male academicians (Stasz Stoll, 1974; Cox, 1976; Frieze, *et al.*, 1978). It has only been in the last ten years or so that some journals have consistently included research about women's issues. However slowly this change is taking place, it is now possible to find articles of relevance to women in most major social science journals. Although many established journalists in the US publish 'token' articles on women's research, some regularly include such research (see *Child Development, Journal of Personality and Social Psychology*, and *Journal of Educational Psychology*). Furthermore, there are several journals which publish research exclusively about women and much of this research is carried out using quantitative methodology (see *Psychology of Women Quarterly* and *Sex Roles*). The issues addressed in much of this recent research are of prime interest to feminists, and include a broad range of topics such as sex discrimination, child care, pregnancy, sex role development, sexual harassment, educational equity, and spouse abuse. In addition, much of this research is carried out from a feminist perspective, and contributes to feminist theory.

Although funding for research on women's issues may be more difficult to secure in the near future, the past several years have seen an increase in research exploring issues of relevance to women. This change probably reflects not only the increased attention which women's issues have received in the popular media, but also the increased numbers of women entering graduate school and the academic job market in the social sciences. While traditional academic 'ethics' dictate the need to be relatively value-free in choosing a research area (Kerlinger, 1979), it is likely that many of these women are choosing research areas which are related to personal interests and values. According to Cox (1976), 'women seem to be more sensitive to the issues of values in social sciences, and without abandoning scientific goals, are more candid about having values that guide them in their work' (p. 13).

Underutilization of relevant social findings

From a political perspective, all quality social research ought to be used in policy decisions. Obviously, this is not what happens. Many social scientists feel that their obligation to research ends with a published document; whether results from their studies have any impact on policy seems to be of little concern. This attitude is reflected in the traditional research process: most educational programs in the social sciences do not include training in the utilization and dissemination of research. In fact, it is a controversial issue as to whether researchers ought to be involved in the decision-making process at all. While there is debate as to the exact role of the researcher in policy-making, few would suggest that all researchers need to become experts in policy formulation.

Tangri and Strasburg (1979) note the importance of both traditional research conducted by researchers and the use of research in policy-making conducted by activists. They believe that while many investigators hope to see their findings utilized in policy decision-making, it is difficult for many already overburdened researchers to take on an additional role as activist. Tangri and Strasburg suggest that there can be an interaction between researchers and activists and that social researchers need not become activists in order to contribute to the political relevance of their work. While the role of the activist is to influence decision-makers, the equally important

> role of the researchers is to contribute knowledge of completed and ongoing studies relevant to the targeted problem; to help the activists frame their questions in research terms; and to develop research designs which incorporate mechanisms for ongoing evaluation (1979, p. 329).

As rare as actual utilization might be, Weiss and Bucuvalas (1977) point out that decision-makers are responsive to recommendations of social scientists when those recommendations support their own views of social issues. The fact that there are a minority of policy-makers who hold values which are consistent with a feminist perspective is not promising for the implementation of policy based on the utilization of social science research which supports feminist goals. Although we need to elect and support policy-makers who are sympathetic to our views and use relevant research data to support their recommendations, as researchers we need more direct strategies.

Tangri and Strasburg (1979) have analyzed the problems of utilization of women's research on policy formulation and offer some recommendations for generating politically useful research. The authors specifically mention that the researcher should be perceived by the policy-maker as 'objective,' and present findings which are statistically significant. This indicates that the use of quantitative research can be an effective tool in influencing policy-makers. These authors also point to the need to (1) make researchers more aware and employ those methods which make their data more useful to activists, and (2) change academic structures so that there is support for the use of these methods. Of course, the latter particularly will not be easy to achieve.

In another analysis of which factors affect the usefulness of research, Weiss and Bucuvalas (1977) identified one factor which consisted of items establishing 'trust' in the research. These items, which concern the methodological quality of the research, were 'statistical sophistication, objectivity, quantitative data, generalizability, validity, and additions to descriptive, causal, or theoretical knowledge' (p. 218).

One important court decision which indicates the potential influence of quantitative data is *Griggs vs. Duke Power Company* (1971), which was argued under Title VII of the Civil Rights Act of 1964. Prior to this case, sex discrimination could be substantiated only if one could prove intent on the part of the defendant. The decision resulting from this case, however, was that discrimination could be indicated by presenting statistics which show a different and unfair impact on a racial, sex or other group covered by Title VII. This decision set a new course for discrimination suits.

Aside from the issue of the *direct* influence of social science research on policy decisions, it is important to consider the indirect effect, that is, the influence on public opinion. Some of the results from social research, particularly those concerning current or controversial issues, find their way into the popular media, such as *Psychology Today*, women's magazines or newspapers. Often these articles, depending on the extent of coverage, influence public opinion to such an extent that, ultimately, policy decisions are also affected. While this type of 'utilization' of social research has less of an apparent effect than a more direct approach, the political efficacy of the research may be more far-reaching, since it can directly affect people's lives. For example, research which indicated the pervasiveness of wife abuse may not have resulted in immediate policy change to combat the practice. However, popular media attention was so widespread that many victims who otherwise would have felt isolated and been self-blaming, instead sought support in centers and community support programs.

Exploitive relationships between project staff and between staff and subjects of study

Many of us who have been research assistants on research projects are aware of the problems of authoritative researchers who treat their staff and/or respondents as commodities. This problem is not unique to the social sciences and often occurs in other research settings where human (and animal) subjects are used. Reinharz (1979) describes the extreme case where research is

> conducted on a rape model: the researchers take, hit, and run. They intrude into their subjects' privacy, disrupt their perceptions, utilize false pretenses, manipulate the relationship, and give little or nothing in return. When the needs of the researchers are satisfied, they break off contact with the subject (p. 95).

In contrast, there are many researchers who are sensitive to these issues and relate well to their staff and respondents. One survey research project, whose director and staff were particularly respectful of the needs of respondents and interviewers, obtained a response rate of 98 per cent, indicating that these values were manifested in the attitudes of the research team. One interviewer, commenting on the project's success, noted the following:

> I do believe one of the reasons for the high response rate of the study is the fact that interviewers do so enjoy working on the study. That is so important in getting people to do a good job. During training the interviewers were so enthused about the questionnaire and the interviewing situation that I feel this enthusiasm was transmitted to the respondents, and they in turn were eager to do their parts (Freedman and Camburn, 1981, p. 24).

Both personality and personal value differences can account for some of this difference in style. However, the authoritative structure of research projects and institutions is contrary to feminist values and one might expect that feminist researchers would be sensitive to these issues. According to Cox (1976), 'Academic feminists question the value of the individualistic, striving, competitive, aggressive style of achievement for either sex. The style of achievement in which feminists would like to work is based on cooperation, mutual respect, inter-dependence' (p. 13). The fact that many feminist researchers who do traditional research are not exploitive of their staff and respondents suggests that the problem of exploitation is not inherent in the traditional research process. The occurrence of exploitation can be reduced by explicitly promoting more humanistic values in research training programs and by setting examples for others through self-evaluation when doing our own research. Furthermore, decisions which affect the funding of researchers should take into account a researcher's treatment of staff and subjects.

Abundance of 'quick and dirty research'

Much of the research in the social sciences is conducted to produce quickly some publishable product. Often this research is not only poorly done but also not comprehensive or thorough enough to test theory adequately. Standards of appropriate research methodology are too often set aside due to high costs or time constraints. In addition, poor quality research is often a result of the researcher not having adequate research skills or training.

The structure of many academic and research institutions perpetuates this practice in several ways. The most obvious are the 'publish or perish' policies of many universities and colleges. The impact of this policy is enhanced by the policy of journals to publish 'significant' findings from 'successful' research projects. These policies often function to reward 'quick and dirty' research. For example, the untenured assistant professor who needs a long list of publications (and these are sometimes not evaluated for quality) may be more likely to use research methodology which produces significant results instead of appropriate methodology and cut corners in using other appropriate research methods since they take more time. There are further pressures from funding agencies, superiors and colleagues. These pressures can act to make good quality research less rewarding than a more expedient, but 'adequate' product.

Another complicating factor is that, as students, we learn in the classroom to view the research process in idealistic terms. We assume that most research projects are carried out 'successfully,' according to the quality standards we have learned in texts or in the classroom.

When we begin to engage in our own research or work with other researchers in training positions, we can become disillusioned and either change our research orientation or discontinue doing research altogether (for example, see Reinharz, 1979).

While we may not want to compromise our ideal standards, the pressures of competition are real and may in fact become more pervasive given the academic job market and the increasing scarcity of funding for social science research. There is no easy solution to this conflict. Although for some feminists the solution may lie in abandoning the research profession, it is important to have women researchers, and especially feminists, in the social sciences. Not only must we insist on high standards of research but we must direct some energy to changing the existing academic and professional structures which often reward the quantity of research and not the quality. This then becomes a political as well as a personal concern.

Tackling the traumas of research can be made easier if one comes prepared. Exposure to *both* the positive and the negative aspects of the research and a realistic appraisal of the difficulties are important in graduate school. For example, researchers who have extensive training and experience will be more likely to estimate correctly the time and cost factors in their research, allowing for the generation of good quality research within these parameters.

Finally, this discussion points up the need for feminists to differentiate between poor and quality research and to educate others to do so as well. Since the purpose of this paper is not to explicate the numerous methods for producing quality research, the reader is referred to social science research texts which cover quantitative research methods, such as Babbie (1979).

The simplistic and superficial nature of quantitative research

Related to the problem of 'quick and dirty' research is the problem of research which takes a simplistic and superficial view of human behavior and attitudes.

The dangers of simplistic quantitative research are well known to feminists. The most obvious examples are studies which ignore sex differences or look only at sex differences as causal factors without exploring other mediating causal variables. Too often the conclusions from these studies suggest some 'inherent' difference between the sexes (see Benbow and Stanley, 1980). For example, a study which looks at *only* sex differences in maths achievement might find correctly that boys do better than girls on certain maths achievement tests. By not exploring explanatory factors, researchers leave open possible reasons for the differences. While the numbers may be accurate, the simplistic nature of the design can be misleading to the public. Although it is impossible to examine all factors related to a behavior or attitude, it is important to collect enough information so that conclusions drawn from the findings are meaningful and advance theory.[3]

Simplistic research is not inherent to quantitative research but often results from sloppy methodology. In fact, quantitative methods make the analysis of complex research designs possible. Sophisticated quantitative methods and computer techniques have been developed in recent years and are being continually brought up to date in order to handle the analysis of complex data — for example, longitudinal designs.

Although qualitative data often seem more complex than quantitative data, it sometimes depends on which questions are asked by researchers. One could imagine qualitative data which, while thoroughly descriptive in regard to an attitude (e.g., boys are more active than girls), offers no insight as to the reasons for these beliefs. Good qualitative and quantitative researchers need to explore issues by asking appropriately complex questions.

While there is a practical limit to the complexity of quantitative data (and thus analysis), the limit for qualitative data seems higher since, at least theoretically, it can be as detailed as possible. For example, the quantification or coding of an open-ended response puts certain limits on the number of different responses. Cost and time factors allow a practical limit on the number of codes used and the kind of dimensions coded. Qualitative data do not necessarily need such reinterpretation before analysis. On the one hand, the more complex qualitative data are, the more difficult and less likely it is for there to be consensus in analysis. On the other hand, the more complex the qualitative data are, the less superficial and potentially more meaningful they are.

No matter how thorough the questions in quantitative research, quantitative data will yield findings which are superficial in nature, *compared to* most qualitative data. Even the most complex and sophisticated quantitative research report cannot impart the same 'in-depth' understanding of respondents as, for example, a thorough case history. This is most likely due to detailed description which is lacking in quantitative research.

It seems apparent therefore that quantitative research could benefit from the addition of qualitative data. Certainly qualitative data can support and explicate the meaning of quantitative research. Every quantitative research project should include some qualitative data, not only for use by researchers to understand their respondents better, but also to include in presentations and publications so that others may gain a deeper understanding of the quantified results.

Objective appearance of quantitative data

Feminists have argued that 'quick and dirty' quantitative social science research often gets interpreted by the public as the 'truth'; the public does not distinguish between good and bad social science. Most researchers would agree that quantitative data appear to be more objective than qualitative data. However, no social researcher can claim that quantitative data are either truly objective or that they measure 'reality.' What they can claim is that 'good' quantitative data (meeting accepted standards of validity) can be used *more* objectively to evaluate theory than qualitative data. This claim is based on the fact that the principles and guidelines for quantitative data analysis have been specifically developed to produce an objective evaluation. This is true to a greater extent than in qualitative research.

To understand this dialogue more clearly it is important to distinguish between objectivity in the research process and objectivity as a part of the analysis of data. First, there can be no such thing as truly 'objective' research in the sense that the product of research is *not* subject to our own value judgments (Babbie, 1979). Personal biases impinge on the research process in many ways, particularly in theory formulation and interpretation, but also in development of design, data collection, and analysis. However, by using accepted standards of research, the final product can be less subject to those biases. Or at least one can more readily identify the biases that may have been operative. Thus while there is no absolute objectivity possible, the research product can be more or less objective and the nature of the bias can be more or less easily evaluated. For example, a research project in which interviewers openly make personal comments on a respondent's answers may produce less objective data than one in which interviewers comment little.

Second, quantitative analysis is, as much as possible, an objective evaluation of data because it is conducted according to generally accepted procedural methods based on mathematical principles.[4] These principles applied to the analysis of data result in a product which is relatively unaffected by personal bias. This is because mathematics is based on logical assumptions that are usually not open for debate. For example, suppose that a researcher is interested in why some women find it difficult to return to work after being full-time homemakers. A quantitative researcher might ask respondents to indicate the importance of various reasons. (A skilled researcher would include a comprehensive list of reasons and allow for unanticipated reasons.) Quantitative analyses could produce statistical evidence that most women feel that lack of good jobs is the most important reason. Further, the analysis could indicate either that no other reasons were important or that several other reasons were marginally or similarly important. The relative degree of importance of various factors could be specifically determined. This interpretation of the data could not reasonably be refuted because the analysis is a logical (mathematical) interpretation of data. Babbie (1979) terms this phenomenon 'intersubjectivity' and defines it as 'two scientists with different subjective orientations arriv[ing] at the same conclusion if each conducted the same experiment' (p. 52).

A qualitative researcher exploring the same issue might ask women why it was difficult to return to work. Many reasons might be given and analysis without quantification might indicate that poor job possibilities was a major one. However, this analysis would be more subject to debate and thus personal judgment because the evaluation was not based on standards as objective as mathematical principles. Another researcher might say that job possibilities was not such an important reason and a third researcher might arrive at an altogether different opinion.

The appearance of objectivity is a powerful tool for changing public opinion. As feminists, we need to monitor closely and publicize the problems with research which appears objective − but in fact may be a product of poor methodology and/or subjective bias. (See Parsons

(1981) and Parlee (1976) for examples of responses to such research.) Furthermore, we can use this power of quantitative research to our advantage to change public or political opinion in support of feminist goals. For example, we can *document* the enormous number of unwanted teenage pregnancies in support of free access to birth control. We can *document* the sex discrimination which occurs in school systems and use it to advocate change. This documentation is possible because of the use of quantitative research methods. (See, for example, Chapter 3 in Stasz Stoll (1974) for a statistical overview of sexism in our society.)

More important than using the *appearance* of objectivity for our benefit is the *actual* objectivity which quantitative methods allow in theory evaluation (i.e., data analysis). As noted earlier, it is imperative for feminist theory to be assessed accurately so it can be used to direct political and research work. For example, there may be differing opinions as to why sexual harassment occurs in the workplace. Our personal values and experiences will influence our opinions as to why it occurs. If we want to combat the practice, we need to understand and assess its causes accurately. High quality quantitative research can best do this, and the findings which result will not likely be debated on the basis of personal view. This is extremely important if we want to create effective programs and policies to reduce the incidence of sexual harassment. Directing our energies toward the correct target problem areas we define as important will help us to achieve our goals. An inaccurate evaluation of the target or problem area will result in wasted energies.

Even if one accepts the argument that quantitative data analysis is more objective than qualitative analysis, and may be important for feminist theory evaluation and for political and public opinion change, one may not accept the idea that objectivity is a valuable goal if the researcher has to be detached from her work. This emphasis on detachment in quantitative research is expressed by Kerlinger (1979):

The mixture of strong commitment and advocacy of political and social programs, on the one hand, and scientific research into the problems of such programs, on the other hand, seem to induce bias and what has been called selective perception. This means that we see what we want or need to see rather what is actually there. So strong is this tendency that I have almost gotten to the point of thinking that behavioral scientists should not do research on the things they passionately advocate. Or better, when they do it, they should conceive and use exceptionally elaborate safeguards against their own biases (p. 17).

Too many social researchers assume that they are 'appropriately' detached if they do not have strong feelings about the issues they study. Often what they do not realize is that their views really indicate a strong commitment to the status quo — which is as potentially biased as any other orientation.

Feminists have argued, and correctly so, that researchers need to become more involved with and concerned about the people they study. It is critically important here to realize that to conduct 'objective' quantitative research, one does *not* have to be detached and unconcerned about the topic. Having a strong opinion about the subject of research does not necessarily mean that research decisions will be any more biased than if those opinions were not held. The use of good research methodology helps to assure against this accusation. None of us can possibly be completely objective toward our research. Therefore our methods must be as objective as possible. This is why there are clear guidelines, codes of ethics, and standards for doing quantitative research. Whatever our position, we should always make clear in our reports and publications our opinions about the subject of our research so that others will know with what initial orientation we began and carried our research.

As a feminist and a social science researcher, I have clear and strong political and personal goals for my research. The topics I choose to study and the theory I use to direct my research are strongly affected by these goals. To evaluate my theories as accurately as possible, I use some traditional research procedures and quantitative methods. Using these methods does not lessen in any way my strong commitment to feminism, or my appreciation of the value of qualitative research. And my commitment to feminism does not necessarily mean that my research is of poor quality due to bias.

Generalizing with quantitative research

One important part of the quantitative research process is generalizing. When researchers study a large group of people, they usually cannot gain information on all the persons in the group due to time and cost factors. They often select a smaller sample of persons from the larger group to furnish the needed information. If the sample is selected so that it is representative of the larger population, then the researcher can correctly (while accounting for small errors) infer that the information found in the sample applies to the larger population. The validity of this inference is obviously important *if* one wishes to make generalized statements. This issue is especially critical in reviewing certain methods of qualitative research since some methods (particularly case history) do not permit generalization. Many aspects of Freudian psychology are good examples of generalization from a non-representative sample.

Generalized statements are important both for advising policymakers of public opinion and deciding on strategies for bringing about change in public opinion itself. This can be useful to feminists, who, for example, need to know the strength of public support for the right to life amendment or the ERA, in order to develop appropriate political strategies for action.

Conclusions

As indicated above, most of the feminist criticisms of the traditional quantitative research process have merit, although an exploration of the issues surrounding these criticisms indicates the need for caution in condemning quantitative research altogether. The discussion of the criticisms also suggests methods for resolving those problems which do arise. These suggested changes in the traditional research process, which increase consistency with feminist values, will obviously not be fully implemented for some time. In the meantime, as feminists we have two plausible options for dealing with existing inconsistencies. We can either reject quantitative research altogether or value it for its benefits and work to change those elements which are antithetical to feminist ideas. (I do not consider ignoring the inconsistencies a plausible option.)

My preference is for the second option, since I believe it is the most effective method for changing the sexist structure of society to a more egalitarian one. There must be appropriate quantitative evidence to counter the pervasive and influential quantitative sexist research which has and continues to be generated in the social sciences. Feminist researchers can best accomplish this. If some of the traditional procedures used to produce that needed evidence are contrary to our feminist values, then we must change those procedures accordingly. In the process of change we not only must remember to view our research in a political context as outlined above in this paper, but we must support one another against the academic and professional pressures to compromise our standards. The better quality research that we do, the more likely that that research will influence others and ultimately help in achieving their goals.

Notes

1 An early version of this paper was presented at the National Women's Studies Association Conference, Bloomington, Indiana, May 1980. I would like to thank Jacquie Eccles Parsons, Marti Bombyk and Shula Reinharz for their valuable comments on the manuscript. I would also like to acknowledge the ideas and suggestions from women in the Feminist Methodology Seminar at the University of Michigan: Nicki Beisel, Marti Bombyk, Sue Contratto, Linda Kaboolian, Eleanor McLaughlin, Cindy Palmer, Paula Rabinowitz, Shula Reinharz and Betsey Taylor.
2 For an interesting analysis of the benefits of and difficulties with women's qualitative research, see Peplau (1977).
3 The criticisms of simplistic research apply mostly to areas of research in which theory is well-developed, since researchers should know and examine the major relevant factors in a study. When research is exploratory, it is more acceptable to produce 'isolated' findings needed to develop theory.
4 Although there is not absolute agreement on which mathematical or statistical method to use, there is consensus as to which methods are appropriate for which kind of data and for the kind of questions being asked of the data.

References

Babbie, Earl R. (1979), *The Practice of Social Research*, Belmont, Wadsworth.
Bailey, Kenneth D. (1978), *Methods of Social Research*, New York, Free Press.
Benbow, C.P. and Stanley, J.C. (1980), 'Sex Differences in Mathematical Ability: Fact or Artifact?,' *Science*, vol. 210, no. 12.
Bogdan, R. and Taylor, S. (1975), *Introduction to Qualitative Research Methods*, New York, Wiley.
Chesler, Phyllis (1972), *Women and Madness*, New York, Doubleday.

Cox, Sue (1976), *Female Psychology: The Emerging Self*, Chicago, Science Research Associates.

Depner, Charlene (1981), 'Toward the Further Development of Feminist Psychology,' paper presented at the mid-winter conference of the Association for Women in Psychology, Boston.

Fox Keller, Evelyn (1978), 'Gender and Science,' *Psychoanalysis and Contemporary Thought*, vol. 1.

Fox Keller, Evelyn (1980), 'Feminist Critique of Science: A Forward or Backward Move?,' *Fundamenta Scientiae*, vol. 1.

Freedman, D. and Camburn, D. (1981), 'Some Techniques for Maintaining Respondent Participation in Longitudinal Studies,' paper presented at the Population Association of America, Washington, DC, March.

Frieze, I.H., Parsons, J.E., Johnson, P.B., Ruble, D.N. and Zellman, G.L. (1978), *Women and Sex Roles: A Social Psychological Perspective*, New York, W.W. Norton.

Glaser, B. and Strauss, A. (1967), *The Discovery of Grounded Theory: Strategies for Qualitative Research*, Chicago, Aldine.

Griggs vs. Duke Power Co. (1971), 401 US 424.

Jaggar, A.M. and Struhl, P.R. (1978), *Feminist Frameworks: Alternative Theoretical Accounts of the Relations between Women and Men*, New York, McGraw-Hill.

Kerlinger, Fred N. (1979), *Behavioral Research: A Conceptual Approach*, New York, Holt, Rinehart & Winston.

Kroeber, Theodora (1969), *Ishi in Two Worlds*, Berkeley, University of California Press.

Levitin, T.E., Quinn, R.P. and Staines, G.L. (1973), 'A Woman is 58% of a Man,' *Psychology Today*, March.

Lewis, Oscar (1961), *The Children of Sanchez*, New York, Random House.

Liebow, Elliot (1967), *Tally's Corner*, Boston, Little, Brown.

McCall, G. and Simmons, J.L. (eds) (1969), *Issues in Participant Observation*, Reading, Addison-Wesley.

Millett, Kate (1969), *Sexual Politics*, New York, Avon.

Parlee, Mary B. (1976), 'The Premenstrual Syndrome,' in S. Cox (ed.), *Female Psychology: The Emerging Self*, Chicago, Science Research Associates.

Parsons, Jacqueline E. (1981), 'Social Forces Shape Attitudes and Performance,' unpublished manuscript.

Peplau, Letitia A. (1977), 'The Hite Report: A Nationwide Study on Female Sexuality by Shere Hite,' *Psychology of Women Quarterly*, vol. 2, no. 1.

Reinharz, Shulamit (1979), *On Becoming a Social Scientist*, San Francisco, Jossey-Bass.

Schatzman, L. and Strauss, A. (1973), *Field Research*, New Jersey, Prentice-Hall.

Stasz Stoll, Clarice (1974), *Female and Male: Socialization, Social Roles and Social Structure*, Iowa, Wm C. Brown.

Tangri, S.S. and Strasburg, G.L. (1979), 'Can Research on Women Be More Effective in Shaping Policy?' *Psychology of Women Quarterly*, vol. 3, no. 4.

Weiss, C. and Bucuvalas, M. (1977), The Challenge of Social Research to Decision Making, in C. Weiss (ed.), *Using Social Research in Public Policy Making*, Lexington Books.

Weisstein, Naomi (1970), '"Kinder, Küche, Kirche" as Scientific Law: Psychology Constructs the Female,' in R. Morgan (ed.), *Sisterhood Is Powerful*, New York, Vintage.

11

Experiential analysis: a contribution to feminist research

Shulamit Reinharz

Introduction

In 1979 I published a book written over several years, documenting existential-methodological problems encountered in the process of becoming a female social scientist (Reinharz, 1979). Using a combined autobiographical, literature review, and theoretical perspective, I described an intellectual journey starting with training in survey research, continuing through participant observation, and culminating in what I call 'experiential analysis.' The purpose of this essay is to delineate further the background of 'experiential analysis,' explain what the method consists of, describe problems which arise in carrying out a project using this method, and suggest further implications such as the relation between 'experiential analysis' and feminist concerns.

Background of 'experiential analysis': the sociology of knowledge perspective applied to the social sciences

Methods and methodology are not simply techniques and rationales for the conduct of research. Rather they must be understood in relation to specific historical, cultural, ideological and other contexts. Methods and procedures for conducting research are in continuous flux, influenced by the kinds of relative proportion of people attracted to or permitted access to given disciplines, the values and philosophy of the social milieu, the conceptual underpinning of common sense at the time, the means of communication and level of technology available, and the discipline's previous history. Thus, when one ponders the questions — what methods will I use in my study? or, why was a certain method used for a given study? — these are not simply technical issues but profound socio-historical-disciplinary concerns.

Within the discipline of sociology, there is a subdiscipline called the 'sociology of knowledge.' Its concern is to explain the relationship between the knowledge produced or accepted in a particular society at any time, and the other dimensions of that society. In the words of Karl Mannheim, a significant contributor, 'the sociology of knowledge seeks to comprehend thought in the concrete setting of an historical-social situation' (1936, p. 3). To do this we have to examine persons 'who have developed a particular style of thought in an endless series of responses to certain typical situations characterizing their common position' (Ibid.). For example, Freud's theory of the formation of female identity centers on their establishing an orientation to men as a product of girls' oedipal transition. Nancy Chodorow shows us that 'feminine heterosexuality in this model has Victorian characteristics that include women's passivity and the subordination of sex to pro-creation' (1978, p. 111). She and others writing today about the formation of femaleness are in turn influenced by the contemporary ideology of feminism.

Mills's (1943) study of the theory of social pathology is another explication of a social theory rooted in the social conditions of its proponents. He studied social pathology as a 'point of entry for the examination of the style of reflection and the social-historical basis of American sociology' (p. 4). He shows that the social pathologists' perspective is linked to the fact that they

> were born in small towns, or on farms near small towns, three-fourths of which were in states not industrialized during the youth of the authors. The social circles and strata in which they have generally moved are quite homogeneous (p. 5),

(i.e., reform groups, colleges, voluntary societies, their spouse's con-nections, etc.). Like the critics of Freudian theory, Mills demonstrates that American sociological theory was grounded in the social position of its theoreticians.

Thomas Kuhn was first exposed to the history of his own discipline, theoretical physics, when he attempted to teach physical science to non-scientists. 'To my complete surprise, that exposure to out-of-date scientific theory and practice radically undermined some of my basic conceptions about the nature of science' (1962, p. v). In reaction, he switched fields from physics to the history of science and explored what it was like to think scientifically in different historical periods. As is well known, he then directed his energy to explaining how different theories and discoveries emerge in response to an accumulation of unexplained anomalies, and how a new paradigm crowds out those that preceded it. Murray Davis (1971) has extended Kuhn's argument in a social psychological way. He claims that ideas are accepted not because they are 'true' but because they have attracted attention and strike people as 'interesting.' The structure of 'the experience of something as interesting,' according to Davis, is the overturning of a commonsensical or previously held idea. When this is dramatic and clear, the new idea takes hold, and eventually a search gets under way for refutations of the now new.

Method and theory preference vary also by national milieu and culture, a subject discussed by Merton (1968) in his comparison of European and American variants of sociological studies. It is interesting to take note of, and then ponder the contexts of these norms. For example, Tesch informs us that today,

> In Germany, interpretative (hermeneutic) studies are the conventional way of conducting research and experimental research is the modern method of the computer age. In the 1950's, experimental research was hardly heard of (except in certain branches of psychology), and even in the 1960's it was considered quite daring to do anything other than what amounted to phenomenological inquiry. The first German statistics book for the behavioral sciences (other than American translations) did not appear until the 1970's. Today, experimentation is an accepted part of behavioral science research, but a methodology book will usually devote less space to it than to observation or 'Interaktionsanalyse,' the content analysis of human interaction (1980, p. 54).

Because of the value clashes and radicalizing events of the 1960s and 1970s in the United States, Alvin Gouldner recognized that the practices and assumptions of the social sciences, particularly sociology, are inconsistent with emerging values and social conditions. He converted the sociology of knowledge perspective, which had hitherto been applied primarily to historic periods or other cultures, into a reflexive sociology which is self-consciously self-critical. He claimed that current circumstances demand 'heightened self-awareness among sociologists' (1970, p. 25), which means that we must ask ourselves questions about why *we* hold our professional and scientific beliefs. Why for instance, do we think that social science should be value-free?[1] He urges us to recognize that 'scientific method,' for example, 'is not simply a logic but a morality' (1970, p. 26). If this is so, then new methods become accessible if one is willing to risk being considered 'immoral' (i.e., not rigorous) by those colleagues who hold that morality is exclusively on their side.[2]

Contemporary social science is part of the fabric of our social life and reinforces the current order and its values. When there have been changes in social values, the social sciences have been influenced by them, but rarely has the process been reversed. Sometimes the timing of social science research publication and public events are all so closely tied that it is difficult to determine which influenced which. For example, 'The Stanford Prison Experiment' was concluded just before the sensational shootouts at San Quentin and Attica. It was publicized in the popular media as well as in professional literature and contributed to mounting demands for prison reform in the early 1970s (Stannard-Friel, 1981).

Jessie Bernard (1975) has applied a sociology of knowledge perspective to the branch of *psychological* research which directly evaluates women — sex differences research. She views that body of research as 'a sociological phenomenon, an institution' (p. 7) and asks why it has selected to investigate certain issues, what are its objectives, what is its methodological and ideological stance? Her by now familiar answer is that the objectives and stance mirror a male-controlled and male-defined environment (see also Weisstein, 1971). Interestingly, when the sociology of knowledge analytic framework has been applied to *sociology*, Dorothy Smith (1974) shows an identical pattern: 'how sociology is thought — its methods, conceptual schemes and theories — has been based on and built up within the male social universe (even when women have participated in its doing)' (p. 7). This corroboration from two disciplines can be viewed as adding credibility to the analysis, although it has also been dismissed on the grounds that the critics have a shared perspective (Levin, 1980).

My own development of 'experiential analysis' as a critical method rooted in this time and place, based on an alternative set of assumptions from the objectivist mainstream morality-methodology, and stemming from perceived contradictions or inadequacies in certain research methods, was possible only within the context of my own continued application of a sociology of knowledge perspective to the social sciences. I asked myself continuously, 'What should I do with all this criticism?' Should I accept, modify or create a methodology? Vaughter answers: 'The response called for is the restructuring of the methods, subjects, apparatus, materials, procedures, discussions, and references' (1976, p. 143). My insights made it difficult to simply 'add on' another method to the existing corpus. Instead, they made me rethink (or if very bold, revamp) the entire enterprise of social science (see also Gould, 1980). This revamping orientation is criticized by some as 'throwing the baby out with the bathwater' (Wallston, 1979), but it is clear to many that sometimes a new baby needs to be born! (Westkott, 1979). It is within this alternative, dialectical rather than cumulative framework that 'experiential analysis' is being suggested.

Toward a new method for a revamped social science

The first step in articulating a new method is to understand that one's personally experienced dissatisfaction with conventional methods is not an intrapsychic, private problem but derives from structural inconsistencies and skewed assumptions underpinning the methods themselves. Thus one begins to sense that there is a gap between the 'experience of the world ... and the theoretical schemes available to think about it in' (Smith, 1974, p. 7). When one's critique is articulated and made public, others will find resonance in their own experiences and thus one's *private* concerns will be redefined as *shared*. Making one's concerns public requires some courage. Being stuck in the extreme dualism of micro- and macro-interpretations of one's thoughts is paralyzing. The challenge is to convert the private concern into a public issue.

Those who fail to have their private insights confirmed by others (in any area, not just social science methodology) receive the social label of mentally ill, incompetent or absurd. To abandon one's insights altogether rather than be so labelled is to become alienated from one's self, a conformist. The difficulty in accepting the validity of one's own experiences is part of our cultural heritage and rigorously perpetuated in our schools (Toby, 1955). Marx's 'false consciousness,' Freud's 'unconscious,' Durkeim's 'social facts' in contrast with personal volition, sociology's 'latent and manifest functions' which undermine the notion that things are as they appear, the substitution of computer-based quantification for individual assessment — all of these dovetail to cast doubt on human interpretations and intentions.

Women's position in patriarchal society casts further doubt on the truth of our ideas. Feminism has partially corrected this imbalance. First, it has *confirmed the experience of women* which had hitherto been denied as real or important. The recovery of experience began in the 'consciousness raising' or 'rap groups' in which women talked 'to each other about their individual experiences and analyzed them communally . . . . From a sociological perspective the rap group is probably the most valuable contribution the women's liberation movement has made so far to the tools for social change' (Freeman, 1973, p. 22). Second, feminism revalues experience as a part of social science methodology (Wallston, 1979). 'One hallmark of the feminist research in any field seems to be the investigator's continual testing of the plausibility of the work against her own experience' (Parlee, 1979, p. 130). The new definition of experience is that it is interesting (not arbitrary), effective (in the sense that our ideas shape our world and are not simply shaped by it), uniquely human, and contextual. Parlee connected the issues of the devaluation of experience and the context-stripping traditional scientific methods when she wrote: 'The commitment to the experimental method . . . functions to . . . obscure the connection between individual experience and social roles and institutions' (1979, p. 133).

The second step in articulating a new method is to specify the assumptions of the traditional framework which are being challenged (see Sherif, 1979; Mishler, 1979). Gouldner (1970) would call these assumptions the values of the traditional morality. Once these assumptions are clearly articulated, one can suggest an alternate set. The following is a product of my attempt:

Table 11.1 Contrasting claims of sociological research models[3]

Mainstream sociology claims to be	An alternative method would acknowledge that it is
Exclusively rational in the conduct of research and the analysis of data	A mix of rational, serendipitous and intuitive phenomena in research and analysis
Scientific	Accurate but artistic
Oriented to carefully defined structures	Oriented to processes
Completely impersonal	Personal
Oriented to the prediction and control of events and things	Oriented to understanding phenomena
Interested in the validity of research findings for scholars	Interested in the meaningfulness of research findings to the scholarly and user communities
Objective	A mix of objective and subjective orientations
Capable of producing generalized principles	Capable of producing specific explanations
Interested in replicable events and procedures	Interested in unique although frequently occurring phenomena
Capable of producing completed analyses of a research problem	Limited to producing partial discoveries of ongoing events
Interested in addressing problems with predefined concepts	Interested in generating concepts in vivo, in the field itself

These two columns closely parallel what Bakan (1966) has referred to as the two basic tendencies of human existence: the agentic and communal. The contrasts he suggests are the following:

Table 11.2

Agency	Communion
Separation (of subject and object)	Fusion
Repression (of feelings)	Expression
Conquest, control, mastery (of others, nature)	Acceptance
Contracted (relationships)	Uncontracted cooperation
Ordering, quantifying	Nonlinear patterning
Masculine	Feminine

Feminist scholars such as Carlson (1972) and Fox Keller (1978) have added elements to the agentic and communal ways of being/knowing:

Table 11.3

Agency	Communion
Hard/dry	Soft/wet
Context-stripped	Situation-embedded, contextualized
Autonomy	Interdependence
Positivism	Grounded observationism of action, words, sentiments
Value-freedom	Value-oriented
Androcentric	Humanistic, egalitarian
Ego-enhancement	Egoboundary diffusion
Objectivity	Subjectivity
Science/mind	Nature

Graham and Rawlings (1980) suggest a tri-partite division among sexist, non-sexist, and feminist assumptions and methods in research. The suggested communal epistemology linked to the communal ontology is 'naturalistic observation' of behavior, 'sensitivity to intrinsic structure and qualitative patterning of phenomena studied and greater personal participation of the investigator' (Carlson, 1972, p. 20); a recent example is Sharff, although she is publicly criticized by a member of the setting, *Psychology Today* (1981).

Releasing oneself from thought structures which isolate 'variables' in supposed unidirectional relation is a good way to begin (Blumer, 1956). Since research has been confined primarily to the agentic mode, Carlson suggested that 'research paradigms with more communal types of research await development and reception' (1972, p. 21; see also Vaughter, 1976). Wallston (1979) reports that a 'transactional methodology' is being developed at George Peabody Teachers College, Vanderbilt University, as an alternative to static, linear models. In the interim, it is important to recognize the 'machismo factor' (Bernard, 1975) in research, and as outlined in step one, to 'achieve liberation from the constraints of agentic modes of inquiry . . . . [B]y developing thoughtfully the communal aspects of content and method, [we] may succeed in bringing forth those new research paradigms needed for the scientific revolution (Kuhn, 1970) of our time' (Carlson, 1972, p. 29). The reason that some feminist scholars talk about liberation from the agentic is that the dichotomy is not one of equals but is asymmetric in terms of credibility and legitimacy (Parlee, 1979).

The third step is to connect these conventional and alternative assumptions into specific components of research procedures. Here is one example:

Table 11.4 Research models in contemporary sociology[4]

	Conventional or patriarchal	Alternative or feminist
Units of study	Predefined, operationalized concepts stated as hypotheses.	Natural events encased in their ongoing contexts.

	Conventional or patriarchal	Alternative or feminist
Sharpness of focus	Limited, specialized, specific, exclusive.	Broad, inclusive.
Data type	Reports of attitudes and actions as in question-naires, interviews and archives.	Feelings, behavior, thoughts, insights, actions as witnessed or experienced.
Topic of study	Manageable issue derived from scholarly liter-ature, selected for potential scholarly contribution, some-times socially signi-ficant.	Socially significant prob-lem sometimes related to issues discussed in scholarly literature.
Role of research: in relation to environment	Control of environment is desired, attempt to manage research conditions.	Openness to environment, immersion, being sub-ject to and shaped by it.
in relation to subjects	Detached.	Involved, sense of commit-ment, participation, sharing of fate.
as a person	Irrelevant.	Relevant, expected to change during process.
impact on re-searcher	Irrelevant.	Anticipated, recorded, reported, valued.
Implementation of method	As per design, decided a priori.	Method determined by unique characteristics of field setting.
Validity criteria	Proof, evidence, statis-tical significance; study must be replic-able and yield same results to have valid findings.	Completeness, plausi-bility, illustrativeness, understanding, respon-siveness to readers' or subjects' experience; study cannot, however, be replicated.

Table 11.4 Continued

	Conventional or patriarchal	Alternative or feminist
The role of theory	Crucial as determinant of research design	Emerges from research implementation.
Data analysis	Arranged in advance relying on deductive logic, done when all data are 'in'.	Done during the study, relying on inductive logic.
Manipulation of data	Utilization of statistical analyses.	Creation of gestalts and meaningful patterns.
Research objectives	Testing hypotheses.	Development of understanding through grounded concepts and descriptions.
Presentation format	Research report form; report of conclusions with regard to hypotheses stated in advance, or presentation of data obtained from instruments.	Story, description with emergent concepts; including documentation of process of discovery.
Failure	Statistically insignificant variance.	Pitfalls of process illustrate the subject.
Values	Researchers' attitudes not revealed, recognized or analyzed, attempts to be value-free, objective.	Researchers' attitudes described and discussed, values acknowledged, revealed, labelled.
Role of reader	Scholarly community addressed. evaluation of research design, management, and findings.	Scholarly and user community addressed and engaged; evaluate usefulness and responsiveness to perceived needs.

Can we create methods which are communal (rather than agentic), and that are grounded in people's experience of the world as well as in our own? Can we create methods without being 'methodolatrous' and without inventing new rigidities which will distort anew that which is being studied? I think the answer to these questions is that these methods already partially exist, but they have been so undervalued that they constantly need to be rediscovered.[5] Also, because they have been increasingly undervalued in our society (Brown and Gilmartin, 1969; McCartney, 1970; Patel, 1972), they have not had the benefit of much refinement (Reason and Rowan, 1981). As each 'rediscovery' or contribution is made, it appears new and gets its own name. For example, Gould reports that 'feminist sociologists are trying oral histories, textual analysis and a more politically self-conscious ethnomethodology' (1980, p. 465). DiIorio is developing 'feminist phenomenology' (1980). She defines the procedure as follows:

> Researchers will utilize first-hand, immediate and intimate contact
> with their subjects through direct observation and reflective analysis,
> drawing upon her or his own experiential information (feelings, fan-
> tasies, thoughts) as well as her or his observations of what others say
> and do in order to relate the subjective and objective dimensions
> (p. 21).

There are calls for qualitative and descriptive studies, taxonomies of situations, systematic analysis of situations (Wallston, 1979) and just plain talking to people and observing them.

People who call themselves 'existential sociologists' also approximate what we have been discussing. 'Existential sociology is defined descriptively as the study of human experience-in-the-world in all its forms' (Douglas and Johnson, 1977, p. vii). They talk about recognizing feelings, not just ideas (see also Hochschild, 1975), about observing, describing and analyzing one's own inner experiences and reflections, as well as those of others. They choose the phrase 'existential' rather than 'experiential' so as to avoid appearing like a distinctively defined method or obscuring the connection with existential philosophy. My own decision to label an alternative method 'experiential analysis' rather than 'existential' or 'phenomenological' was (1) to avoid inheriting prejudiced reactions of those who already dissociate themselves or are unfamiliar with existentialism or phenomenology, (2) to avoid

connotations of rigidity likely to be connected with a specified philosophical school, and (3) to create a term that was descriptive of an
activity, i.e., analysis of experience. In recently completed doctoral
dissertations at the University of Michigan, students are carrying this
line of reasoning further: one has devised a method called 'dialogic
retrospection' (Kieffer, 1981) which he defines as an open and active
exchange between the researcher and participant in a partnership of
co-research.

Elements of an experiential analysis

In order to break away from the linear model which would describe
a research method as a progression of steps, I would like to present
'experiential analysis' as a collection of interacting components:
*assumptions, personal preparation, problem formulation, data gather-
ing and stopping, data digestion and presentation, policy questions.*

The following discussion is divided into sections elaborating on
each of these components. As a guiding framework, I suggest that
research within the experiential mode has three distinct purposes:
it should represent growth and understanding in the arena of *the
problem* investigated, *the person(s)* doing the investigation, and *the
method* utilized. Such a triple achievement yields deep insight into
the study's subject matter, new personal knowledge about the investigator him/herself, and further innovations with regard to method.
This integrated approach to research (Vaughter, 1976) guides problem selection so as to make personal growth likely. It begins to fashion
a non-masculine or non-conventional reflexive model and vocabulary
of research. All three yields should be communicated. Another criterion
for evaluation of research is its social value — what impact does it have
on the distribution of power and resources?

Assumptions underlying an experiential method overlap with those
of symbolic interactionism (Blumer, 1962), social construction of
reality theories (Berger and Luckman, 1967), and humanistic philosophy (Roche, 1973). In these theories, people are intentional beings
who create and discover meaning; they are not simply actors carrying
out meanings given in an objective reality. In addition, humans are
defined as processes in continuous development over time, and in
continuous interaction with environments in space. Morgan and Smircich

(1980) have provided a very useful table of the range of assumptions which underlie different research methods in the social sciences. The assumptions I outlined cluster in what they call the 'subjectivist' in contrast with 'objectivist' approaches. Lest these assumptions appear strange, however, Roche reminds us that these assumptions 'are very much those of everyday common sense' (1973, p. 297). An additional assumption is that disciplinary boundaries in academia have no counterpart in social reality, so a researcher is better off drawing on multiple disciplines than confining her/himself to only one. The above assumptions have been part of the interpretive tradition in social science (Westkott, 1979).

Personal preparation for 'experiential analysis' borrows from phenomenology in the sense that phenomenologists attempt to suspend preconceptions about the matter they are about to study. Among phenomenologists this is called 'epoché' (Husserl, 1931). Practically, this means that experiential researchers will not do an extensive literature search *before* an investigation but rather *after* it, so as not to create self-fulfilling prophecies in their research. The researcher attempts to avoid bringing a priori categories to the project[6] and therefore eliminates 'front-end instrumentation' (Miles, 1979, p. 590). 'The rigor of the research is thus dependent on its ability to maintain the "strangeness" and purity of the presuppositionlessness of experience' (Kieffer, 1981).

At the same time, the researcher investigates his/her own previous experiences, intentions, hopes, prejudices to try to understand what s/he is bringing to the study (some researchers recommend psychoanalysis as appropriate preparation; see Reinharz, 1979, p. 13). S/he also keeps a personal diary throughout the research process, keeping close touch with changing attitudes (e.g. Johnson, 1977). The record of the researcher's feelings and ideas is also data, a clue to the nature of the social environment being studied (for examples, see Reinharz, 1979, pp. 336-53). This record also draws one's attention to the researcher as a human being, not a replaceable object, or in Phillips's term, 'a data-collecting machine . . . (so that) another machine would obtain the same results' (1971, p. 142). Many of one's predispositions, when known, can be questions put to the persons one is studying — they need not be discarded.[7] They are only 'biases' if they are not acknowledged or explored, as is almost always the case in positivist research.

Finally, one tries to ground oneself in a rich array of experiences so that one has comparisons on which to draw in understanding the thing being studied, so that one is not naive. This requirement combined with the previous one yields the following question — are you, the researcher, willing and able to experience the thing being studied or its environment? Are you motivated to do the study because of the hoped-for beneficial impact of the findings on your own life and the lives of others?

Problem formulation has two necessary components: first that the research question be of sincere concern to the *researcher* and that it be of sincere concern to the *subject(s)* so that they will collaborate in uncovering the phenomenon.[8] (For a discussion of the appropriateness of the terms 'researcher' and 'subject,' see p. 180). We should develop a 'participatory model' which 'engage(s) the constituents of science (the public) and the participants in research (the subjects) in the scientific enterprise, that is, in the establishment of research priorities, data collection and data interpretation' (Vaughter, 1976, p. 145). Hessler and New have provided a model of how such collaboration can be accomplished. They created a 'research commune in Boston's Chinatown in which community residents were partners in research' (1972, p. 13). Formulating a problem in a way that is unalienating to the researcher can be accomplished if the researcher carried out a serious process of value-clarification[9] in which s/he asks: what is a significant issue, why do I want to study this, what do I want to discover, what will I do if I discover something very different, who will help, what help do they really need; what experience of mine does this research question reflect?

To formulate a question of concern and interest to the 'subjects' makes it likely that they will collaborate.[10] If this is the case, the subject is likely to be interested in investing the time necessary to work through what is being learned in the project. This is likely if the research *process* provides an opportunity for catharsis or self-discovery, or if the research *product* is likely to provide resources or answers to pressing problems in living. Such a reconceptualization of the 'subject role' places demands on the investigator to seek appropriate subjects, tapping into networks where subjects are recommended or referred only when one's own trustworthiness as a researcher has been examined by referring persons. A revised notion of sampling becomes apparent. Since the trustworthiness of the researcher must be established in the eyes of the subject (as every participant observer learns in the field since s/he does not control the environment), the experiential researcher can facilitate this process by providing clear opportunities to be interviewed, scrutinized and questioned by the subjects even after they have agreed to collaborate. One's trustworthiness is not confined to what one says, of course, but also to how one acts and who one is. Collaborative problem formulation obviously precludes subject deception[11] and completely alters the issue of human subject research reviews. Collaborative problem defining sometimes demands several problem redefinitions until the problem is suitable for joint researcher-population investigation. In other words, meaningful research builds on finding out what is meaningful to oneself and one's research collaborators. Having subject input also minimizes researcher bias since it includes diverse points of view.

The second component of problem formulation is that the question posed should be suitable for experiential analysis. Some appropriate formats include: what is the experience of ————, what is it like to be a ————, what happens in such an environment, what are the kinds of reactions to ————, what does ————mean to people, how do certain persons talk about ————, what does a certain group think is significant about ————, etc. This type of question is open-ended and relatively unstructured. It allows the subject to demonstrate how s/he constructs his/her reality. It focuses on 'what's' rather than 'why's' (Valle and King, 1978), although, *why* can be asked later. From the material one collects, other questions can then be superimposed retrospectively.

Data gathering is the foundation of the research enterprise in the sense that one's interpretations depend on how one's information was obtained in the first place (Phillips, 1971). The exact conditions of data gathering are typically under-reported or frequently reported in a standardized manner obscuring a complete picture of what occurred. The more information is gathered by specific instruments designed to gather data, the more likely that we have created special 'miniature social situations' with their own characteristics (Hyman, 1949). The data collected in those situations tell us about behaviors, attitudes, etc., in those situations, not necessarily in others. This is a general epistemological dilemma in the sense that all knowledge is contingent on the situation under which it is formed.

Recognizing that there is no absolute way to overcome the Heisenberg principle, the Hawthorne effect, artifact effects, response effects, reactivity or artificiality, an experiential analysis strives to know others under multiple conditions that in combination approximate their lived reality. Thus experiential analysis strives to gather data in the natural setting(s) of the persons studied (Willems, 1969) and draws on participant observation research. Experiential analysis raises the question about whether we should study populations or networks rather than aggregated samples, recognizing that a 'complete group' has different merits from those of a 'large n.' Experiential research, as contrasted with positivistic research, relies on 'small n's' since statistical tests need not be applied when interpreting meaning. Involvement in natural settings forces or allows one to be aware of environmental, architectural, climatic, botanical, etc., factors which are significant parts of people's experience, but not frequently asked about in other methods.

Similarly, gathering data in natural settings allows the researcher to play a background rather than foreground role — one is not manipulating the environment but is part of it. One can observe how people speak and act with each other rather than rely entirely on how they respond to you (Brandt, 1972). Several researchers have found major 'discrepancies' between people's reports to researchers about their behavior and the behavior the researcher sees the same people engage in when primarily in their own company (see Cole, 1976, pp. 163-4). An experiential analysis does not define these differences as 'discrepancies' but uses them as leads into the complex process of the construction of reality and/or the influence of social situations on people's expression of beliefs or even perception (Asch, 1952). The data thus are of people's being, not in the world of phenomenologists, but in situations to which they *give* meaning and which shapes their making of themselves and of meaning.

The findings or interpretation of an experiential study requires a detailed ethnographic (Crowle, 1976) or ethological (Vaughter, 1976) description of the conditions under which the information was gathered. Experiential analysis does not utilize instruments such as psychological tests, checklists or coded questionnaires which do not use the subject's categories of thought and action, but it can be aided by technologies that record audially or visually what is occurring. Many such researchers use tape recorders while conversing with people and then analyze the transcripts while listening to the recording (Cole, 1976). Such equipment frees the researcher from recording the conversation by hand while it is occurring or laboriously reconstructing it afterward. The tape recording allows reliving the experience afterward and helps the researcher to understand her/his own contribution to the conversation. The transcript allows the researcher to present interpretations drawing on the language of subjects.

Data gathering in natural settings can alert the researcher to the presence of information that is already available in the setting such as archives, reports, newspapers, posters, letters, diaries, photo albums, etc. — material that historians typically use. Data gathering in the experiential mode is not exclusively data creating, but can really be 'gathering up' what is already there.

Experiential data are not confined to talk but can/should include meaningful action that persons engage in, the processes and activities that compose people's lives. As we examine human living in ordinary settings we will uncover new kinds of data that can be collected — many of these unobtrusive measures have not been imagined yet. An analogy here is psychoanalysis which retrieved dreams, slips of the tongue, jokes, etc., from the domain of triviality and brought them center-stage as crucial data for understanding the self. Thus experiential analysis is self-consciously methodologically innovative, continuously seeking new types of data and varied types of natural settings (e.g. Whyte's use of bowling scores in Whyte, 1943).

To begin to appreciate the range of settings which constitute people's lives, one need only look to the work of Barker (1968) or follow a subject around his/her day. We certainly must be aware of the fact that one's own race, class, religion and gender predispose us to consider some settings more interesting and important than others, even though this half-conscious evaluation might be entirely discordant with the views of the subject. As various researchers have noted, researchers often do not understand the diversity of settings and niches in which people perform well (friendship networks, neighbors, church relationships, voluntary associations) and focus instead on settings designed and controlled by professionals.

The research process that includes researcher exposure to the settings in which people live does not fit the hierarchical research model which consists of a team of numerous persons earning differential pay and charged with varying tasks. Roth (1966) has shown that the data gathered by subordinates tend to be distorted by their alienation. Reliance on such teams can result in situations where the principal researcher completes a study without ever having encountered the studied phenomenon. It is this direct contact with the subjects' experienced reality which is the occasion of the researcher's experiential knowledge about the phenomenon (e.g., Coles, 1974). To insist upon the direct involvement of the principal researcher with the research participants would change the research process: the sample would be smaller, the opportunities for apprenticeships would be fewer (since the principal investigator would take on more tasks), and perhaps, unfortunately, researchers who are less physically mobile would be more restricted in their selection of research topics. But the decrease in project scale would make research less dependent on and therefore less influenced by major funding sources, an important consideration in the coming years. For those projects that nevertheless require a team, the drawbacks of multi-person research can be reduced if collectivist organizational principles are followed (Rothschild-Whitt, 1979) and if the persons doing the writing have been in the field and have engaged in joint reflective encounters with the subjects. The creation of noncompetitive, collaborative teams, particularly if they are interdisciplinary, is very difficult, indicating the extent to which the opposite features are endemic to our relationships (e.g., Bronfenbrenner and Devereux, 1952; Vidich and Bensman, 1971). To this end, feminist researchers have begun to set up research collectives.

The collaborative relation among researchers is mirrored in the collaborative relation between the researcher and subjects. The very use of the terms 'researcher' and 'subject' is awkward here in that they are part of the traditional model. Our language shapes our world so it is important to consider other language. The conventional view of the subject is one on whom research operations are performed, rendering him/her passive, in essence 'an object,' or in Buber's words, an 'it,' or in other words a 'not I.' Perceiving others as submissive objects complements mechanistic means of knowing about those objects. Because researchers have prestige and other kinds of power (e.g., they are more likely to be white, male, middle class, articulate, and are definitely more likely than their subjects to be in control of the research setting), the likelihood exists that the research subject will be manipulated and the data s/he gives will be colored by that state. The Milgram study of obedience to the authority of the researcher (1963) is a clear example of this phenomenon. Daniels's essay (1967) about her inability to gain control of the research situation because she was a woman studying the military (a role she calls the low-caste stranger) illustrates the limits of researcher power. 'Dehumanized knowing implies treating other men (sic) as objects' (Collins, 1977, p. 63). By contrast the researcher stance which perceives the 'subject' as collaborator produces 'communication through dialogue with others to determine how they experience reality' (Ibid.). Knowing which does not reflect the reality lived by others, which is anti-dialogical, is artificial and incomplete.

To translate these ideas into the activity of experiential analysis is to adopt a non-hierarchical, non-authoritarian, non-manipulative, humble relation to the 'subject' — perhaps the attitude of student rather than expert is a useful analogy. Wolff (1971) uses the term 'surrender' to characterize the researcher's stance of receptivity to anything the subject offers. Vaughter describes the relation as one of 'equality, sharing and trust' (1976, p. 146). Such a relation needs to be prepared, explained and developed, since the two parties begin as strangers. In the case of the 'research commune,' Hessler and New write, 'Our first task was to write a paper establishing the structure and function of the commune' (1972, p. 13). Beyond these formalities, relationships must be cultivated by sharing experiences. The relation is more likely to develop as an I-thou dialogue if the 'subject' is as eager to explore his/her own way of constructing meaning as is the researcher, and if s/he feels as much in control of the situation as does the researcher. These are the elements of collaboration. Similarly, the researcher as student rather than expert must remember to convey this stance in personal, direct, colloquial speech, particularly in being open and 'owning' one's statements. In Freire's view (1970) both researcher and 'subject' are students.

The data gathering process, which is a recording of meaning as it is constructed in the dialogue, comes to an end when both or all parties (if there is a group) feel saturated, depleted, complete. The time required to achieve this cognitive-emotive state varies with the person. Frequently the orienting open-ended questions posed by the researcher have been addressed or redefined by the subject, additional topics are raised which are of significance to the subject; these then are explored further by both, until the subject matter (and the persons) is exhausted. A break of a few days, weeks or even longer can be used and then another meeting can take place in which the previous dialogue is reviewed to see if the researcher has adequately understood and if further explorations should take place (see Coles, 1974). Since the researcher uses the assumption that meaning is being constructed rather than information simply given, time and context have to be provided in a flexible way for the meaning to be clarified. A phrase to describe this process could be 'multiple depth conversations.' A phrase to describe the continuous clarification of the emergent meaning would be 'shared feedback loops' or 'joint interpretation of meaning' or 'unpredictable discovery based on intersubjectivity' (Westkott, 1979).

The role of the subject in conventional research is confined to 'giving data' or extends to receiving the report or feedback after the researcher has performed the analysis. In collaborative experiential research the subject's role expands to all phases of research. It begins with shared topic formulation — the participants acting as partners or consultants in shaping the research focus, selecting research procedures and their implementations; collaborating in data analysis and publication, or at least monitoring publications before their dissemination. Although Hessler and New (1972) describe an actual instance of this collaboration, in some sense complete partnership remains an ideal type like complete detachment, which is approximated but never entirely achieved. The presently constituted research ethics of privacy and confidentiality are not what is needed alone. Rather there should be a new research ethic of participation.

Data analysis is typically described by theorists of participant observation as proceeding concurrently with data collection. If it does not, then questions which arise in the data analysis phase will have to remain unanswered. If the two proceed together then the researcher will have a project-specific indication as to when to stop collecting data, i.e., when s/he and her/his collaborators better understand the phenomenon being studied.

Data analysis is an activity based on a cognitive mode different from data gathering: reflective rather than active, solitary rather than interactional. The recorded experiences, conversation transcripts, pieces of information are compiled, reduced and examined for their interactions (patterns) and basic themes. The more significant is extracted from the less significant within a system of meaning. Parts are strung together to make new wholes — simplicity is sought beneath the complexity. The somewhat imprecise preceding statements are intended to convey the reflective analytic stance taken toward the data, which is humanistic rather than mechanistic. Perhaps it draws on a feminine cognitive style — not in the pejorative sense of sentimental, irrational or unscientific, but in the positive sense of artistic, sensitive, integrated, deep, intersubjective, empathic, associative, affective, open, personalized, aesthetic, receptive.

The feminine mode draws on the interplay of figure and ground rather than on the dominance of either; on the contextualized, not dissociated. As interpretations are made and recorded, the remaining data are examined to see if and how they corroborate or refute the ongoing analysis. There are no rules for data analysis except one — that the analysis draw heavily on the language of the persons studied, i.e., that it is grounded. The language of the researcher, which holds the analysis together, must be evocative and communicative, not jargon. It produces a document that is readable and usable. It addresses a second audience with the intention of fostering a dialogue — whereas the first audience was the subject, the second is the reader. If it succeeds it will create a 'felt response' (Gendlin, 1965-66), an encounter with the reader.

Although new questions arise during data collection, data analysis refers back to the original questions which propelled the study — what is it, why is it this way, what does it mean, how do its parts connect, etc.? Simultaneously, it integrates other research literature and points out similarities and differences.

The analysis also proceeds with participation from the research subjects. Here is yet another source of validity built into the orientation. Since throughout the project meaning is assumed to be a constructive, ongoing process, there is no final interpretation valid 'for all times' but simply an adequate interpretation which is endorsed by participants, confirmed by readers and cognitively satisfying the researcher. An adequate interpretation, ironically, does not give definitive answers but keeps the dialogue going.

Finally, as the analytic phase draws to a close, the self-reflective phase assumes prominence. In addition to posing questions to oneself such as — how have I grown in this process; how have my values deepened or changed, etc. — one also asks 'sociology of knowledge' questions — what cultural values does my analysis reflect, what are the sociopolitical conditions illuminated by the interpretation, what is the impact of my age, race, sex or other attributes on what I believe I have found? These questions draw on reflections after writing the analysis but also on the research diary kept throughout the project.

Experiential analysis: insights from another research project

The parameters and ingredients of the 'experiential analysis' method have been described briefly as an ideal type of research process. In my own experience I have not yet been able to implement the procedures completely, but nevertheless in the process of trying, I have learned my limitations as well as those of the method and of a particular setting. In my last extensive research project (fieldwork 1979-80) it was very difficult to establish a collaborative relation with the community as a whole, although it was possible to do so with the individuals who constituted the community. Many times I experienced community pressure to act like a conventional researcher and do the work myself rather than ask for extensive collaboration. Similarly some individuals expressed interest in serving as collaborators while others would not participate at all if others did. Thus researchers working in natural settings become part of the political web of those settings, and the procedures they have prepared in advance in the sanctity of academia can not be neatly operationalized. Similarly I learned that some people expect researchers to fulfill expectations of what a researcher does — ask a set of prepared questions, quantify results, etc. Whenever I encountered people who wished me to behave in ways that did not suit the purpose at hand, I wondered if I should 'educate' them as to the merit of the alternative method, or should I become flexible and respond to each 'subject' as s/he wished?

A second set of problems concerned data analysis — the problem is that since the materials have to be carefully digested, some time is required. To the extent that one's research is problem-oriented, the time lag may allow the problem to have changed before the interpretation has been fully articulated, let alone converted into an implemented solution. The experiential method appears thus more likely to produce an informed understanding of the nature of the phenomenon than a quick overview or remedy for a given problem. This limitation of the experiential method could discourage feminists who are interested in documenting policy relevant issues in ways that convince even skeptical others of the presence of discrimination or harassment against women (or another group) or who would like to demonstrate that women's (or another nondominant group's) abilities are equivalent to men's under equally supportive circumstances.

Much more discussion needs to take place, however, about what in fact has been policy-affecting research. Just because research appears to be conducive to shaping policy does not mean that it does so. Riesmann (1972) has shown, for instance, that social science and the development of social policy operate in time cycles that are out-of-sync. To what extent do 'policies' (e.g., preventing discrimination based on sex, etc.) actually break down the patriarchal or oppressive nature of society, or is it factors of another kind (e.g., economic) that are more likely to produce such effects? Has it not been true that making the private consciousness public and consequently empowered has transformed society more than trying to protect people by transient public policies?

The problems I encounter as I attempt to implement the emerging 'experiential analytic' methodology seem minor in comparison with the quality of relations that I develop with people involved in the study and the quality of the understanding that emerges from those relations. The end of a project does not mean the end of those relations, but does mean the cessation of the in-depth conversations which I experience as a deep loss. The publication by feminist scholars at a prolific rate of their criticisms of conventional methodology, the presentation of symposia at conferences, the development of courses and seminars on alternative methodologies,[12] lend not only *support* to the continuing effort to fashion an alternative research method but also contribute *new ideas* for its refinement. After spending several years in private contemplation of my distress with social-science research strategies, it is an unimaginably gratifying experience to engage in dialogues with other feminist researchers who help clarify my thinking and share this perspective. These are good omens for further methodological breakthroughs.

Notes

1 One way to answer this question is to consider a society's approved knowledge and way of knowing as the quintessential embodiments of the society's basic orientation. Parsons developed a vocabulary for discussing these basic orientations, calling them 'pattern variables.' As we all are taught in introductory sociology, our modern culture is characterized by affective neutrality, collectivity orientation, particularism, achievement (or performance), and specificity, rather than affectivity, self-orientation, universalism, ascription (or quality), and diffuseness (Parsons and Shils, 1951). In my

judgment, the mainline methodologies of sociology and psychology embody the former orientations, whereas the alternative methodologies proposed by feminist and other critics of the social sciences build on the latter orientations.

2 One also risks being considered immature. Mullin writes that adulthood favors the positivist characteristics of certainty and stability whereas adolescence favors immersion and awe (1981, p. 120). Since, of course, the scientific attitude is not the typical stance of research subjects, it is likely that researchers consider their subjects immature too!

3 From Reinharz (1979, pp. 11-12).

4 From Reinharz (1979, pp. 14-15).

5 There are already at least nine textbooks on the subject of qualitative research: Bruyn (1966); Glaser and Strauss (1967); McCall and Simmons (1969); Filstead (1970); Glaser (1978); Runkel and McGrath (1972); Schatzman and Strauss (1973); Bogdan and Taylor (1975); Smith (1975). There are also many monographs and collections of retrospective accounts of qualitative field research, e.g., Adams and Preiss (1960); Vidich, Bensman and Stein (1971); Bowen (1964); Powdermaker (1966); Golde (1970); Wax (1971); Reinharz (1979); among others.

6 For a description of a project that suffered because of a lack of a predetermined framework and an argument that there needs to be one, see Miles (1979).

7 A very clear and productive use of this procedure can be found in the dissertation of Barry Wolff (1979).

8 For numerous examples see Reason and Rowan (1981).

9 For a report by one feminist researcher who carried out these procedures, see Marti Bombyk (1981) unpublished paper, available from the author.

10 This complementarity of sincerity as an essential ingredient in research is similar to a discussion by Argyris. Stimulated by Carl Rogers, Chris Argyris writes that people who behave in accordance with their values are behaving genuinely. They then are sometimes able to behave genuinely in a way that encourages others to behave genuinely. If genuineness is experienced by both parties, the relationship is called authentic. As researchers, we should be interested only in information derived from authentic relations.

11 To eliminate deception means to *preclude deliberately misinforming subjects*. Still acceptable, in my view, is to tell subjects that one is interested in understanding people's spontaneous behavior. In order to maintain spontaneity without being deceptive, the researcher may choose not to specify which behavior is of interest. To inform people of one's exact observational focus is to dramatically intervene in their behavior. For an insightful related discussion of how subjects deceive researchers and researchers deceive themselves, see Crowle (1976).

12 For example, the First Annual National Summer Institute in Women's Studies (1981) held in Ann Arbor, Michigan, trained a group of women's scholars from an international pool in a 'Feminist Transformation of the Curriculum.' An element of the training program is a feminist research methodology workshop.

References

Adams, R., and J. Preiss (eds) (1960), *Human Organization Research: Field Relations and Techniques*, Homewood, Illinois, Dorsey Press.

Asch, Solomon (1952), *Social Psychology*, Engelwood Cliffs, Prentice-Hall, Ch. 16.

Bakan, Paul (1966), *The Duality of Existence*, Chicago, Rand McNally.

Barker, Roger (1968), *Ecological Psychology: Concepts and Methods for Studying the Environment of Human Behavior*, Stanford University Press.

Berger, P., and Luckman, T. (1967), *The Social Construction of Reality*, New York, Doubleday.

Bernard, Jessie (1975), *Women, Wives, Mothers: Values and Options*, Chicago, Aldine.

Blumer, Herbert (1956), 'Sociological Analysis and the "Variable",' *American Sociological Review*, vol. 21, pp. 683-90.

Blumer, Herbert (1962), 'Society as Symbolic Interaction,' in A. Rose (ed.), *Human Behavior and Social Processes*, New York, Houghton Mifflin, pp. 179-92.

Bogdan, R., and Taylor, S. (1975), *Introduction to Qualitative Research Methods*, New York, Wiley.

Bombyk, Marti (1981), 'Planning a Research Strategy to Study Social Parenting,' presentation to Feminist Research Methodology Seminar, University of Michigan, Women's Studies, 2 April.

Bowen, Elizabeth (1964), *Return to Laughter: An Anthropological Novel*, New York, Harper & Row.

Brandt, R. (1972), *Studying Behavior in Natural Settings*, New York, Holt, Rinehart & Winston.

Bronfenbrenner, U., and Devereux, E.C. (1952), 'Interdisciplinary Planning for Team Research on Constructive Community Behavior,' *Human Relations*, vol. 5, pp. 187-203.

Brown, J., and Gilmartin, B. (1969), 'Sociology Today: Lacunae, Emphasis and Surfeits,' *American Sociologist*, vol. 4, pp. 283-90.

Bruyn, Severyn (1966), *The Human Perspective in Sociology: The Methodology of Participant Observation*, Engelwood Cliffs, Prentice-Hall.

Carlson, Rae (1972), 'Understanding Women: Implications for Personality Theory and Research,' *Journal of Social Issues*, vol. 28, no. 2, pp. 17-32.

Chodorow, Nancy (1978), *The Reproduction of Mothering: Psychoanalysis and the Sociology of Gender*, Berkeley, University of California Press.

Cole, Stephen A. (1976), *The Sociological Method*, Chicago, Rand McNally.

Coles, Robert (1974), 'The Method,' in R.J. Lifton and E. Olson (eds), *Explorations in Psychohistory: The Wellfleet Papers*, New York, Simon & Schuster.

Collins, Denis (1977), *Paulo Freire: His Life, Works and Thought*, New York, Paulist.

Crowle, A.J. (1976), 'The Deceptive Language of the Laboratory,' in R. Harré (ed.), *Life Sentences: Aspects of the Social Role of Language*, New York, Wiley.

Daniels, Arlene K. (1967), 'The Low-caste Strange in Social Research,' in G. Sjoberg (ed.), *Ethics, Politics, and Social Research*, Cambridge, Schenkman.

Davis, Murray (1971), 'That's Interesting! Toward a Phenomenology of Sociology and a Sociology of Phenomenology,' *Philosophy of the Social Sciences*, vol. 1, pp. 309-44.

DiIorio, Judith (1980), 'Toward a Phenomenological Feminism: A Critique of Gender Role Research,' paper presented at the 2nd Annual Women's Studies Association Conference, Bloomington, Indiana, 18 May.

Douglas, J., and Johnson, J. (eds) (1977), *Existential Sociology*, New York, Cambridge University Press.

Filstead, William (1970), *Qualitative Methodology: Firsthand Involvement with the Social World*, Chicago, Rand McNally.

Fox Keller, Evelyn F. (1978), 'Gender and Science,' *Psychoanalysis and Contemporary Thought*, vol. 1, pp. 409-33.

Fox Keller, Evelyn F. (1980), 'Feminist Critique of Science: A Forward or Backward Move?,' *Fundamenta Scientiae*, vol. 1, pp. 341-9.

Freeman, Jo (1973), 'Women on the Move: Roots of Revolt,' in A. Rossi and A. Calderwood (eds), *Academic Women on the Move*, New York, Russell Sage.

Freire, Paulo (1970), *Pedagogy of the Oppressed*, New York, Seabury.

Gendlin, Eugene (1965-66), 'Experiential Explication and Truth,' *Journal of Existentialism*, vol. 22, pp. 1-33.

Glaser, Barney (1978), *Theoretical Sensitivity: Advances in the Methodology of Grounded Theory*, Mill Valley, Sociology Press.

Glaser, B., and Strauss, A. (1967), *The Discovery of Grounded Theory: Strategies for Qualitative Research*, Chicago, Aldine.

Golde, Peggy (ed.) (1970), *Women in the Field: Anthropological Experiences*, Chicago, Aldine.

Gould, M. (1980), 'The New Sociology,' *Signs*, vol. 5, no. 3, pp. 459-68.

Gouldner, Alvin (1970), *The Coming Crisis of Western Sociology*, New York, Basic Books.

Graham, D.L.R. and Rawlings, E. (1980), 'Feminist Research Methodology: Comparisons, Guidelines, and Ethic,' paper presented at APA, and NWSA.

Hessler, R., and New, P. (1972), 'Research as a Process of Exchange,' *The American Sociologist*, vol. 7, no. 1, pp. 13-14.

Hochschild, Arlie (1975), 'The Sociology of Feeling and Emotion: Selected Possibilities,' in M. Millman and R. Kanter (eds), *Another Voice: Feminist Perspectives on Social Life and Social Science*, New York, Doubleday, pp. 280-307.

Husserl, Edmund (1931), 'The Thesis of the Natural Standpoint and Its Suspension,' in *Ideas: General Introduction to Phenomenology*, London, Allen & Unwin, pp. 27-32.

Hyman, Herbert (1949), 'Inconsistencies as a Problem of Attitude Measurement,' *Journal of Social Issues*, vol. 5, pp. 40-1.

Johnson, John (1977), 'Fusion of Thinking and Feeling in Sociological Research,' in J. Douglas and J. Johnson (eds), *Existential Sociology*, New York, Cambridge University Press, pp. 201-28.

Josephson, Ed (1970), 'Resistance to Community Survey,' *Social Problems*, vol. 18, pp. 117-29.

Kieffer, Charles (1981), 'The Emergence of Empowerment: The Development of Participatory Competence Among Individuals in Citizen Organizations,' unpublished doctoral dissertation, University of Michigan.

Kuhn, Thomas (1962), *The Structure of Scientific Revolutions*, University of Chicago Press.

Levin, Michael (1980), 'The Feminist Mystique,' *Commentary*, pp. 25-30.

Mannheim, Karl (1936), *Ideology and Utopia*, New York, Harcourt, Brace.

McCall, G. and Simmons, J.L. (1969), *Issues in Participant Observation: A Text and Reader*, Reading, Addison-Wesley.

McCartney, J. (1970), 'On Being Scientific: Changing Styles of Presentation of Sociological Research.' *American Sociologist*, vol. 5, pp. 30-5.

Merton, Robert (1968), *Social Theory and Social Structure*, New York, Free Press.

Miles, Mathew (1979), 'Qualitative Data as an Attractive Nuisance: The Problem of Analysis,' *Administrative Science Quarterly*, vol. 24, pp. 590-601.

Milgram, Stanley (1963), 'Behavioral Study of Obedience,' *Journal of Abnormal and Social Psychology*, vol. 67, pp. 371-8.

Millman, M. and Kanter, R.M. (eds) (1975), *Another Voice: Feminist Perspectives on Social Life and Social Science*, New York, Doubleday.

Mills, C. Wright (1943), 'The Professional Ideology of Social Pathologists,' *American Journal of Sociology*, vol. 49, pp. 165-80.

Mishler, Eliott (1979), 'Meaning in Context: Is there any Other Kind?,' *Harvard Educational Review*, vol. 49, pp. 1-19.

Morgan, G. and Smircich, L. (1980), 'The Case of Qualitative Research,' *Academy of Management and Review*, vol. 5, no. 4, pp. 491-500.

Mullin, Jay (1981), review of *The Social Construction of Mind: Studies in Ethnomethodology and Linguistic Philosophy* by Jeff Coulter, *Contemporary Sociology*, vol. 10, no. 1, p. 120.

Parlee, Mary Brown (1979), 'Psychology and Women,' *Signs*, vol. 5, no. 1, pp. 121-33.

Parsons, T., and Shils, E. (1951), *Toward a General Theory of Action*, Cambridge, Harvard University Press.

Patel, N. (1972), 'Quantitative Collaborative Trends in American Sociological Research,' *The American Sociologist*, vol. 7, pp. 5-6.

Phillips, Derek (1971), *Knowledge from What?*, Chicago, Rand McNally.

Powdermaker, Hortense (1966), *Stranger and Friend*, New York, W.W. Norton.

Psychology Today (June 1981), 'Letters,' p. 6.

Reason, P., and Rowan, J. (eds) (1981), *Human Inquiry: A Sourcebook of New Paradigm Research*, New York, Wiley.

Reinharz, Shulamit (1979), *On Becoming a Social Scientist: From Survey Research and Participant Observation to Experiential Analysis*, San Francisco, Jossey-Bass.

Riesmann, L. (1972), 'The Solution Cycle of Social Problems,' *The American Sociologist*, vol. 7, pp. 7-9.

Roche, Maurice (1973), *Phenomenology, Language and the Social Sciences*, Boston, Routledge & Kegan Paul.

Roth, Julius (1966), 'Hired-hand Research,' *American Sociologist*, vol. 1, pp. 190-6.

Rothschild-Whitt, Joyce (1979), 'The Collectivist Organization: An Alternative to Rational-Bureaucratic Models,' *American Sociological Review*, vol. 44, pp. 509-27.

Runkel, P. and McGrath, J. (1972), *Research on Human Behavior*, New York, Holt, Rinehart & Winston.

Schatzman, L. and Strauss, A. (1973), *Field Research: Strategies for a Natural Sociology*, Englewood Cliffs, Prentice-Hall.

Sharff, Jagna W. (1981), 'Free Enterprise and the Ghetto Family,' *Psychology Today*, March, pp. 41-8.

Sherif, Carolyn (1979), 'Bias in Psychology,' in J. Sherman and E. Beck (eds), *The Prism of Sex: Essays in the Sociology of Knowledge*, Madison, University of Wisconsin Press.

Smith, Dorothy (1974), 'Women's Perspective as a Radical Critique of Sociology,' *Sociological Inquiry*, vol. 44, no. 1, pp. 7-13.

Smith, H. (1975), *Strategies of Social Research*, Englewood Cliffs, Prentice-Hall.

Stannard-Friel, Don (1981), *Harassment Therapy: A Case Study of Psychiatric Violence*, Boston, G.K. Hall.

Tesch, Renata (1980), *Phenomenological and Transformative Research: What Are They and How to Do Them — A Guide to the Planning of Naturalistic Inquiry*, California, The Fielding Institute.

Toby, Jackson (1955), 'Undermining the Student's Faith in the Validity of Personal Experience,' *American Sociological Review*, vol. 20, pp. 717-18.

Valle, R., and King, M. (1978), 'An Introduction to Existential-Phenomenological Thought in Psychology,' in R. Valle and M. King (eds), *Existential-Phenomenological Alternatives for Psychology*, New York, Oxford University Press, pp. 3-17.

Vaughter, Reesa (1976), 'Psychology,' *Signs*, vol. 2, no. 1, pp. 120-46.

Vidich, A.J. and Bensman, J. (1971), 'The Springdale Case: Academic Bureaucrats and Sensitive Townspeople,' in A. Vidich, J. Bensman and M. Stein (eds), *Reflections on Community Studies*, New York, Harper & Row.

Vidich, A.J., Bensman, J. and Stein, M. (eds) (1971), *Reflections on Community Studies*, New York, Harper & Row.

Wallston, Barbara (1979), 'What are the Questions in Psychology of Women: A Feminist Approach to Research,' Presidential Address, Division 35, Psychology of Women, American Psychological Association, New York.

Wax, Rosalie (1971), *Doing Fieldwork: Warnings and Advice*, University of Chicago Press.

Weisstein, Naomi (1971), 'Kinde, Küche, and Kirche as Scientific Law: Psychology Constructs the Female,' in V. Gornick and B. Moran (eds), *Woman in Sexist Society: Studies in Power and Powerlessness*, New York, New American Library.

Westkott, Marcia (1979), 'Feminist Criticism of the Social Sciences,' *Harvard Educational Review*, vol. 49, no. 4, pp. 422-50.

Whyte, William F. (1943), *Street Corner Society*, University of Chicago Press.

Willems, E.P. (1969), 'Planning a Rationale for Naturalistic Research,' in E.P. Willems and H.L. Rousch (eds), *Naturalistic Viewpoints in Psychological Research*, New York, Holt, Rinehart & Winston.

Wolff, Barry (1979), *Adolescent Substance Abuse: A Social-Phenomenological Investigation*, doctoral dissertation, University of Michigan.

Wolff, Kurt (1971), 'Surrender and Community Study,' in A. Vidich, J. Bensman and M. Stein (eds), *Reflections on Community Studies*, New York, Harper & Row.

12

'Back into the personal' or: our attempt to construct 'feminist research'

Liz Stanley and Sue Wise

Our feminist research

Like most academic feminists, we are involved in a search for a way of doing research, and of writing about this, that will encapsule 'feminism.' We attempt to relate feminist principles and beliefs to living feminism within everyday life, to living as feminists doing research, and we have written about this in our book, *Breaking Out* (1983). The purpose of this paper is to draw together more succinctly some of our ideas about why and how such links between beliefs, life and research might be made. Although this sounds somewhat grandiose, we see it as one of the prime tasks of academic feminism in the social sciences.[1]

For us, feminism is a way of living our lives rather than a set of beliefs or a style of revolutionary rhetoric or a means of analysis. Indeed, we believe that it is only within the *doing* of feminism that any feminist revolution lies. By this we mean that 'the feminist revolution' isn't anything that'll occur some Thursday (or Saturday or . . .) in March (or September or . . .). It *is* occurring — now. It occurs as and when women, individually and together, hesitantly and rampantly, joyously and with deep sorrow, come to see our lives differently and to reject externally imposed frames of reference for understanding these lives, instead beginning the slow process of constructing our own ways of seeing them, understanding them, and living them. For us, the insistence on the deeply political nature of everyday life and on seeing political change as personal change is, quite simply, 'feminism'.

'Women are oppressed' is a truism which we believe needs critical explication because, while self-evident to feminists on one level, on another it hides a multitude of complexities, ambiguities, and contradictions. This, and similar truisms, need examining through a close scrutiny of the fabric of our everyday lives. It doesn't need yet more generalised statements and assumptions made *about* it but instead examination *of* it. We believe that the present style of feminist theory, with its vast generalisations about 'the family,' 'patriarchy' and other structural abstractions based on yet more vast assumptions about 'women's' experiences (always *other women's*) has landed us with theory, research, and a style of doing both, that is traditional, structural, and fundamentally anti-feminist.

Feminism is no unitary phenomenon and within the feminist body politic there are, to put it mildly, disagreements. Feminists can treat those women who don't agree with us as falsely conscious, stupid, malicious, as not 'real,' 'right-on' feminists. Or we can start off from the assumption that they're probably just as sensible and well-meaning as we are, and try to examine how such disagreements arise. And as we say this about disagreements between feminists, so we say it about those between women who define themselves as feminists and those who don't. We believe that these arise from material differences in women's lives. By 'material differences' we mean real events and experiences in women's lives. Our materialist analysis isn't one which separates off the 'subjective' social world from the 'objective' one, idealism from materialism, nor involvement and emotion from reason and analysis.[2] Therefore, we find preferable a definition of 'material' which accepts as axiomatic that if something is real in its consequences then it is real to the person experiencing those consequences.[3]

Closely connected to these ideas is our understanding that the notion of 'false consciousness', with its underlying assumption of lower and higher states of consciousness, is basically positivist in nature. In brief, 'positivism' is an ontological approach, a way of seeing and constructing the world, which insists that 'physical' and 'social' worlds are in all essentials the same. Positivism claims that in any occurrence there is one true set of events ('the facts') which is discoverable by reference to witnesses of various kinds, including people as 'eye witnesses' and material evidence of other kinds. It describes social reality as 'objectivity constituted' and so insists that there is one true 'real' reality. And it suggests that researchers can objectively find out this real reality because they remove themselves from involvement in what they study.

Basic to these assumptions is the 'subject/object' dichotomy. Positivism sees what is studied as an 'object'. 'The subject' is the researcher, and she can stand back from the object/s of study (people), can look at it/them objectively and dispassionately. And sometimes implicit, but frequently explicit, within the positivist canon of belief is also a sanctification of the power relationship between researcher and researched. Positivism sees the researcher/theoretician as more competent, because more 'objective', in understanding other people's lives (always *other* people's) than are the people who live them. The ability to do this is seen as the prerogative of only 'the scientific mind', trained and operating within a scientific ethic which insists on scrupulous removal of commitment and value.

Closely associated with this is positivism's negative orientation to 'the particular', the specific, and to lived experience of all kinds. It eschews the particular, seeing it as *over*particular and thus as incapable of generating generalisations from the few to the many. It sees individual experience as essentially subjective and therefore not properly 'scientific' unless collected together to produce generalizations.

Both as feminists and as social scientists we find these aspects of positivism objectionable. Few of our objections, if any, are unique to us and derive from a flourishing critique of positivism within the social sciences. We reject the idea that scientists, or feminists, can become experts in other people's lives. And we reject the belief that there is one true real reality to become experts about. We feel that feminism's present renaissance has come about precisely because many women have rejected other people's (men's) interpretations of our lives. Feminism insists that women should define and interpret our own experiences, and that we need to re-define and re-name what other people (men, experts) have previously defined and named for us. And so feminism argues that 'the personal', lived experience, is intensely political and immensely important politically. Each of these aspects of feminism stands in opposition to the basic tenets of positivism. Feminism either directly states or implies that the personal is the political; that the personal and the everyday are important and interesting and must be the subject of feminist inquiry; that other people's realities mustn't be downgraded, sneered at or otherwise patronised; that feminists must attempt to reject the scientist/person dichotomy and, in doing so, must endeavour to dismantle the power relationship which exists between researchers and researched.

And as we see feminism so we see, and try to construct, feminist research. We not only want to do research, we also want to 'be researchers' in the same way that we try to 'be feminists'. We don't see our feminism as something which we simply add into an established way of doing *anything*, including research. We believe that feminist research should be the doing of feminism in another context. We don't believe that 'doing feminist research' requires activities or procedures other than those which we ordinarily use in ordinarily understanding ourselves as people and as feminists in the social world.

Other feminist researchers are attempting to grapple with the self-same problem of how to do feminist research.[4] Interesting and insightful though these attempts are, they leave out any detailed account of the process by which research is carried out. We don't mean what 'technique' was used when, in order to find out what, but rather the interaction that takes place between the researcher and the researched (whether other people, or books, or statistical tables or . . .), including the ways in which researchers come to know and understand what we do. The position of the researcher, as the source of 'what we, the readers, know about this research', is left inviolate.

Feminist research must confront these issues. 'The personal' must be included as much more than data fodder, for understanding our experience of our everyday lives is crucial in understanding our oppression. And 'everyday life' is after all what we spend our lives doing. What people spend their lives doing must obviously be the subject of research; what all women (including feminists) spend our lives doing must obviously be the subject of feminist research.[5]

Closely connected to this is our belief that the process of research must be central to any account of 'feminist research'. This is because without including an account of this process the sources of the researcher's knowledge are hidden from scrutiny. We don't know how or why she claims to know what she does; and she remains hidden although central. A consequence of prime importance for feminism is that here the power relationship between researcher and researched remains fundamentally unchanged and unchallenged.

We feel very strongly that these issues are crucially important. Firstly, our belief that 'the personal is the political' demands that we take a principled stand on them. Secondly, we believe that without confronting them the most important, and certainly the most interesting, aspects of research are omitted from 'the research' as it is reported and made public. For us an explication of how/why (we see these as indivisible) researchers come to know what we do is the most intellectually demanding feature of any research. It is also within such an explication of the bases of knowledge that alternative means of using 'the personal' are to be found.

But of course in order to examine 'the personal' in this way it's necessary to locate not only the researched but also the researcher, thus making her extremely vulnerable in ways usually avoided by researchers like the plague. We now try to explain this 'vulnerability' in more detail as it is central to later sections of this paper.

Feminist research as we envisage it wouldn't be concerned with replicating existing social science through the inclusion of women. It would instead explore the bases of our everyday knowledge as women, as feminists and as social scientists. It would do this by starting from the experiences of the researcher as a person in a situation. Researchers, like all new members of situations, have to find out what's going on in them. How we find out, how we come to know what members of it know, is what feminist research should be concerned with. And in doing this we must make available to others the reasoning procedures which underlie the knowledge produced out of 'research'. We must say *how* we find out what we do, and not just *what* we find out.

Traditionally, social science identifies people's understandings of their experiences as deficient or incompetent. The only certain way to avoid doing this is to move away from presenting 'them' as the focus of the research and instead present ourselves in the form of our understandings about what's going on, by examining these in any given context. We must make ourselves vulnerable and not hide behind what 'they' are supposed to think and do.

'Vulnerability' thus makes absolutely explicit the centrality of researchers in all research processes. All research necessarily comes to us through the active and central involvement of researchers, who necessarily interpret and construct what's going on. There is no other way to 'do' either research or life.

We find such an approach to research preferable to any other, but not because we claim for it any greater facility in getting at 'truth', at real reality. We find it preferable because it openly eschews any allegiance to ideas about truth, instead being concerned to present 'this, how I understand it'. This is what is frequently written off as subjectivity, although we don't see it as in any way inferior to or even very different from what's presented to us as 'objectivity'.

We aren't suggesting research concerned only with the researcher as an atomised individual, nor with recording her innermost sensations and feelings. We believe that people are social beings and that 'the individual' is rather to be seen as a *member* of society. It has been suggested to us that what we're proposing is mere self-indulgence. While rejecting the 'mere', we also believe that it is self-indulgent to do anything other than what we suggest. Most social science research, and most feminist research, has been riddled with the self-indulgences of people who have refused to face up squarely to their own active involvement within the central processes of *constructing* research. Vulnerability, as we see it, is no easy, sloppy or self-involved exercise in relating inner thoughts, feelings and fantasies. It involves us in a disciplined, scholarly and rigorous explication of the bases of our knowledge by tying in such an explication to a detailed analysis of the *contexts* in which such knowledge is generated.[6]

'The personal is the political' rules, OK?

We've argued that to omit 'the personal' is to omit the central intellectual and practical experiences of research. This is particularly regrettable in feminist research, for research which involves women necessarily involves the feminist researcher in issues concerning her relationship with them,[7] and research which involves men necessarily involves the feminist researcher in experiences of sexism. Our particular research involved men and experiences of sexism of the grossest kind, being concerned with obscene phone calls. However, even in less extreme situations similar, although more subtle, experiences of sexism occur. That we discuss a particularly gross example of sexism in no way invalidates the point we make; rather it makes the point particularly clearly because it uses such an extreme example. We believe that wherever research involves people, whether in the flesh or in books, issues about sexism arise and similar possibilities for exploring these exist.[8]

Our experiences of obscene phone calls weren't produced as part

of any academic exercise. Their occurrence was linked to our involvement in the gay movement in Britain. Between 1971 and about 1976
our home telephone number was a contact number for several local
gay groups, and for most of this time it was a contact number for the
local lesbian group we were involved in. The obscene calls originate
from the time it became exclusively associated with the lesbian group.
For a period of time in 1975 and 1976 our number was very widely
advertised and during this time we received up to forty obscene calls
a day.[9]

The obscene phone calls dominated our lives. They could, and did,
occur at any time of the day and night and thus, in a purely physical
sense, intruded on our lives to a very marked degree. The calls dominated our lives in another sense too, because to be subjected to a constant barrage of obscenity and sexually-objectifying threats and remarks
is to experience 'sexism' and 'women's oppression' in a very direct
way indeed. Few women who have not experienced them can appreciate exactly how threatening and disturbing is the sexual assault that an
obscene call constitutes. We spent a great deal of our lives thinking
about the obscene calls and in particular what they told us about the
nature of the oppression of lesbians, what they told us about the
oppression of women generally and what they told us about the links
between the two.

A lot of people appear to see obscene phone callers as sexually
frustrated and pathetic little men, as men who are in some sense not
responsible for their actions. Some indeed see their activities as victim-
precipitated.[10] However, we came to see that the men who rang us
were in no way pathetic or to be pitied. We insist that what such men
say must be treated absolutely seriously at its face-value, as presented
to us by them. Obscene phone callers deliberately and consciously
choose to verbally assault particular women in the most violent ways.
In doing so, they mouth absolutely clearly their utmost contempt for
all women. They insist that all women are nothing but objects, holes
between legs, cunts, to be used. The publication of our telephone
number gave them the opportunity to articulate this contempt in
anonymity and so with no repercussion in the rest of their lives.

Initially we saw the calls simply as an expression of the threat
that many heterosexual men feel about lesbians. Later we were astonished to find that many gay men too experienced them as sexually
arousing. In confidence, and usually in less immediately objectionable

terms, many men of all sexual orientations told us how they too found the calls sexually exciting, how they too were turned on by them. Soon it began to appear as though just about every man who heard about them shared the callers' feelings, not about lesbianism but about the relationship between sex and violence and the total desirability of a, the, any, erect penis.

From women the reaction was different but often no less disturbing to us. Most lesbians, whether homosexual or bisexual, feminist or not, saw elements of their own experiences with men reflected in the calls. But many heterosexual women we talked to have said that, while they can see that the calls may have been annoying or intrusive, they believe our feelings about the calls, and our analysis of them, are 'extreme' — over-reaction, paranoia from (man-hating?) lesbians. Such reactions from other feminists were very upsetting to us; they seem so very similar to the responses that people make to the feminist insistence that women are oppressed. Our feeling is that these women see our interpretations of the calls as not only invalid for *them* but also invalid for *us*. Our decision to end the research was partly due to our feelings about heterosexual 'sisters'' reactions as well as our weariness at being used as total sexual objects by callers.

Because of these research experiences our analysis of the basis of women's oppression changed. Our original understanding of women's oppression was a thorough-going idealism. It involved the belief that 'patriarchy' is an ideology reflected in institutions and negotiated through interactions. We came to adopt a 'materialist' theory of women's oppression as promulgated and presented to us by the callers themselves. We now think that women's oppression is derived from phallocentrism. The obscene phone callers identify power and the penis as in some sense synonymous. They also express very clearly indeed their belief that those without penes, those who are or who can be penetrated by penes, are without power and therefore are the legitimate objects of their contempt, there merely for use by those who have the penis and thus power. In a very real sense indeed the callers see penis-possessors as 'people' and those without them as less than fully human.

We 'adopted' this theory because we came to understand that people's stated motives and interpretations are, because they're stated, important to them. Because of this, they are to be taken seriously and studied. Our feeling is that sexist men are a perfectly valid, and very useful, source of information about sexism. In other words, we came to take other people and their understandings as seriously as we take our own.

We see this shortened account of our research on obscene phone calls as an appropriate means of conveying, as immediately and convincingly as we know how, that the researcher's 'personal' is absolutely central to the research process. We believe that discussions of experience grounded in a context do this more successfully than any abstract account can. An abstract account would have been very different. For a start it would have excluded us as lesbians, which would have fundamentally altered many aspects of what we said and how we said it. It would also have excluded any account of the many ways in which we changed our opinions, actions and theoretical understandings, including our understanding of women's oppression, for without including 'us' as 'subjective' persons there would have been nothing to center this around.

What we've described here is a very crude and superficial way of examining 'the personal'. All we've outlined have been some of the more obvious things that occurred in our work on obscene phone calls. However, it is absent from most research, most feminist research too, although it constitutes only a minimal way of accounting for 'the personal' and is a first step only.

We now go on to briefly examine how and why feminist research can go further in recovering the personal. In essence, we see this as *going back into* the everyday in order to explicate all the many features of it, rather than the call to 'go beyond' the personal (as though this were possible) demanded by some.[11]

Back into the personal

We've stated, as clearly and unequivocally as we can, our conviction that the essence of feminism lies in its re-evaluation of 'the personal' and its insistence on the location of 'politics' and 'revolution' *within* the minutiae of the everyday. If we take this insistence on the importance of the everyday seriously, and we believe that feminists ought, then we need the *means* to research it. Part of this 'means' lies within what is already immediately available to us — our consciousness of ourselves as women and feminists within sexist society;[12] the other lies within more technical aspects of explicating the personal. However, both the ambivalent relationship between academic feminism and the WLM in Britain[13] and the assumption that consciousness-raising and exploring 'the personal' are synonymous, has occasioned a general reluctance (to put it no stronger) to look for, examine, try out, other means of explicating the everyday. We believe there's been a general flight of academic feminists into 'theoretical' and eminently traditional forms of analysis.

In case there's any misunderstanding about this, we should say we're in no way opposed to theorising as such. We've already said that all people (even academics) theorise out of the stuff of our everyday lives. What we *are* opposed to is what we call 'de-corticated' theory. This kind of theory is based on general principles arrived at independently of any detailed examination of the facts or phenomenon to be explained. It is essentially speculative and concerned with abstractions, not knowledge grounded in living experience. For us, such an approach yields over-generalised mush. It sounds clever and academically respectable because of what it talks about and how it talks about it, but it determinedly mystifies and is applicable to no one and nothing in particular.[14] As an alternative to this we're looking for an approach which combines the analysis of substantive work with theory which arises out of this, rather than seemingly separating theory and experience. We say 'seemingly' because of course all theory is experientially based, although this uncomfortable fact is normally bracketed away. And so we're particularly interested in looking to those approaches which share with feminism its interest in the personal and in focusing on the everyday as a topic in its own right.

There are a number of existing social science approaches which start from people's experiences of and within everyday life and which treat these absolutely seriously. By 'seriously' we mean that they accept that experiences and understandings are absolutely valid for the person providing them. Of course these approaches contain their own share of sexism. However, we feel that their basic assumptions about the validity and importance of the everyday have much more in common with our kind of feminism than structural and other positivist approaches do.

We feel that academic feminism has gratuitously dismissed the possible contribution of those perspectives which focus on the personal, accept the validity of experience, and see the need to concentrate academic work on the everyday as a topic in its own right. Of course we recognise that any 'alliance' between feminism and any other perspective is fraught with danger, particularly the danger of (attempted or successful) takeover, of the colonisation of feminism. And so we aren't proposing any such alliance. We're first, foremost, and last, feminists; not feminist-phenomenologists, feminist-marxists or feminist hyphen anything else. Our interest and concern is with feminism and feminist revolution. And because of this we believe that feminism should borrow, steal, change, modify and *use* for its own purposes any and everything from anywhere that looks of interest and of use to it, but that we must do this critically.

Both of us arrived at our ideas about 'recovering the personal' through explicating our everyday experiences by using various ideas and insights from ethnomethodology, drawn out of our initial interest in symbolic interactionism.[15] Symbolic interactionism is concerned with everyday life and with face-to-face relationships of all kinds, whether these are interactions on the street, within institutions, between lovers or those which lead to changes in interest rates and the mobilisation of armies. It adopts a non-deterministic attitude towards social life and interaction. Because of this it rejects the idea that people's actions are the result of 'imprinting', 'instinct' or 'socialisation'. Instead it sees social action as the result of *interaction*, in which people make decisions — decisions about what to do, how to do it, what to say, how to react, taking into account as they do so the impressions they make on other people. Another key feature of interactionism is that it insists that structures are to be found *within* these processes. It doesn't see 'structure' as any mechano-like thing hovering around, above and within us. Instead it sees social structures as social constructions produced within and by everyday interactions. It rejects the idea that 'structure' is somehow more than 'social life'.

Symbolic interactionism was the means of sensitising us to a view of reality we'd never come across before. And this is one in which 'oppression' isn't seen as any once and for all event, explained by events 'back there', in childhood, in infancy, or any other 'stage'. Within interactionism people are seen as actively constructing, negotiating, interacting — not just passively 'enacting'. However, while learning a great deal from interactionism, we later came to feel that many versions of it retain a positivist adherence to 'science' and 'objectivity' and insist that a clear distinction can and must be made between the objective researcher and the people she studies. An approach which seemed, and seems, to avoid these grosser aspects of interactionism, which was both 'there' and available to us when we were searching for an alternative, was ethnomethodology.[16]

Frequently, ethnomethodology is seen as over-jargonised or else simplistic, irrelevant and concerned with bourgeois trivia. Sometimes it is downgraded as 'fag sociology' — 'sociology without balls' seems to be the message here. For this reason alone it is attractive to us. Something which so arouses the scorn and disgust of social scientists because of its 'effeminacy' is an obvious candidate for feminism's interest and support. Why other social scientists feel so threatened we can only guess at. Our guess is that ethnomethodology's concentration on the everyday brings social science a bit too close to home. And particularly so because it also insists that 'social science methods' are the methods all of us use in making sense of the everyday (what ethnomethodology calls 'the documentary method of interpretation'). As long as social science remains about 'structure', 'theory' and 'other people' like car workers, middle management and so forth, then it remains a profession like any other, a job based on specialised knowledge and specialised techniques. But when it focuses on more personal concerns, then it also promises to turn some attention on social scientists ourselves. And when it also suggests that mere people, untrained, unspecialised people, use essentially scientific methods in going about their everyday business, then it 'goes too far'.[17]

Ethnomethodology takes the everyday as both the topic of its research and also the resource with which it works. It uses the everyday, through the documentary method of interpretation, in order to find out about and understand the everyday. It doesn't lay claim to special expertise over other people's lives, nor does it attempt to falsify people's experiences by downgrading them as 'false consciousness'. In doing this it argues that most social science has confused 'topic' with 'resource'. Conventional social science, it suggests, uses 'data' provided for it by members of society as a resource for building academic theory.

Ethnomethodology instead argues that 'data' should be used as a topic in its own right. This idea suggests that we shouldn't use people and their lives as unexplicated data; we should instead explicate these. We should examine in close detail how people provide themselves and others with the accounts that they do. The emphasis in ethnomethodology is on understanding how people construct (not interpret) reality. That is, it is on understanding how we 'do' everyday life.

In explaining how ethnomethodology sees the researcher going about this 'explication', the term 'members' is crucially important. This is because 'membership' involves the idea of a shared body of knowledge about the social world, shared in common between the people who are party to it. And so 'membership' stems from one of its most basic propositions. This is that the social world is seen and experienced by us all as a 'factual reality', as an objective reality existing outside ourselves which constrains our behaviours. It isn't saying that there are sets of concepts inside of us, 'internalised', which we simply release in interaction; nor does it say that we all share exactly the same 'objective reality'. It goes beyond this to argue that such concepts and beliefs are used by us and others in appropriate ways in appropriate settings, and that by 'doing' these we both give accounts of them and at the same time we so construct the reality these are accounts of.

How researchers go about understanding the data that is life is, ethnomethodology insists, precisely the same way that all other members of society go about knowing what they know and doing what they do. We use the documentary method. This is a members' method, one used by all of us all the time, although it may be (perhaps) used more consciously and deliberately by us-as-social-scientists than by us-as-members. The idea of the documentary method suggests that we look for 'evidence' of what's going on, of what the events in hand are and what we should be doing within them as competent members. We use events, conversation, ways of looking, and a whole variety of other material evidence as precisely *evidence*; and we use this as 'evidence which stands on behalf of . . .' a whole body of knowledge which we deduce from this small part.

To suggest that social science methods are 'merely' members' methods is, of course, totally unacceptable for many, perhaps most, social scientists. Most of us have an enormous amount invested in our 'professional expertise' and use of technical procedures seen as far superior to anything which 'people' can muster. This expertise is seen by many social scientists as setting us apart from the people we do research 'on'. People 'do life' but social scientists understand, interpret and use it. However, ethnomethodology rejects the notion that there is any sharp distinction between members' and social science approaches; there are no dichotomies, only gradations. And this we view very sympathetically because we feel it accords well with the egalitarian ethos of feminism.

We believe that feminist social science must begin with the recognition that 'the personal', lived experience, underlies all behaviours and actions. We need to find out what it is that, as women and feminists, we know. We need to re-claim, name and re-name our experience and thus our knowledge of this social world that we live in and daily help to construct, because only by doing so will it become truly *ours*, ours to use and do with as we will. The social world we presently inhabit is one we conceptualise through a worldview provided by a sexist society and a thoroughly androcentric social science. We need to construct our own; and we see this process beginning from an explication of women's experiences of women's social realities. Without starting here we believe we can have no truly feminist social science; we can have only a social science in which women's lives are researched and analysed using the same old conceptual frameworks, methods of research and analytic models.

Women are social beings. We live in a social world with other social beings and merely living requires that we behave in social ways. We interact with other people at all times, both physically and in our minds. It is all of these social actions which should properly be the concern of a feminist social science. 'The self' is a social self and feminist research should be concerned with the social processes we're immersed within and help construct. As we go about our lives we do the things we do for good reasons, reasons which are ordinarily accessible to ourselves and to other people for critical examination and analysis. This is what we ordinarily do as ordinary members of society. We see the present process of becoming a professional social scientist as a training in how to disguise or dismiss this.

Feminist social scientists must relearn how to do this, but to do it deliberately and without shame. Instead of bracketing such processes away, pretending that they don't happen, we need to explore what it is that we know about the social world and how we behave and relate within it. These things become accessible to us as we go into situations and try to find out what's happening in them. We can write this accessibility out of our research but we believe that in doing so we lose a great deal, and a great deal that is of paramount importance in the achievement of feminist revolution.

We need to know how, in minute detail, all facets of the oppressions of all women occur, because if we're to resist oppression then we need to understand how it occurs. We believe that liberation has to start somewhere. We can't, and we won't, leap into a liberated world overnight, after the revolution. We must necessarily effect many small liberations in many small, seemingly insignificant, aspects of our lives or we shall never start 'the revolution' nor even recognise it happening around us.

Feminist research as we envisage it would explore the basis of our everyday knowledge as women, as feminists and as social scientists. It would recognise that each of these is inextricably linked rather than trying to separate off one of these facets of 'us' within research reports. It would go about this by starting from the experiences of the researcher as a person in a context. How we find out must be what our research is concerned with; and 'how' must be as central to how we write feminist research as it is to how we do it. We feel strongly about this because we believe that a major consequence of making available the reasoning procedures which underlie the knowledge produced out of research is 'vulnerability'. We believe that this is the only satisfactory — because effective — way of tackling fundamental features of the power relationship existing between researchers and researched that we have yet come across. This relationship must, whatever and whoever 'the researched' are, reflect feminist principles and beliefs. And we believe 'vulnerability' as we've described it does indeed reflect these principles and beliefs.

Notes

1 We've chosen to restrict our discussions to the social sciences for a number of reasons. By trade we're both social scientists and we want to address ourselves to issues of interest to and a part of this trade. We haven't written about the natural sciences because our involvement in these, except within everyday life, is minimal and we try to stick to writing about what we know about first-hand. We haven't written about literature and 'the arts' for different reasons. We don't accept any easy distinction between 'fact' and 'fiction' or between 'literature' and 'science,' and in some ways we see the products of social science as 'fictional' (or the products of literature as 'science'). But to expand our discussions away from the social sciences would produce something unmanageable in the space of a short paper.

2 We see the origins and use of these dichotomies as essentially sexist, for reasons which we discuss in Stanley and Wise (1983). Our discussion there owes much to Dale Spender (1978).

3 This argument is fundamental to the symbolic interactionist and pheno-

menological approaches within the social sciences. We think it significant for our general argument in this paper that British academic feminism has been, and is, largely blind to this strand of thinking and working in the social sciences. We see these approaches as very much in sympathy with feminism's insistence on the importance of 'the personal' and draw our own conclusions about academic feminism's propensity for structural analyses from them.

4 We've discussed these attempts to construct 'feminist research' in Stanley and Wise (1983) especially in chapter one.

5 In saying this we've been accused of advocating research that's concerned with 'bourgeois trivia'. We find it odd that revolutionaries seem to have such a profound distaste for the everyday lives of ordinary people. We also welcome the association with Trivia, the three-headed goddess of ambiguity and contradiction who stood at crossroads and confused men who asked the way! That 'Trivia' has become 'trivial' is itself sufficient comment on the sexism of such insults.

6 In relation to our use of terms such as 'scholarly' and 'rigorous', we must emphasise that we *don't* mean them as they're conventionally seen — removed, detached and so forth. We have in mind models like the disciplined rigour of Dorothy Richardson's *Pilgrimage* sequence of novels (Richardson, 1979) or the novels of Virginia Woolf, recast in social science terms and concerned with social science issues.

7 Nancy Kleiber and Linda Light's (1978) discussion of their research on and for a Women's Health Collective illustrates these issues very clearly. Their research involved women who were feminists. Similar issues and possibilities of course exist with research on/for other women, but may be more difficult to see, given that Kleiber and Light were in a sense forced to confront them by their 'research population', who simply refused to be objectified in the traditional way.

8 Many feminists discuss feminist research largely in terms of problems. We see *possibilities*, possibilities which should be gratefully grasped and explored.

9 This research is discussed in detail in Stanley (1976a), Stanley (1976b), Wise (1978), Stanley and Wise (1979), Stanley and Wise (1983), as are the reactions to our public presentations of it from gay groups, academic colleagues and feminists.

10 One interpretation of obscene phone calls is to view them as consensual sexual acts between callers and receivers, and the women who are their victims are instead seen as fully consenting sexual partners. See Russell (1971), Nadler (1968).

11 See Mitchell and Oakley (1976), Brunsdon (1978) and Himmelweit *et al.*, (1976). Mitchell and Oakley reject 'sisterhood' and its ideas about personal experience, arguing that feminists mustn't be involved in wholesale rejection of existing social practices, and in particular they say that changes in lifestyle are 'politically pretty useless'. We believe that within what they say can be detected the reappearance of 'subjectivity' and 'objectivity' as dichotomous categories, with subjectivity being seen as limited and

inadequate as a basis for theorizing. While appreciating something of why they feel as they do, we reject both their answer ('going back to the drawing board') and their statement of the problem; our reasons for doing so are embodied in the text of this paper.

12 We are deeply indebted to the work of Dorothy Smith in illuminating for us more precisely what the possibilities are for using 'ourselves' as women and as feminists in this way. See Smith (1974a, 1974b, 1978a, 1978b, 1980).

13 And also the insistence of some women, speaking on behalf of 'feminism', that the WLM owns all ideas and statements produced by women who call themselves feminist. See Leeds Revolutionary Feminist Group (1979).

14 Margrit Eichler has made this point in relation to feminist work on 'gender role' (Eichler, 1980), while here we're making it more widely.

15 Some useful introductory reading include Manis and Meltzer (1967), Rose (1962), Douglas (1972), Turner (1974). We owe particular thanks to a number of people for sparking off trains of thought which led to our ideas changing in this direction, some of whom at least would be horrified to hear of it. We thank Michael Smith, John Phillips, Gill Burrington, Ken Plummer, Alison Kelly, Rod Watson, and most of all each other.

16 Our account of ethnomethodology here is extremely basic. Our purpose isn't to introduce all its many complexities but more simply to emphasize those ways in which we view it as in sympathy with, and so usable by, feminism.

17 Robin Morgan (1978) uses this term to discuss how feminists are seen to 'go too far.'

References

Brundson, Charlotte (1978), 'It Is Well Known That by Nature Women are Inclined to Be Rather Personal', in Women's Studies Group (eds), *Women Take Issue*, London, Hutchinson, pp. 18-34.

Douglas, Jack (ed.) (1972), *Understanding Everyday Life*, London, Routledge & Kegan Paul.

Eichler, Margrit (1980), *The Double Standard*, London, Croom Helm.

Garfinkel, Harold (1967), *Studies in Ethnomethodology*, Engelwood Cliffs, Prentice-Hall.

Himmelweit, Susan *et al*. (1976), 'Why Theory?' in Women's Publishing Collective (eds), *Papers on Patriarchy*, London, WPC/PDC, pp. 1-5.

Kleiber, Nancy and Light, Linda (1978), *Caring for Ourselves*, Vancouver, University of British Columbia.

Leeds Revolutionary Feminist Group (1979), 'Every Single Academic Feminist Owes Her Livelihood to the WLM,' unpublished paper, WRRC Summer School, Bradford.

Manis, Jerome and Meltzer, Bernard (eds) (1967), *Symbolic Interaction*, Rockleigh, Allyn & Bacon.

Mitchell, Juliet and Oakley, Ann (1976), 'Introduction', in J. Mitchell and A. Oakley (eds), *The Rights and Wrongs of Women*, Harmondsworth, Penguin, pp. 7-15.

Morgan, David (1981), 'Men, Masculinity and the Process of Sociological Enquiry,' in H. Roberts (ed.), *Doing Feminist Research*, London, Routledge & Kegan Paul.

Morgan, Robin (1978), *Going too Far: The Personal Chronicle of a Feminist*, New York, Vintage Books.

Nadler, Raoul (1968), 'Approach to Psychodynamics of Obscene Telephone Calls,' *New York State Journal of Medicine*, vol. 65, pp. 521-7.

Richardson, Dorothy (1979), *Pilgrimage* (4 vols), London, Virago.

Rose, Arnold (ed.) (1962), *Human Behaviour and Social Processes*, London, Routledge & Kegan Paul.

Russell, Donald (1971), 'Obscene Telephone Callers and Their Victims,' *Sexual Behaviour*, pp. 80-6.

Smith, Dorothy (1974a), 'Women's Perspective as a Radical Critique of Sociology,' *Sociological Inquiry*, vol. 44, pp. 7-13.

Smith, Dorothy (1974b), 'Some Implications of a Sociology for Women,' in W. Glazer and H. Youngleson Waehrer (eds), *Woman in a Man-Made World*, Illinois, Rand McNally, pp. 15-29.

Smith, Dorothy, (1978a), 'K Is Mentally Ill,' *Sociology*, vol. 12, pp. 23-53.

Smith, Dorothy, (1978b), 'A Peculiar Eclipsing,' *Women's Studies International Quarterly*, vol. 1, pp. 281-96.

Smith, Dorothy (1980), 'No One Commits Suicide: Textual Analysis of Ideological Practice,' unpublished paper, Ontario Institute for Studies in Education.

Spender, Dale (1978), 'Educational Research and the Feminist Perspective,' unpublished paper, British Educational Research Association Conference on 'Women, Education and Research', University of Leicester.

Stanley, Liz (1976a), 'On the Receiving End,' *OUT*, vol. 1, pp. 6-7.

Stanley, Liz (1976b), 'Obscene Phone Calls,' unpublished paper, British Sociological Association, Sexuality Study Group, Manchester.

Stanley, Liz (1981), 'The Problems and Problems of Working with Gay Men,' WRRC Conference on 'The Women's Liberation Movement and Men,' London.

Stanley, Liz and Wise, Sue (1979), 'Feminist Research, Feminist Consciousness and Experiences of Sexism,' *Women's Studies International Quarterly*, vol. 2, pp. 259-379.

Stanley, Liz and Wise, Sue (1983), *Breaking Out: Feminist Consciousness and Feminist Research*, London, Routledge & Kegan Paul.

Turner, Roy (ed.) (1974), *Ethnomethodology*, Harmondsworth, Penguin.

Wise, Sue (1978), 'Labelling Theory and Societal Reactions to Lesbianism,' unpublished dissertation, Manchester Polytechnic.

13

Women's Studies as a strategy for change: between criticism and vision

Marcia Westkott

Underlying the current dialogue concerning alternative methods for practicing Women's Studies lies the fundamental question of purpose: why study women, their historical contexts and their created works? The answer to this question cannot be logically deduced from any theory or method, but lies outside of the scholarly process. It is rooted in the personally defined intentions of the scholar-teacher herself. The answer which one gives to this question is decisive, for the methods of study that she selects can be judged to be appropriate only in reference to the purpose. To begin with the question of method, rather than that of purpose not only is irrational ('I don't know why I'm doing this, but at least I'm doing it well,' i.e., following the rules), but also contributes to what Mary Daly (1973) has termed the 'invisible tyranny' of method.[1]

An early definition of Women's Studies linked the purposes of Women's Studies scholarship to the aims of the feminist movement: to the eradication of all forms of sexism and thus to the liberation of women. Women's Studies was defined by the founders of the National Women's Studies Association as an 'educational strategy' for change, not because of some abstract principle that change is good in itself but because the founders recognized that we live in a sexist world in which women are devalued, subordinated, and in other ways oppressed. They held that it is that world that needs to be changed and that Women's Studies is a means to this end (*Women's Studies Newsletter*, 1977).

To participate as scholar-teachers in changing a sexist world we do more than describe or distill that world. We simultaneously understand and oppose it. Whether we engage in historical analysis, literary criticism, sociological investigation, or interdisciplinary studies, our relationship to our material is critical, because our purpose is to change the sexist world that we are also seeking to understand. We assume, therefore, in our development of knowledge a critical sensibility that holds that coming to knowledge and making judgments are not separate processes, but that (in Flannery O'Connor's phrase) 'judgment is implicit in seeing' (Walker, 1979, p. 49). In this we affirm the power of the full range of our sensibilities, rejecting the belief that forms the basis of the male-defined intellectual tradition, a belief that holds judging and seeing to be necessarily separate processes. Separating seeing from judging dilutes the power of 'seeing' so that it becomes an enfeebled process of blind observation and bland description. Thus released from the full range of human perception and understanding, judgment itself becomes trivialized as mere 'opinion.' We reject this enfeebling approach not simply because it bores us intellectually, but also because it violates the vehemence with which we oppose the sexist world that devalues us.

The development of this feminist critical approach to knowledge begins with an awareness of our relationship to the historical contexts in which we live. Those who teach Women's Studies courses are familiar with the process of developing this awareness. It begins with the fact that in Women's Studies courses women students are no longer studying material that is totally outside themselves, but are learning about the ways in which their social contexts have shaped them as women. In this process social knowledge and self-knowledge become mutually informing. Not only can students illuminate knowledge of themselves through understanding their social contexts, but also they can test interpretations of their social contexts from the perspectives of their own experience. For them the personal becomes intellectual, and the intellectual, personal.[2]

The great possibility of such courses where knowledge of the social world becomes personalized is the chance of connecting psyche and history. These are the moments when we discover that buried parts of ourselves are held in common with others. These 'experiences of consciousness-in-history' are exciting not only because they reveal to us knowledge of ourselves that we have buried and 'forgotten,' but also because they link us to others through the experiences that we hold in common. To study the history of women, especially as it is recorded through the consciousness of women themselves, is to set the opportunity for discovering how one's life experiences are connected to those of other women. Psyche and history are thus joined in the discovery of the ways that one's personal life has been shaped by being born a woman.

The feminist consciousness that emerges from this connection between psyche and history becomes critical when a student discovers patterns in her own and other women's lives that are not created freely, but are determined by restrictive, male-dominated structures. Through reading critical analyses and examining her own life, a student discovers the ways in which she has been victimized because she is a woman: regarded physically as a non-person, an 'other' who mirrors and validates men (de Beauvoir, 1952); encapsulated and domesticated within the family as mother, where she is regarded as a totally self-less caretaker, an 'it' (Dinnerstein, 1976); denied access to historically created spheres of power, wealth, and social prestige, where she is regarded as an incompetent child who needs to be protected (Gornick, 1971); and perhaps most devastatingly, cut off from her own bodily and personal power as an autonomous human being (Ehrenreich and English, 1979). These discoveries of subordination and victimization, because they are personal as well as historical, often generate anger. Paradoxically, however, the discoveries that produce anger also intensify understanding. Putting one's own struggles in historical context enables a student to distance herself from her personal experiences of victimization at the same time that she learns to uncover these parts of herself and feel them deeply.

Judging what we see is rooted in our personal connection to the object of our understanding as well as our distancing ourselves from it. To reflect upon the historical oppression of women and to assert that 'it need not be' (Rich, 1976) presumes both the ability to take the oppression of women as an object of understanding as well as to feel the oppression in a deeply personal way. Moreover, this refusal to tolerate the conditions that we discover proceeds from the historical consciousness that the world could be different. It assumes that alternatives are possible to the historically created male-dominated structures that presently oppose the freedom of women. By clarifying that which we oppose, we set the groundwork for creating a vision of that for which we long.

Because this alternative vision emerges from one's own sense of devaluation and struggle as a woman in a male-dominated society, it is fundamentally a personal vision of one's life freed from these constraints. The dream of freedom for oneself in a world in which all women are free emerges from one's own life experience in which one is not free, precisely because one is a woman. The liberation of women is thus not an abstract goal tacked onto the creative process, but is the motive for that process. Individual freedom and the freedom of all women are linked when one has reached the critical consciousness that we are united first of all in our unfreedom. Hence, the personal dream of freedom is also the feminist vision of liberation.

We know from our classes in Women's Studies the importance of pushing our criticism past itself to the visions that the criticism suggests. Unless we do that, we offer no hope for directing the anger that is often generated by the critical awareness, and we are left with paralyzing fury or hopeless resignation ('Is this another moan course?', a Women's Studies major asked on the first day of class). To push beyond criticism, however, is not to relinquish it, but to hold it in tension with vision. The criticism indicates to us an absence or a problem which our imagination can transcend. This transcendence is a visionary transformation of the conditions which we oppose, a new world view rather than a mere extension or rearrangement of present structures. Feminist vision is thus, not a feasibility study, but an imaginative leap that stands opposed to sexist society. As negations of the conditions that we criticize, visions both reflect those conditions and oppose them. In the words of Josephine Donovan, 'The feminist critic is thus on the cutting edge of the dialectic. She must, in a sense, be Janus-headed: engaged in negations that yield transcendences' (1975, p. 80).

By engaging in 'negations that yield transcendence' our Women's Studies classes are 'educational strategies' for change. First, by articulating that which we oppose and by envisioning alternative futures, we identify the goals and strategies for action; that is, we clarify what it is we want to move *away from* as well as what it is we want to move *toward*. Change is thus informed by purpose and goal. Second, through the classroom process itself we create changes in the forms of learning: in student-teacher relationship, in the personal-intellectual mediation, in the dialogue and negotiations from which critical perspectives and transcending visions emerge. In the processes of creating these changes in the classroom itself, we not only produce models for other contexts, but also learn about processes for creating feminist change. We learn, for example, that criticism and vision are not static ideations but are related in a continuing mediation in which they themselves are changed. Hence, the very processes of creating alternative possibilities changes the way in which we understand the problems we criticize; and to the extent that we realize our visions, the problems themselves will be transformed.

Thus, to play upon the dialectic implied in Flannery O'Connor's aphorism, through teaching Women's Studies as an educational strategy for change we affirm that 'judgment is implicit in seeing' *and that seeing is implicit in judging.* Refusal to accept the conditions which oppose us is the ground upon which we both understand those conditions and imagine alternatives to them. Our negations ground our seeing.[3] To be a feminist seer is thus to appropriate the full range of human possibilities of seeing and to give them new meaning. We experience *and* understand, discover *and* create, judge *and* envision, grasp *and* take care of. This process teaches us to move beyond the male definitions and dichotomies that falsify our experiences and possibilities, to creating spheres of thought and action where we can simultaneously discover and create ourselves and the world in which we live.

We bring the criticism-vision dialectic to our classrooms with an intensity and frequency that is less visible in our scholarship. The reasons for this difference, if not happy, are at least intelligible. They are rooted, first of all, in the process and criteria for judging academic acceptability of our work. Published research and not teaching has become the activity *sine qua non* for survival and advancement within the academy. Hence, because it is judged to be less important for academic success, classroom teaching affords greater freedom for responding to issues and creating alternative approaches to knowledge that may transcend the male-defined tradition of education. In addition, Women's Studies students frequently goad us into confronting pertinent issues and devising methods that are appropriate to those issues, thus reminding us of the Women's Studies commitment to change for women. Conversely, our publications are for the male-defined intellectual tradition because our survival within the academy is dependent upon their acceptability within that tradition. In this lies our problem. First, the male-defined tradition has institutionalized the 'tyranny of method' as the requirement for 'good' scholarship.

To violate the canonized methods of our disciplines through employing the critical-visionary approaches appropriate to feminist change is to risk certain rejection by the academic gate-keepers. Second, the anti-feminism that is implicit in the above approach is rendered explicit in the academy's judgment of scholarship that has women as its subject and is published in Women's Studies journals. Regardless of its adherence or lack thereof to the institutionalized methods, scholarship about women is viewed with suspicion for its perceived lack of seriousness, importance, and contribution to 'the field'.

It is no wonder that many academic women have decided that if they wish to continue studying and writing about women while pursuing an academic career, the realistic course of action is the cautious one: writing about women, their historical contexts and creative works, but employing scrupulously the established methods of the male-defined intellectual tradition. This cautious resolution to the dilemma that the academic woman faces is unfortunately a compromise that robs our work of the Women's Studies commitment to feminist change. By producing information about women as the male traditions would 'see' us, we may slip through the immediate academic personnel hoops at the expense of tacitly supporting present conditions of female oppression and distortions of our experiences. By choosing not to see and judge but only to 'observe' and describe, we reify the conditions of our own — and thus all women's — oppression and further entrench the male-defined tradition which imposes the methodological tyranny.

And yet, criticizing this compromise taken by some academic women does not remove the underlying dilemma that women in the academy face. To have a woman-centered university (Rich, 1979) requires at the very least having women in the university, and beyond that, having women in positions of power to make changes for women. To criticize the culture, history, and procedures that undergird the institution through whose ranks we seek to advance, and to expect that our criticism will be accepted as a valid means to that advancement, is to face a tough problem, indeed. How we personally mediate the various contradictions inherent in this problem cannot be prescribed, but emerges from our own commitments and needs as well as the conditions that we face.[4] Whatever the specific risks and compromises that we may choose, whether we leave the academy or attempt to advance or survive within it, the goal of creating change *for* women guides us in our struggle.

To choose to apply our scholarship to this purpose is to employ the dialectical approach to knowledge which we employ in our classes. Like the classroom activity, our scholarship can criticize and imagine alternatives to conditions outside of itself (i.e., sexist institutions and practices), and thus suggest goals and strategies for changing those conditions. It can study as models the lives of women from the past who engaged in this struggle and who can teach us today. Moreover, just as the pedagogy of Women's Studies classes is itself a means for creating change, so scholarship about women can change the means by which we understand ourselves and the world in which we live. To change the forms through which our experience is mediated — especially that of language — is to break through the tyranny of the ultimate method by which our selves and our possibilities are made known to us.

The transformation of categories and concepts is basic to our capacity to engage in 'negations that yield transcendences.' To imagine a different world requires first of all the ability to perceive the world differently and to open ourselves to formerly denied possibilities. The taken-for-granted-world mediated by familiar categories is not a natural 'given' but consists of historically created forms that define feelings and give meaning to experience. The given categories not only define conscious processes, but also permeate the unconscious, creating what Herbert Marcuse has identified as the 'false automatism of immediate experience' (1969, p. 39). This link between psyche and symbol, thus, binds us deeply to the perceptions and purposes of the symbol makers, i.e., those who have the power to define their symbols as universal and absolute. Today this means that our conscious and unconscious processes are informed by categories and concepts that, in the words of Monique Wittig, 'teach us about ourselves through the instrumentality of specialists' (1980, p. 107). We are defined, and come to regard ourselves as means through which others' purposes are realized, as objects for manipulation and control, and as interchangeable parts in an apparatus that has no plan. Thus, we are defined not only *in terms of* the instrumentality, but we *become* the instrumentality of those who perpetuate the tyranny of method.

To rupture these categories is to break the limitations upon perception and to create new ways of seeing and of expressing that perception. It is also to reclaim ourselves as our own ends as we refuse to accept being the means for others. It should come as no surprise to us that it is the feminist poets who are taking the greater risks in shattering those old forms and creating new ones: in critically uncovering the cultural meanings of the categories that take women as instrumentalities (Griffin, 1981) and in creating new categories that simultaneously touch and liberate our experience.[5] Those who transform categories risk confronting experience in itself as they reject the familiar signposts to its meaning. In the words of Adrienne Rich 'No one who survives to speak / new language, has avoided this: / the cutting-away of an old force that held her / rooted to an old ground' (1978, p. 25).

As we reject the 'old ground,' we should also reject its assumptions that only the poets who inspire us have the license to cut the conventions that once appeared to hold us down. The very definition of scholarship as uncritical and unimaginative, and therefore unable to be a strategy for change is a pretentious weight that holds us to this 'old ground.' To negate and transcend it, we must risk cutting ourselves free from its familiar but false categories and promises.

Notes

1 'The tyranny of methodolatry hinders new discoveries. It prevents us from raising questions never asked before and from being illumined by ideas that do not fit into pre-established boxes and forms. The worshippers of Method have an effective way of handling data that does not fit into the Respectable Categories of Questions and Answers. They simply classify it as nondata, thereby rendering it invisible' (Daly, 1973, p. 11).

2 See, for example, Rutenberg, 'Learning Women's Studies,' this volume Chapter 5.

3 The idea of the negation of domination giving rise to alternative possibilities derives from the concept of 'critical theory' associated with the work of those of the Institute for Social Research at Frankfurt. While the idea of negation is a useful one for feminist critical theory, the content and promise of that negation is not derivative from the male critical tradition, but is grounded in women's concrete, lived experience.

4 A collective strategy is no less complex, but it does create power in union that may be lacking in individual rank. For an excellent analysis of an example of successful campus organizing, see Karen Childers, Phillis Rackin, Cynthia Secor, and Carol Tracy, 'A Network of One's Own,' unpublished paper.

5 For an excellent analysis of Adrienne Rich's work from this perspective, see Diehl (1980).

References

Blau Du Plessis, Rachel (1975), 'The Critique of Consciousness and Myth in Levertov, Rich and Rukeyeser,' *Feminist Studies*, vol. 3, no. 1, 2, Fall, pp.199-221.

Daly, Mary, (1973), *Beyond God the Father*, Boston, Beacon Press.

de Beauvoir, Simone (1952), *The Second Sex*, New York, Knopf.

Diehl, Joanne F. (1980), '"Cartographies of Silence:" Rich's Common Language and Woman Poet,' *Feminist Studies*, vol. 6, no. 3, Fall, pp. 503-46.

Dinnerstein, Dorothy (1976), *The Mermaid and the Minotaur*, New York, Harper & Row.

Donovan, Josephine (1975), 'Afterword: Critical Re-Vision,' in J. Donovan (ed.), *Feminist Literary Criticism: Exploration in Theory*, University Press of Kentucky, p. 80.

Ehrenreich, B. and English, D. (1970), *For Her Own Good: 150 Years of the Experts' Advice to Women*, New York, Anchor Press/Doubleday.

Gornick, Vivian (1971), 'Woman as Outsider,' in V. Gornick and B.K. Moran (eds), *Woman in Sexist Society*, New York, New American Library, pp. 126-44.

Griffin, Susan (1981), *Pornography and Silence: Culture's Revenge Against Nature*, New York, Harper & Row.

Marcuse, Herbert (1969), *An Essay on Liberation*, Boston, Beacon Press, p. 39.

Rich, Adrienne (1976), *Of Woman Born: Motherhood as Experience and Institution*, New York, W.W. Norton, p. 14.

Rich, Adrienne (1978), 'Transcendental Etude,' *The Dream of a Common Language: Poems 1974-77*, New York, W.W. Norton, p. 75.

Rich, Adrienne (1979), 'Toward a Woman-Centered University,' *On Lies, Secrets, and Silence: Selected Prose 1966-1978*, New York, W.W. Norton, pp. 125-55.

Walker, Alice (1979), 'One Child of One's Own,' *Ms.*, vol. 8, no. 2, August, p. 49.

Wittig, Monique (1980), 'The Straight Mind,' *Feminist Issues*, vol. 1, no. 1, Summer, p. 107.

Women's Studies Newsletter (1977), 'Constitution of the NWSA,' vol. 5, no. 1, 2, p. 6.

14

In praise of theory: the case for Women's Studies[1]

Mary Evans

One of the most obvious results of contemporary feminism has been the establishment of a new academic subject: that of Women's Studies. None of the courses can be said to have been welcomed with wild enthusiasm by the male academic establishment: at best a benign tolerance has allowed academics to teach courses about that half of the population which has been generally invisible in much of traditional scholarship. Yet at the same time as those of us teaching Women's Studies have been arguing with the more articulate battalions of male chauvinism, we have also been faced with a more problematic form of opposition, in the shape of criticism from other feminists who have voiced either misgivings or outright hostility to the mere idea of Women's Studies, and have condemned Women's Studies as incompatible with feminism. These criticisms have often been far more difficult to deal with than those of the academic arrière-garde since they are often better arguments and are capable of including those acute fits of sisterly soul-searching which can paralyse all further activity. Disagreeing with Professor D.E.D. Wood is one thing, disagreeing with a woman who prefaces all her remarks with an invocation of sisterhood is another, and far more fearful, experience.

The argument put forward by some feminists suggests that Women's Studies represent either the exploitation or the de-radicalization (or both) of feminism and the women's movement. By becoming part of what is an elitist, and essentially male system of higher education, it is argued that those who teach (and presumably also those who study)

Women's Studies only serve their own professional interests and those of patriarchy and the male ruling class. The energies that should be directed towards the transformation of social and sexual relationships are, it is suggested, dissipated in narrow scholastic battles which serve only to perpetuate those hierarchies of control and authority to which the women's movement is opposed.

Inevitably this argument poses the crucial question of whether or not Women's Studies — as a distinct area of study within the academy — is feminist in any meaningful sense. Many feminists would agree that a distinction must be made between Women's Studies and feminist studies, and that only the latter is a viable and defensible form of feminist activity. As I shall argue in this paper I do not think this is the case.

Women's Studies is feminist studies

My major reason for supposing that no distinction exists between Women's Studies and feminist studies is two-fold: first, because Women's Studies and feminist studies both challenge male intellectual hegemony. In asserting, describing and documenting the existence of women, both women's studies and feminist studies propose a radical change in the theoretical organization of the universe. To quote Maurice Godelier, himself paraphrasing Marx:

> We might say that the dominant ideas in most societies are the ideas of the dominant sex, associated and mingled with those of the dominant class. In our own societies, a struggle is now under way to abolish relations of both class and sex domination, without waiting for one to disappear first (1981, p. 17).

Women's Studies is part of that struggle: a self-conscious determination to show that both the content and form of existing knowledge is related to the unequal distribution of social power between men and women. The second reason that I would propose for there being no distinction between feminist and Women's Studies is that the distinction often rests upon a falsely homogeneous view of feminism. Women's Studies is seen as the reactionary, incorporative, pro-status quo activity whilst feminism is always radical, always antithetical to existing society.

Yet feminism — as everyone in the women's movement knows — comes in a variety of forms, some of which are far from incompatible with industrial capitalism as we know it. To suppose, therefore, that feminism and feminist studies, has an inevitable theoretical coherence and radicalism which Women's Studies lacks is to run the risk of reifying a quite mythical unity.

There are, then, two forms of feminist attack on Women's Studies. The first, outlined above, is that Women's Studies are not feminist studies. The second, to be discussed here, is that neither feminist studies nor Women's Studies are desirable. It is thus argued by some feminists that any academic study of women is divorced from the interests of the women's movement, that it engages energies that would be better used elsewhere and that it serves the interests of a small, élite group of female academics.

Theory versus experience

A further argument, derived in part from a hostility to theoretical speculation that is a well-documented feature of British life, deserves less detailed attention. Nevertheless, it does demand mention. It is the contention — argued most passionately by some feminists — that there is no necessary difference between reported, subjective experience and theoretical and analytical work. This position would therefore assign the same importance, both practical and theoretical, to the work of a feminist theorist (by which I mean someone who has attempted a coherent analysis of her situation and that of other women) and any statement about her situation by any woman. This is emphatically not to say that a woman expressing horror or dislike at her situation does not have the same right to express that dislike or the same claim to be taken seriously as the theorist with a range of five-volume arguments at her disposal, but that a distinction has to be made between the analysis of subordination of all women and the subjective and personal reaction to that subordination by one woman.

Yet analysis of the situation of women is in some ways deeply problematic for the women's movement, since the first phenomenon that meets us when we attempt to analyse the situation of women is that it is many and varied. Thus we confront a fundamental issue within the women's movement: exactly what constitutes the oppression of women and who decides if it exists? It is clear from the reaction of many women (both in this country and in the Third World) that Western feminism has often made too many, too ethnocentric judgements about the nature of oppression.

In our attempt to achieve objective analytical accounts of the situations of women we are, therefore, stuck with theory. If this can be tolerated — and clearly some feminists do not tolerate it, seeing theory as a masculinization of that apparently exclusively female virtue of feeling — the existence of theory still poses problems for feminists. Three difficulties about the existence and elaboration of feminist theory and analysis come to mind. The first is the issue of the accessibility of theoretical discussion about women to all women, with the implication that it is possible that feminist theory may become the preserve of a small élite, which occasionally issues statements on what to think and how to think it, to the rest of the women's movement. The second issue is the problem of how feminist energy should be directed, and whether or not the intellectual and indeed practical resources that are directed into the development of feminist theory and Women's Studies would not be better employed in other ways, such as participation in grass-roots organizing. The third problem concerning feminist theory is the criticism that the development of feminist theory serves the career and professional interests of those involved in its development, makes experts of a small group and — this is related to the first point — denies the rank and file of the movement access to decision making and control of the formulation of policy.

Whilst these issues are common to the Left as Western Europe has known it, they are also a large part of feminism's dissatisfaction with traditional Left wing parties and organisations. Indeed, as Sheila Rowbotham, Lynn Segal and Hilary Wainwright have argued, it is essential to feminism that it should organize in a much more democratic and less authoritarian way than the traditional male Left. The contribution of feminism to the Left has been, they argue, the demonstration that political power does not have to ossify in the hands of a small élite and that it is possible for radical, left-wing organizations to be both effective and democratic. It is arguable that Rowbotham and her co-authors place too much emphasis on disillusionment with the authoritarian male Left in explaining the commitment to democracy within the women's movement since that very Left which is castigated in *Beyond the Fragments* has not been without its own democratic impulses recently. Nevertheless, whatever the origin of its democratic ideals, the British women's movement is deeply hostile to, and suspicious of, institutionalized power in any shape or form, be it intellectual or organizational. Yet despite this suspicion, British feminism does have an indigenously produced theoretical tradition of some sophistication, within and related to a women's movement which is deeply suspicious of all forms of élitism.

To return to the three problems about Women's Studies and feminist theory which I posed earlier. The first issue which I identified is whether or not feminist theory will become the exclusive activity of a small élite. The issue is a particularly crucial one in the case of Britain, where an exceptionally élitist system of higher education restricts the means of theoretical production to a very small number of people, and an even smaller number of women.

But it would be wrong to suppose that there is a *single* kind of feminist theory: some feminist writing, of great theoretical complexity, is accessible and readily comprehensible, whilst other feminist writing is virtually indecipherable to anyone without immense resources of time, patience, imagination and encyclopaedias on French intellectual practice. Nor is there any single home of those guilty of theoretical obscurantism; they lurk amongst feminist Marxists, feminist psychoanalysts and structuralists of all kinds and persuasions. Whilst some feminist Marxists write with great clarity and precision, others plunge their readers headlong into debates and definitions of shattering incomprehensibility. However, whilst I do not defend the deliberate use of obscure language in order to perplex, mystify and induce feelings of inadequacy, I would argue that there might be a case in some instances for the development of a highly precise theoretical language. Marxist feminist accounts of the economy, or the class structure, are one instance where the use of what is in a sense a technical language could be justified.

But there is no necessary reason within the practice of producing theory why a precise theoretical language, or theory itself, should become the preserve of a small élite. Theory is much more likely to become élitist for reasons outside itself; that is, the social conditions in which intellectual life takes place produce the possibility of élitist theory, rather than the theory itself. To condemn theory because of the possibility, however small, that it will remain the preserve of an élite, suggests a quite uncritical, and indeed reactionary, acceptance of a society in which access to higher education and critical thought is denied to many people. The implication of a claim that all analysis must be understood by all, is that those committed to change must accept the given divisions within any society and not attempt to do anything to change those divisions except in terms of those existing divisions. Thus we would have theory for graduates, the school-leavers with O levels, the almost illiterate and so on. The production of all these different theories would satisfy those who want to make feminism accessible to everyone, yet they would do nothing to challenge existing inequalities or hierarchies.

The risks of anti-theoreticism

Perhaps the crucial problem of feminist theory is not, however, its accessibility but about the resources that its production commands. The second issue about feminist theory is, therefore, the criticism that producing theory drains the women's movement of energy and talent that might be better spent elsewhere. Feminism (like socialism), it is argued, faces the appalling spectre of being so pre-occupied with interpreting events in the light of theory that it is rapidly overtaken by events and becomes the victim, rather than the vanguard, of history.

Yet an equally awful prospect is that feminism, in refusing to develop a coherent theory, remains at that stage of primitive subjectivism that is characteristic of some of the most reactionary social organizations in existence. That is not to say that all theories are necessarily right, but that the exercise of the construction of a rational case is the first step towards a real understanding of the social world. It is not for nothing that Jane Austen identified 'mean understanding' as one of the most unhappy states for human beings to live in. She well understood the horror of having to live in a circumscribed social world in which people — but perhaps most particularly women by virtue of their domestic seclusion — were constantly in the presence of over-developed opinion and quite under-developed understanding. Of the great nightmare characters of fiction, Jane Austen created perhaps the most vivid representatives of that state of existence in which self-interest, personal inclination and unreflective feeling could, in its human embodiment, create hell for other people. It may seem strange to cite the work of Jane Austen as relevant to the problems of contemporary feminism, but I would argue that she warns us against one of the risks which anti-theoretical feminism runs: that of refusing the accumulated knowledge of the past two thousand years. When some of Austen's more headstrong romantic heroines either throw themselves, or threaten to throw themselves, into some absurd romantic venture, they are cautioned by the author or a more careful character, to consider what has happened to other individuals who have followed too much the devices and desires of their own hearts. The heart, and all kinds of spontaneous feeling, was not, Austen realized, necessarily the best guide to the form of action most likely to produce the greatest happiness for the greatest number. To assert, therefore, as do some feminists, particularly in the United States, that women should 'get in touch with their own feelings' and 'reclaim their own subjectivity', is to follow a path which could lead to the most closed and unproductive of dead ends.

Feminist theory can, hopefully, lead us away from the blind alley of subjective feeling and subjective action. Yet the case against theory makes a great deal of the distinction between the production of theory and action which seems to suggest a theory of knowledge in which thought and action have no effect on each other. This view invokes a picture of human beings as headless chickens: the head, full of theory, lies inert and ineffective, while the headless body, empty of direction, rushes around in mindless circles. This dichotomy between theory and practice leads to some bizarre conclusions about the social world: that 'action' or practice is in some way separable from thought and that theory is always the soft option and action always the role of the true believer. It is seldom allowed that human beings have not only achieved a practical mastery of nature, but have also created most elaborate systems of thought, belief and ideology, which have critical effects on the material conditions of life of millions of people. The production of counter-ideologies may, therefore, be as much part of a struggle of the oppressed as any other.

Profiteering feminists?

The final criticism of feminism theory which has been named here is that the production of theory by feminists is motivated exclusively by the desire for self-aggrandisement of some kind. Protagonists of this argument go on to suggest that the production of feminist theory is in itself often suspect, in that it increases the discrepancy between highly educated women — able to write, and presumably understand, theory — and those women with little or no higher education.

The first part of this criticism of feminist theory — that it enhances the status, and the wealth, of those women producing it — is difficult to accept as a measured or rational criticism. It is undeniable that a few — a very few — women have grown rich by writing feminist, or quasi-feminist books, but in comparison to these quite exceptional cases there are literally hundreds of women in schools, universities and various other institutions who have battled, and are battling, to suggest that women do have special interests, and that the discussion and consideration of these interests merits attention. Furthermore, a brief look at those women who have written best-selling feminist works shows us that even feminist riches are intensely problematic. Poor Kate Millett, racked by guilt and conscience, beset by requests for help and money, exposed to every scurrilous intrusion of a totally irresponsible mass media, is a creature worthy of great feminist sympathy and understanding rather than a somewhat mean-minded envy for the income which her writing generated. Simone de Beauvoir received serious critical attention for the essays and novels which she wrote before the publication of *The Second Sex*, but as soon as that book was published she, like Kate Millett, was discussed and pilloried as a figure of fun and curiosity. The moral of these two cases is therefore, that successful feminists (or feminists who are successful in terms of the market place of capitalist production) cannot hope to enjoy that success. For a woman to write critically about her situation guarantees notoriety and hostility. Should that feminist criticism strike a sympathetic and resonant note in a large audience — as did *The Second Sex* and *Sexual Politics* — the more likely that the author will be submitted to every intrusive device of mis-representation of which the media is capable.

But many other feminists do not, of course, write best-sellers. We toil away in more prosaic and limited ways: proposing courses on Women's Studies, attempting to do feminist research or to encourage women students to set their sights above the given limits of female achievement. We must ask if these activities prolong élitism, or serve our professional interests. Suppressing, at this stage a desire to launch into biographical anecdote, I would argue that this is emphatically not the case: in most cases our professional interests would be best served by keeping well away from Women's Studies, let alone feminism.

But the reasons for saying that this is the case are more complex than might be supposed. The simple answer — and indeed an important part of the answer — is that Women's Studies is seen by many male academics as both a personal and an intellectual threat. It is very difficult to demonstrate this in academic terms: that is, I cannot say that you should turn to journal X or Y to see an example of this blatant prejudice. Academics are generally loathe to put on paper something which might correspond to an unsubstantiated opinion, or prejudice. The bias against women is much more subtle therefore than blatant, clear sexism, and frequently takes the form of the exclusion of women rather than bias against them.

So many male academics simply didn't see women as part of the social world, rather than taking a conscious decision to exclude them from it. To be asked, therefore, to make a conscious decision about *including* women, is something of a problem for individuals who have previously refused to recognize that the issue exists. It takes an effort of will to appreciate that the boundaries of a particular subject are neither as accurate nor as inclusive as has been hitherto supposed. Feminism poses, therefore, a genuine instance of a paradigm shift — a shift which like many other shifts is inevitably resisted by those committed to the modes and practices of thought and existing knowledge.

Sex-blind disciplines?

In resisting the discussion of women in the curriculum, academics (of both sexes) generally fall back on two arguments. First, that the existing literature on women is inadequate and second, that although it is conceded that it may be necessary for women to occupy a more central place in the disciplines than previously, the central issues of all subjects are sex-blind, and will remain untouched by the discussion of women.

The denial of the relevance of the study of women, and the specificity of the female case, to the central issues of a subject has important practical and intellectual consequences within the academy, one of which is the possibility of the pejorative labelling of women who produce work on women as narrow specialists in esoteric fields, whilst more conventional studies become important works of scholarship.

The history of theoretical feminism in Britain and the United States has yet to be written. However, when it is documented it would seem likely on the evidence so far available that women engaged in feminist research do not profit by that exercise in any orthodox sense, either inside or outside the academy. There are few indications at present that British or North American universities see Women's Studies as anything other than a peripheral or temporary phenomenon. Whatever the indications that the subject might be popular or lively it remains — as do its practitioners — in an outer courtyard, far removed from the real centres of academic power and authority. Given these factors it is unlikely that those who decide to accept feminism, and work for it, will be able to ignore the consistent marginality and academic deviance of their position.

The undeniable contextual importance of the struggle to assert women's voice within the academy and the intellectual community should not allow us to forget the nature of those worlds and their relationship to the general social formation. By this I do not just mean that those teaching Women's Studies should not turn our backs on the women's movement, but that we should confront the part that intellectual life can play in industrial capitalism. It is important that we should examine critically the reasons why, and the means by which, knowledge in our society is produced, assessed and distributed. Women's Studies has a most important part to play in ensuring that knowledge, itself a form of social power, is not produced solely in the interests of the powerful and the influential.

Notes

1   The complete version of this paper was previously published in *Feminist Review*, February 1982. I am extremely grateful to members of the *Feminist Review* collective for their comments on an earlier draft of this paper. I would also like to acknowledge the help of David Morgan and to thank Marion Shaw for inviting me to give the lecture at the University of Hull on which this paper is based.

References

Godelier, Maurice (1981), 'The Origins of Male Domination,' *New Left Review*, no. 127, pp. 3-7.

15

Selected annotated bibliography of articles on theories of Women's Studies[1]

Gloria Bowles, Renate Duelli Klein
and Taly Rutenberg

'Alice in Campusland,' (1979), *MS*, September, pp. 37-74.
A survey of current issues for women in higher education. This
report includes the results of a questionnaire distributed to forty
undergraduates on various campuses, as well as articles on privilege,
power, careers, returning adult women students, stopping out,
athletics, a campus newspaper takeover, and an overall look at
feminism on United States campuses.

Ballou, Pat (1977), 'Bibliographies for Research on Women,' *Signs*,
vol. 3, no. 2, pp. 436-50.
Ballou reviews and lists available bibliographies in eight areas:
general bibliographies, history, literature, anthropology and area
studies, economics and employment, education, politics and law,
sociology, psychology and health.

Bartky, Sandra L. (1978), 'Toward a Phenomenology of Feminist Consciousness', in M. Vetterling-Braggin, F. A. Elliston, and J. English
(eds), *Feminism and Philosophy*, Totowa, Littlefield, Adams, pp.
22-34.
According to Bartky, feminist consciousness is an immediate, personal consciousness arising from a combination of an awareness
of existing socioeconomic conditions with an awareness of real
possibilities for change; it allows what were previously seen as 'facts'
to be seen as 'contradictions' requiring resolution. Primarily a

consciousness of women's victimization, it gives one a paranoia-like wariness and a preparedness for struggle in any situation. It also places one in a perpetually 'ambiguous ethical situation' in the course of everyday life, leaving one constantly uncertain as to how to reconcile 'consciousness' with one's own feelings and with the demands and desires involved in living with others in the world as it is. Although it is an uncomfortable and ambiguous consciousness of alienation from society and self, it allows a truer understanding of things which in turn makes change possible. (JA)

Benson, Ruth C. (1972), 'Women's Studies: Theory and Practice,' *AAUP Bulletin*, vol. 58, no. 3, pp. 283-6.
An overview of Women's Studies including theory, structure, staffing and classroom issues. An introduction to issues in an article that is now of particular historical interest.

Blumhagen, Kathleen and Johnson, Walter (eds) (1978), *Women's Studies*, Westport, Greenwood Press.
A collection of essays addressing the theoretical, administrative and pedagogical aspects of Women's Studies. Contributors include: Ellen Boneparth, 'Evaluating Women's Studies: Academic Theory and Practice,' Sarah Hoagland, 'On the Reeducation of Sophie,' and Sarah Slavin Schramm, 'Women's Studies: Its Focus, Idea Power, and Promise.' (TR)

Bose, Christine, and Priest-Jones, Janet (1980), 'The Relationship Between Women's Studies, Career Development, and Vocational Choice,' *Women's Studies Monograph Series*, US Department of Health, Education and Welfare, The National Institute of Education.[2]
This monograph is one in a series of eight, commissioned by NIE. It reviews research on women and career aspirations, cites the available data on Women's Studies graduates and urges that programs compile more comprehensive data and make a concerted effort to link the undergraduate Women's Studies BA with career planning. In addition, the monograph defines specific needs for future research and outlines possible strategies for its accomplishment. (GLB)

Bowles, Gloria (1979), 'Women's Studies and the World: Promoting

Equity for the Other Half,' *Proceedings of the Women's Center Conference on the Impact of the Bakke Decision and Proposition 13 on Equity for Women in California Higher Education*, Berkeley, University of California, pp. 146-51.
The author traces the development of Women's Studies at UC Berkeley and makes a case for its innovative power in content as well as form.

Bowles, Gloria (1983), 'Is Women's Studies an Academic Discipline?', in G. Bowles and R. Duelli Klein (eds), *Theories of Women's Studies*, London, Routledge & Kegan Paul, pp. 32-45.
A detailed examination of the validity of Women's Studies as an academic discipline. Bowles critiques the disciplines as they have evolved while asserting the usefulness of higher education. She argues that Women's Studies is linked to the original principles of the disciplines and to the growing critique of academe from within and without the academy. She cites a definition of the variations of *disciplinary* (cross-, multi-, inter-, and trans-) and comments on the relation of Women's Studies to method and theory. Finally she suggests that, when challenged as to their legitimacy, those involved in Women's Studies should return the challenge, by demanding both a redefinition of terms and fulfillment of the professed aims of the university.

Boxer, Marilyn (1982), 'For and About Women: The Theory and Practice of Women's Studies in the United States,' *Signs*, vol. 7, no. 3, pp. 661-95.
Boxer's article is a survey of the literature about Women's Studies as a field in American higher education: its history, political issues, theories and structures. She documents not only our unifying vision of a society free of all oppression, but examines the internecine conflicts which arise from Women's Studies' struggle to survive as a radical critique of the university system which supports it. Boxer delineates the tenuous balance between scholarship and politics which academic feminism must maintain. Other major issues she considers include: the adaptation of feminist principles to the classroom, the feminist attempt to transform academic structures and curricula, the struggles against racism and homophobia inside and outside of Women's Studies, the accountability of academic feminism

to the larger women's liberation movement and the struggle for Women's Studies to remain a viable transformative force with the power to actually effect female consciousness and change the conditions of women's lives, the difficulties of interdisciplinarity in a discipline-based university; the current autonomy vs. integration debate, and the formation of feminist methodologies appropriate to Women's Studies as an autonomous discipline and as a force for social change. (HK)

Brush, Lorelei, Gold, Alice Ross and White, Marni (1978), 'The Paradox of Intention and Effect: A Women's Studies Course,' *Signs*, vol. 3, no. 4, pp. 870-83.
The authors describe the procedures, problems and results of a study of students taking a one-semester Women's Studies course. The intent of the study, which can be replicated in other institutional settings, was to evaluate the effect of the course upon students in relation to commitment to a feminist ideology, self-concept and sex-role stereotyping.

Building Feminist Theory. Essays from Quest (1981), Quest Staff and Quest Book Committee (eds), New York, Longman.
As Gloria Steinem says in the foreword, 'This book pulls together in permanent, portable form the works of a group of feminists who have spent most of the past decade thinking about subjects that may still be considered "new": class divisions experienced by women as both workers (unpaid or paid in the work force) and as the most basic means of production (the means of reproduction); the varying realities of race and culture; redefining power and the polarized options allowed by patriarchy; the politics of sexuality and spirituality; new forms of organizations, leadership, strategy and communication; and perhaps most of all the integrity of the process of change as part of the change itself.' The essays reflect the vision of the Quest staff which sees theory vital to the success of activism.

Bunch, Charlotte (1979), 'Not by Degrees,' *Quest*, vol. 5, no. 1, pp. 7-18.
Bunch emphasizes the development of feminist theory as a framework for analysis crucial to the survival of feminism and to the realization of educational and political goals of the activist women's

movement. She proposes a theoretical model involving four inter-related steps: description, analysis, vision and strategy. In addition, Bunch emphasizes the importance of literacy and the development of analytical skills for both understanding and creating theory. She attempts to 'demystify' theory by showing a link between theory and action and encourages theorizing as a means of intellectual and personal growth for women. (AB-P)

Callaway, Helen (1981), 'Women's Perspectives: Research as Re-vision,' In P. Reason and J. Rowan (eds), *Human Inquiry*, London, Wiley, pp. 457-71. In one of only two female contributions to this book on 'human' research, Callaway provides an overview of research on and by women and points out the new approaches in 'methodology, theory construction, and modes of expression' with which feminists work towards new paradigms. Hers is a strong case for the need to re-visit all previous knowledge, draw attention to research results in which women are judged according to criteria created by men, and continue our work of re-vision, looking ahead, anticipating, imagining. (RDK)

'Campus Special: Where Our Future Is Coming From' (1980) *Ms.*, vol. 9, no. 3, pp. 45-62.
This college issue introduces 'Women in the Think Business,' including an interview with Catharine Stimpson discussing women as academics, a description of the twelve women chosen to advise *Ms.* on women's issues and their status in academia, an interview with Frances 'Sissy' Farenthold (the first woman president of Wells College in New York), and a humorous look at the difficulties encountered as a feminist on campus. In addition, employment advice is offered to graduating seniors. (DB-A)

Coyner, Sandra (1983), 'Women's Studies as an Academic Discipline: Why and How to Do It,' in G. Bowles and R. Duelli Klein (eds), *Theories of Women's Studies*, London, Routledge & Kegan Paul, pp. 46-71.
The author asks Women's Studies practitioners to imagine the perfect program of the future, as she examines the various definitions of 'academic discipline,' ideas of 'objectivity' and Kuhnian 'paradigms' and argues that interdisciplinarity and an emphasis on influencing

existing disciplines is perhaps the wrong way for Women's Studies to proceed. Rather, Coyner insists that Women's Studies should be building its own distinct discipline. She goes on to describe her vision of that new discipline as it develops paradigms for study.

Du Bois, Barbara (1983), 'Passionate Scholarship: Notes on Values, Knowing and Method in Feminist Social Science,' in G. Bowles and R. Duelli Klein (eds), *Theories of Women's Studies*, London, Routledge & Kegan Paul, pp. 105-16.
Du Bois underlines the ways in which belief has informed scientific 'fact.' The 'process of science making,' says Du Bois, 'involves interpretation, theory-making, and thus values, in each of its phases.' Because of the androcentric bias of social science, women have not only been 'unknown, but virtually unknowable.' Once outside androcentric social science, we can begin to think in utterly new ways about our purposes and methods and we must do this because 'we literally cannot see women through traditional social science theory.' Ours is a communal search dedicated to process, and to complex, contextual analysis which opposes dichotomized thought, including the polarity of the knower and the known. Du Bois advocates 'passionate scholarship,' the 'passionate participation of the knower in the act of knowing.' (GLB)

Duelli Klein, Renate (1983), 'How to Do What We Want to Do: Thoughts about Feminist Methodology,' in G. Bowles and R. Duelli Klein (eds) *Theories of Women's Studies*, London, Routledge & Kegan Paul, pp. 88-104.
Until recently, the development of feminist methodology has been given little attention. Thus, as Duelli Klein claims, the use of nonfeminist methods in some research resulted in research *on* women rather than research *for* women. She says the goal of feminist research should be social change and that our methods should reflect this goal. Using a German research example, she discusses criteria for feminist methods and proposes some theoretical and practical ways to advance the development of feminist methodology and empower feminist scholarship.

Duelli Klein, Renate, Nerad, Maresi, Metz-Göckel, Sigrid (eds) (1982) *Feministische Wissenschaft und Frauenstudium*, Ein Reader mit

Originaltexten zu Women's Studies, Hamburg, AHD.
The intent of this collection of translations of original US papers on Women's Studies is to introduce European readers to the development of Women's Studies in the US. In addition, the editors provide an overview of the US system of higher education and draw parallels between North American Women's Studies and the development of feminist studies and research in Germany.

Duggan, Lisa (1979), 'Lesbianism and American History: A Brief Source Review,' *Frontiers*, vol. 4, no. 3, pp. 80-6.
Duggan explains that history is, for her, a tool to understand the present by illuminating the past. She is dismayed to realize how little history of lesbians exists. She briefly describes attitudes toward lesbians during several historical periods: colonial, nineteenth century, turn of the century, and twentieth century. Duggan suggests the need for a more creative approach in order to uncover facets of lesbianism which have been hidden or ignored. She includes an extensive bibliography which is intended as a guide for the researcher in lesbian history and includes work in this field as well as work in women's history, homosexual history, and general sex history.
(DB-A)

Elovson, Allana (1980), 'Women's Studies in the Community Colleges,' *Women's Studies Monograph Series*, US Department of Health, Education and Welfare, The National Institute of Education.[3]
Elovson asserts the revelance of Women's Studies classes and programs for women in community colleges by reviewing both demographic (changing age compositions, changing female/male ratios) and non-demographic factors (increased self-awareness and understanding) that make their continued existence within the community college system important. She reviews the existing literature on Women's Studies at community colleges and concludes that ' . . . our survey of both formal and informal sources yielded no data of the kind we sought. There is still a dearth of organized information in this area . . . .' In addition, she summarizes the comments of individuals involved in Women's Studies at the community college level with regard to these and other topics: (1) what makes Women's Studies courses possible, (2) the kinds of assistance needed, (3) the role of the instructors and the governance structure, and (4) the

goals of Women's Studies courses. Her recommendations include: (1) articulation of a federal policy of support, (2) collection of basic statistical data, (3) provision of money and support for needs assessment studies, (4) evaluation of the impact of Women's Studies on students, faculty, college curriculum, community, and relevant others, (5) provision of technical assistance in setting up programs. Finally, she provides a brief assessment of the future of Women's Studies in the community colleges. (JH)

Farley, Jennie (1974), 'Faculty Reaction to Women's Studies,' *Women's Studies*, vol. 2, no. 1, pp. 115-19.
Farley relates the history and results of the attempt at Cornell University to set up a Female Studies Program. In particular, she describes faculty participation in and reaction to the program, ending with an exhortation to proponents of Women's Studies Programs to 'put high priority on finding faculty backers.'

Fausto-Sterling, Anne (1980), 'Women's Studies and Science,' *Women's Studies Newsletter*, vol. 8, no. 1, pp. 4-7.
An introduction to a feminist critique of science, Fausto-Sterling addresses the hierarchical structure of scientific teaching as well as the concept of science itself. She suggests that science perpetuates male values through the traditional practice of solitary rather than communal work and with its emphasis on analysis rather than synthesis. She discusses concrete ways in which these negative aspects of science might be challenged and changed within the context of the university, particularly within the science classroom. Fausto-Sterling sees Women's Studies as the force for the breakdown of traditional divisions and categories of knowledge and thus disagrees with an approach which would 'add on' feminist thought to existing forms of knowledge. She concludes that changes in science, like changes in society, happen slowly and on many different levels. (LM)

Fitzgerald, Ann (1978), 'Teaching Interdisciplinary Women's Studies,' *Great Lakes College Association Faculty Newsletter*, March, pp. 2-3.
Fitzgerald relates her experiences in teaching interdisciplinary Women's Studies courses, and illustrates many of the difficulties of both Women's Studies and interdisciplinary approaches. As she shows, 'Women's Studies confronts head-on the two shibboleths of

the traditional curriculum: disciplinary specialization and apolitical objective knowledge. Women's Studies, in contrast, is necessarily interdisciplinary and frankly political.'

Freeman, Jo (1979), 'The Feminist Scholar,' *Quest*, vol. 5, no. 1, pp. 26-36.
Freeman states that feminism is not compatible with academia. She examines the structure and values of academe, and cites as its purpose the production of prestige. She discusses the 'publish or perish' and 'publish *and* perish' bind of professors, and the difficulties feminists face in attaining tenure. Freeman does not see the university or Women's Studies programs as the ideal or practical home for the feminist scholar. (PK)

Garside Allen, Christine (1975), 'Conceptual History as a Methodology for Women's Studies,' *McGill Journal of Education*, vol. 10, no. 1, pp. 49-58.
The author looks at the structure and content of Women's Studies programs. She defines the components and functioning of an interdisciplinary course, and suggests a methodology — conceptual history — for examining concepts and archetypes of women in western cultural history. She analyzes various literary texts to illustrate the conceptual approach, and concludes by emphasizing the necessity of innovative methodologies and the interdisciplinary approach for Women's Studies.

Gilbert, Sandra and Gubar, Susan (1979), *The Madwoman in the Attic*, New Haven and London, Yale University Press.
The book analyzes nineteenth century women's literature from a feminist perspective. The opening chapter establishes the theory upon which the remainder of the book rests: men have traditionally been the authors, the pen like a penis, a male tool for creation. Women, then, as creators, as writers, have been without tools, without authority. They have had to write their vision of the world in terms of the pervading masculine world view; much of women's work is about the dilemma of being a female artist. The remaining chapters address specific authors — Austen, Shelley, Eliot, Dickinson, and the Brontë sisters — showing how the particular conditions under which they wrote influenced what they wrote. (RW)

Gordon, Linda (1975), 'A Socialist View of Women's Studies,' *Signs*, vol. 1, no. 2, pp. 559-66.
Gordon explains her own socialist perspective on Women's Studies. She distinguishes between Black Studies and Women's Studies, and between the oppression of black people and the oppression of all women. She expresses her belief that Women's Studies can transform both scholarship and methodology, and thus finally describe the human experience. She ends with the assertion that the 'liberation of all women lies in the socialist transformation of the whole society.'

Gould, Meredith (1980), 'The New Sociology,' *Signs*, vol. 5, no. 3, pp. 459-67.
Gould asserts that although the concept of a sociology which is more responsive to women has made some gains in recent years, a male-centered tradition still dominates sociological analysis. She concentrates her review on what she thinks are the emerging theoretical and methodological issues in sociology: 'the terminological debate over "sex roles," the critique of androcentrism in sociological theory, the reevaluation of traditional methodologies and renewed interest in the sociology of knowledge.' (JH)

Grossman Kahn, Diana (1978), 'Interdisciplinary Studies and Women's Studies: Questioning Answers and Creating Questions,' *The Structure of Knowledge*, Proceedings of the Fourth Annual GLCA Women's Studies Conference, pp. 20-4.
The author briefly looks at the methods and the questions of the disciplines, illustrating her points with a hypothetical new discipline, Grockology, and personal experiences in dealing with a single discipline. She advocates the interdisciplinary approach for Women's Studies as the one most likely to give a complete view of women's experience and most able to provide a broad perspective for problem-solving.

Guttentag, Marcia, *et al.* (1978), 'Evaluating Women's Studies: A Decision-Theoretic Approach,' *Signs*, vol. 3, no. 4, pp. 884-90.
In a new approach for evaluating the effects of Women's Studies courses, the authors discuss evaluative methods in detail, and contend that their approach is particularly appropriate to Women's Studies because it can be adjusted to any program or course.

Harding, Sandra G. (1976), 'Feminism: Reform or Revolution?', in
C. C. Gould and M. W. Wartofsky (eds), *Women and Philosophy*,
New York, Putnam, pp. 271-84.
This article asks whether feminism is a reformist or revolutionary
movement. Harding suggests that it is both: feminism's reformist
approach works toward a revolution which will eventually eliminate
oppression. To support her theory, the first half of the article confronts four arguments which suggest that 'the kinds of changes
[reformist] feminists are claimed to propose are not merely useless,
but, even worse, dangerous and regressive with respect to achieving
significant social and moral change.' Harding refutes this statement
by pointing out the flaws in each of the four arguments against
reformist feminism. In the second half of the article, Harding deals
directly with the reform/revolution dichotomy. She identifies four
arguments condoning a revolutionary approach and condemning a
reformist one. She carefully responds to each argument, pointing out
the problems of a purely revolutionary movement. (RW)

Hechinger, Fred (1980), 'Black Studies Come of Age,' *New York
Times Magazine*, 13 April, pp. 48-51, 62-8, 73-6.
Hechinger gives an historical synopsis of the progress of Black
Studies and discusses the pros and cons of having a separate Black
Studies department within an academic institution. The author interviews selected present-day Black Studies faculty and gives examples
of courses offered at Yale, Stanford, Berkeley and others to illustrate the shift in emphasis from political activism to 'pure' academic
scholarship. The tone of the article disparages the necessity or
legitimacy of having a separate department for this 'non-traditional'
program unless it is linked to an existing department. This is of
interest to Women's Studies because of the parallels between the two
disciplines both recently founded studies with roots in social movements. (MP)

Hersh, Blanche G. (1980), 'Re-entry Women Involved in Women's
Studies,' *Women's Studies Monograph Series*, US Department of
Health, Education and Welfare, National Institute of Education[4]
This monograph examines re-entry women, their changing profile,
and the vital need Women's Studies and re-entry women have for
each other. Hersh discusses the growth and interrelationship of

Women's Studies and continuing education for women. She makes seven recommendations to facilitate further research on re-entry women and women's centers. (ML)

Hoffman, Nancy (1977), 'Seven Years Later: A Review,' *The Radical Teacher*, Special Issue: Women's Studies in 1977, pp. 54-7.
A review of Florence Howe's study of fifteen Women's Studies Programs. Hoffman expands on some of Howe's themes, such as the degree of 'feminism' in the programs and the influence of a white, middle-class bias. Particularly, she looks at program governance and considers the problems involved in decision-making as it relates to the structure of power and authority in the university.

Howe, Florence (1975), 'Women and the Power to Change,' in F. Howe (ed.), *Women and the Power to Change*, pp. 127-71.
Howe explores the relationship between women and power. She looks at the kinds of power that women actually have had and at the kinds of power that various writers have claimed that women have. She explains how power has been thought of, and used. She then presents her own view of power, and the potential changes she sees which feminists can bring about in the manner of wielding power.

Howe, Florence, (1977), *Seven Years Later: Women's Studies Programs in 1976*, a report of the National Advisory Council on Women's Educational Programs, Washington, DC.
A comprehensive study of fifteen Women's Studies Programs in colleges and universities in the United States. Howe's report discusses: curriculum and the classroom, students, faculty and administration, the impact of Women's Studies as a strategy for change, issues for the future, and recommendations. Two appendices outline program curriculum and present demographic profiles of the fifteen campuses.

Howe, Florence (1978), 'Breaking the Disciplines,' *The Structure of Knowledge*, Proceedings of the Fourth Annual GLCA Women's Studies Conference, pp. 34-7.
In the opening address to the 1978 GLCA Conference, Howe outlines the history of the academic disciplines, revealing how revolutionary and threatening these 'new' disciplines, the sciences, were to

the educators of the 1880s. She examines the fragmentation of the 'traditional' disciplines and their claims of objectivity and truth. Howe explains how the development of Women's Studies parallels the development of the 'traditional' disciplines, and yet how Women's Studies differs in its perspective on the structure of knowledge.

Howe, Florence and Ahlum, Carol (1973), 'Women's Studies and Social Change,' in A. Rossi and A. Calderwood (eds), *Academic Women on the Move*, New York, Russell Sage, pp. 393-423.
A detailed article on the situation of Women's Studies in 1973 in terms of the social, educational, and historical context of its development. The authors discuss Women's Studies courses, disciplinary and interdisciplinary approaches, the effect of Women's Studies on graduate and professional schools, and the difficulties faced by the new programs. The article concludes with an examination of the structure and goals of Women's Studies. Throughout, Howe and Ahlum provide data on the size of programs, number of courses, etc.

Huber, Joan (1979), 'Review Essay for Sociology,' *Signs*, vol. 1, no. 3, pp. 685-97.
Recent scholarship has begun to fill in the gaps in economic, educational, political and religious contexts where women were formerly invisible to the sociologist. Huber describes four categories of study: (1) documentation that sexism dominates society and social science, (2) new perspectives on traditional theories about women in the areas of marriage and family, (3) research on women in different social classes, and (4) a synthesis of existing material in order to develop a theory of sex stratification. Before 1970, little information on women was available, since then the field has exploded; Huber cites over seventy-five articles and books. (WG)

Hull, Gloria T., Scott, Patricia B. and Smith, Barbara (eds) (1982), *All the Women Are White, All the Blacks are Men, But Some of Us Are Brave: Black Women's Studies*, New York, Feminist Press.
This book is both a testament to the existence of a strong black feminist tradition and a response to the invisibility of black female experience in either the Women's Studies or Black Studies classroom. The editors envision Black Women's Studies as a 'feminist, pro-woman perspective that acknowledges the reality of sexual

oppression in the lives of black women, as well as the oppression of race and class.' They see Black Women's Studies as a metaphor for the essential revolutionary message of Women's Studies — profound social and political change can occur only when the experience of black women is immediately accessible to all women. In this way Black Women's Studies would serve as a 'transformer of consciousness' not only for black women, but for Women's Studies in general. The text includes: theoretical, sociological, literary and pedagogical essays, extensive bibliographies, Black Women's Studies course syllabi, and photographs. (HK)

Jaggar, Alison (1977), 'Political Philosophies of Women's Liberation,' in M. Vetterling-Braggin, F. Elliston, and J. English (eds), *Feminism and Philosophy*, Totowa, Littlefield, Adams, pp. 5-21.
Jaggar states that although equality is the basic goal for feminists, subgroups of different feminist theories and strategies exist within the women's movement. She describes in detail current ideologies which are most influential: the conservative view, liberal feminism, classical Marxist feminism, and radical feminism, and then cites two 'new directions' in which feminism has continued: lesbian separatism and socialist feminism. She maintains that a theoretical overview approach, rather than an isolationist method, will be more effective in resolving feminist issues. (DB-A)

Jayaratne, Toby Epstein (1983), 'The Value of Quantitative Methodology for Feminist Research,' in G. Bowles and R. Duelli Klein (eds), *Theories of Women's Studies*, London, Routledge & Kegan Paul, pp. 140-61.
Jayaratne responds to the critique of quantitative research made by feminist social scientists. She says that we should not throw out quantitative research, but reform it for our use, and employ it along with qualitative research for the purpose of improving the lives of women. She explains quantitative methodology as it is used in survey research and argues that, since feminists are thought of as subjective, we should take advantage of this form of research to be as 'objective' as possible. (GLB)

Kelly-Gadol, Joan (1976), 'The Social Relation of the Sexes: Methodological Implications of Women's History,' *Signs*, vol. 1, no. 4, pp. 809-23.

Joan Kelly-Gadol explores the theoretical significance and implications of women's history for historical study in general. By questioning the three basic concerns of historical thought — periodization,
categories of social analysis and theories of social change — women's
history has 'shaken the foundations of historical study.' Feminist
historiography has recently unsettled these preconceived notions
of historical periods, social categories and ideologies for social
change, and reexamined their effects on women. At the core of this
disruption is an idea which is basic to feminism: women's relationship to men and our position in society is not natural but a social
construct. She approaches each of these three basic concerns by
describing the traditional outlook and then discussing the problems
raised by women's history. The article lists almost one hundred
other sources of information in the field of women's history. (WG)

Kipp, Rita (1978), 'The Feminist Critique: Plans and Perspectives,' *The
Structure of Knowledge*, Proceedings of the Fourth Annual GLCA
Women's Studies Conference, pp. 49-53.
In the conference's closing speech, Kipp examines feminism, feminist criticism and feminist scholarship. She points out to those involved in Women's Studies that feminism *is* an ideology like other
ideologies and that we must apply feminist criticism to our own
feminism. She asserts that in order to transform social structures,
feminism must always be self-critical instead of assuming its own
truth and adapting information and methods to fit ideology, as the
other disciplines have done.

Kuhn, Thomas S. (1970), *The Structure of Scientific Revolutions*, 2nd
edn enlarged, University of Chicago Press.
Kuhn portrays the history of science not as a gradual accumulation
of knowledge leading to closer and closer approximations of truth
but rather as a continuing series of revolutionary shifts in world
view, each of which changes the nature of scientific truth and work.
Scientists function in the context of 'normal science,' their work
based on the theories, precedents, problems, and methods accepted
by the current scientific community, or, in Kuhn's terms, on a 'paradigm.' The major work of normal science is problem-solving, the
reconciliation of the paradigm with acknowledged anomalies.
Periodically, however, anomalies become irreconcilable to the point

of 'crisis,' and new theories or paradigm candidates emerge. The gradual adoption of a new paradigm, usually by a rising generation of scientists, places previous work in a new light, and, based often on only slightly different ideas of what is significant, allows new discoveries; a qualitatively different science emerges with each of these revolutions. Though Kuhn restricts it to the natural sciences, his theory implies, for many disciplines, that 'knowledge' is extremely malleable and largely dependent for its nature, as well as its extent, on the academic community concerned with it. The theory is interesting for Women's Studies practitioners engaged in a kind of scientific revolution. (JA)

Lamphere, Louise (1977), 'Review Essay: Anthropology,' *Signs*, vol. 2, no. 3, pp. 612-27.
Lamphere provides a concise and useful review of the arguments and frameworks of analysis on sexual asymmetry and women's roles in anthropological literature. She cites four major trends: (1) the clarification of different positions on the issue of women's universal subordination versus the existence of sexual equality in some societies, (2) the search for an appropriate cross-cultural framework for the analysis of sex-roles and women's status, (3) regional studies, often interdisciplinary, making controlled comparisons of women's roles within the same historical and cultural influences, (4) the need to analyze change, both historical and contemporary, with attention to colonialism, migration, 'development,' and revolution. Lamphere gives a valuable critique of the implications and limitations of the positions surveyed. She emphasizes the need for a better model of society in order to assess evidence on sexual asymmetry, and for a better framework for cross-cultural comparisons of women's roles in different kinds of communities. (SH)

Lanser, Susan and Torton Beck, Evelyn (1979), 'Why Are There No Great Women Critics and What Difference Does It Make?,' in J. A. Sherman and E. Torton Beck (eds), *The Prism of Sex: Essays in the Sociology of Knowledge*, Madison, University of Wisconsin Press, pp. 79-91.
Lanser and Beck question the conspicuous lack of feminist critics

at a time when feminist writers are being recognized. Accounting tor this discrepancy, they explain that women have been acknowledged as writers because they share common traits with artists — sensitivity, expressiveness, sensuality — but have been denied recognition as critics because woman as critic, theorist, thinker is considered a contradiction in terms. Lanser and Beck insist there have been women critics. They examine women who were both novelists and critics, yet perceived exclusively as novelists. They also examine distinguished male writers who relied heavily on female criticism, yet failed to credit the women. Finally, they contrast traditional male criticism with feminist criticism, calling for a re-evaluation of criticism: a renaming and reclaiming of that which patriarchy has falsely named for us. (RW)

Lerner, Gerda (1972), 'On the Teaching and Organization of Feminist Studies,' *Female Studies*, vol. V, pp. 34-7.
In this short article, Gerda Lerner looks at Women's Studies from two perspectives. First, she states that Feminist Studies are and should be interdisciplinary since they involve the students' whole beings (body, mind and emotions) and in order to reveal the entire range of women's experiences. Second, the methods used in teaching must have as their *intent* the search/discovery of this full range of experiences. Women's Studies should also challenge the assumption that man is the measure and instead put forward the notion that both women *and* men are the measure. Lerner believes that a new academe could emerge through Women's Studies as it has the potential to break the artificial separation that now exists between theory and practice. However, she warns that in our development we do not create new dogmas and ideologies for 'we do not need to replace the old myths with new ones.' (PA)

Lerner, Gerda (1980), 'Placing Women in History: A Theoretical Approach,' paper delivered at the Organization of American Historians, San Francisco.
Lerner examines the traditional attitudes toward women in history and the recent renaissance of information on women's unique experience and culture. She says that women's oppression is rooted

in our lack of a cultural history; because we have not known about our role in history, we have felt ahistorical and unimportant. Traditional history has relegated a marginal position to women of the past; to reclaim our past, Lerner suggests we emphasize *h*istory ('lived past reality') as opposed to *H*istory ('as recorded in books.). She describes an alternative historiography for women's history which refutes patriarchal methodologies. (WG)

Lopata, Helena Z. (1976), 'Review Essay in Sociology,' *Signs*, vol. 2, no. 1, pp. 165-76.
This article centers around sociological work on sex roles within the family. Recent sociological studies of marriage and the family have examined role conflicts experienced by working women, the problems facing single parents and the low status of the housewife. Gerontology in a sociological context is also examined. Lopata points out that there has been a 'burst of new perspectives and knowledge' in theories about the family, and her review essay lists more than seventy sources of this new information. (WG)

Martin, Wendy and Briscoe, Louise (1974), 'Women's Studies: Problems in Research,' *Women's Studies*, vol. 2, no. 2, pp. 249-59.
This two-part article addresses topics and problems in feminist literary criticism and research. Martin lists areas of study and encourages more innovative, creative research on subjects heretofore unexamined by feminist scholars. Briscoe looks at the trends, assumptions, strengths and weaknesses of feminist criticism of literature and language.

Mies, Maria (1983), 'Towards a Methodology for Feminist Research,' in G. Bowles and R. Duelli Klein (eds), *Theories of Women's Studies*, London, Routledge & Kegan Paul, pp. 117-39.
Maria Mies, a German social scientist, says that if Women's Studies wants to take an active part in the struggle against women's oppression, then we must fundamentally reconceptualize all stages of doing research. Only when women go beyond the initial consciousness raising process and become actively involved in changing our own

lives will we understand the social causes of our individual oppression and devise strategies for changing the status quo. Mies puts forward seven methodological postulates for doing feminist research and discusses their implementation on a project with battered women in Cologne, Germany. Although aware of difficulties, she also suggests the applicability of these postulates in developing countries. She hopes both for a crossing of cultural barriers and a healing of the split between ivory tower theory and praxis in life. (RDK)

Mies, Maria and Reddock, Rhoda (eds) (1982), *National Liberation and Women's Liberation* and Mies, Maria (ed.) (1982), *Fighting on Two Fronts: Women's Struggles and Research*, both Institute of Social Studies, P.O. Box 90733, 2509 LS The Hague, Holland, each Dfl. 10. Two collections of workshop papers under the sponsorship of the MA course 'Women and Development' set up to exchange experiences of women who were involved in both activist struggle and feminist research. The papers investigate the problems in developing alternative research methods, the relationship between women's emancipation and national liberation and feminist struggles in the US and Europe. The first volume contains papers about feminist activities in Jugoslavia, Bangla Desh, Nicaragua, Zimbabwe and South Africa (Azania) as well as a comparison of women's experiences in Indian and Chinese post-liberation society. A group discussion 'what happens to women after the revolution?' is particularly informative – highlighting the need for autonomous women's organizations – and an international annotated bibliography with a strong emphasis on Third World Countries concludes the book. The second volume focuses on how to do feminist research and contains accounts of research experiences in Tanzania and India as well as reflections on Oral History and work in a Theatre Collective: Drama for Struggle and Research. The discussion section mentions some of the especially important areas for feminist research, e.g. the relationship between the researcher and the researched, in particular if they are '1st world' and '3rd world' women (this is important also for researcher/researched relationships); problems involved in field work among 'other' women; funding for research projects; the political context of action and research, etc. The annotated bibliography lists over 80 publications concerned with feminist research again with an emphasis on third world countries. (RDK)

Millsap, M., Bagensatos, N. and Talburtt, M. (1979), *Women's Studies Evaluation Handbook*, US Department of Health, Education and Welfare, The National Institute of Education.[5]
This handbook is intended to aid Women's Studies program directors and faculty. It provides information on program objectives, selecting research designs, deciding on instruments, analyzing data, reporting results, and utilizing other resource materials. (KM)

Morgan, Ellen (1978), 'On Teaching Women's Studies,' *Ann Arbor Papers in Women's Studies* (Special Issue), pp. 27-34.
Morgan exhorts Women's Studies teachers to be aware of and deal with the alienation that Women's Studies students can come to feel. If Women's Studies students are going to be agents of change in our society, they must learn — and instructors should teach — about the psychology of alienation and about the methods which oppressed peoples have historically used to improve their position. Thus students can develop a deepened comprehension of the changes they go through, the society around them, and possible strategies for change. This can greatly mitigate the alienation and immobilizing estrangement from society.

Okerlund, Arlene N. (1979), 'Will Women's Studies Survive?', *The Chronicle for Higher Education*, vol. 18, no. 8, p. 80.
Writing for a general educational audience, Okerlund points out the need for Women's Studies as a catalyst to a traditional curriculum that frequently excludes women or portrays them as they are perceived by men, giving examples from the study of English literature. She fears that the economic cuts faced by educational institutions will affect Women's Studies more than any other department since it is less powerful than the traditional disciplines, but insists that Women's Studies is needed in the university because it permits a 'feminine perspective in a masculine world' and ensures the survival of 'those highly revered, but frequently neglected, academic principles of . . . truth and honesty.' (Letters responding to Okerlund's article appear in the 18 June 1979 issue of *The Chronicle*.) (PA)

Parsons, Kathryn P. (1979), 'Moral Revolution,' in J. A. Sherman and E. Torton Beck (eds), *The Prism of Sex: Essays in the Sociology of Knowledge*, Madison, University of Wisconsin Press, pp. 189-227.

Parsons's examination of the philosophical underpinnings of the abortion issue is relevant to Women's Studies people for her depiction of the interrelated manner in which economics, science, and philosophy gain merit and confirmation from each other. She is highly critical of the male and property owning class dominance embodied within moral thinking. She uses the philosophy of an illegal abortion clinic called 'Jane' as the basis for constructing a moral theory which challenges theories embodied within current moral thinking. (PK)

'Politics and Culture in Women's History: A Symposium' (1980), *Feminist Studies*, vol. 6, no. 1, pp. 28-54.
This symposium is a debate on the historical significance and character of a distinct 'women's culture.' The contributors include Mary Jo Buhle, Ellen DuBois and Gerda Lerner. Buhle views the relationship between women's culture and feminism as crucial to contemporary feminist scholarship. She emphasizes the need for historians to integrate this knowledge to produce theories capable of explaining women's lives. The concept of women's culture, according to Buhle, is one of the most significant theoretical contributions of feminist analysis in recent years. It is instrumental in explaining the development of women's consciousness and the formation of the contemporary women's movement as well as feminism of the past. She reminds us that women's culture and feminist consciousness must be viewed within its social and economic context.

DuBois emphasizes the importance of researching and evaluating history from a feminist perspective. It is important that feminist scholarship focus on the political significance of feminism when developing theoretical concepts to place women in history and to induce social change. She criticizes women's history of the 1960s for focusing too heavily on the theme of oppression and on the existence of a separate women's culture. She attempts to clarify the concept of women's culture and assess its political and theoretical significance. DuBois views the relationship between the history of feminism and the history of women's culture as dialectical.

Lerner discusses the problem of redefinition for feminist scholars in search of appropriate conceptual frameworks. She believes that the terminology we use defines the questions we are able to ask because they either sharpen or dull distinctions between various concepts. We must engage in a process of redefinition in order to move beyond traditional meaning. To begin this process, in relation to women's history, Lerner distinguishes between 'women's rights' and 'women's emancipation.' The former is a movement concerned with winning equality for women in the status quo, a reformist goal. The latter concerns women's freedom from oppressive restrictions imposed by gender toward greater autonomy and self-determinism, implying a radical transformation. Lerner also feels we must distinguish between research done in a male-defined context and in a female-defined context. From a women-centered perspective, all of women's activities and goals in a patriarchal world can be defined as 'women's culture,' including feminism. (AB-P)

Prewitt, Kenneth (1979), 'Annual Report from the President,' *Annual Report 1978-1979*, New York, Social Science Research Council. This report is relevant to Women's Studies because the president of the Social Science Research Council openly acknowledges that the social sciences are suffering from a credibility gap that threatens them both politically and financially. He identifies the 'two research traditions in the social sciences' as quantification ('. . . frequently cited as its single most important achievement . . .') and narration (recognition of the cultural and historical roots of events and behavior in society). While noting the importance of adding narration to social science research in order to increase its legitimacy, he continues to affirm the value of scientific methods. He suggests that quantification should be tempered by narration in order to produce more quantification and more scientific data for policy formulation. (JH)

Rapp, Rayna (1979), 'Review Essay: Anthropology,' *Signs*, vol. 4, no. 3, pp. 497-513. Surveying works employing differing assumptions and methods, Rapp sees current work in the anthropology of women as a continuation of the debate on the universality of sexual asymmetry. Refinements in the argument focus on the historical aspect of gender relations and on greater investigation of small contemporary cultures, exploring 'the ambiguous nature of specific contexts of sexual subordination.' Rapp argues for a more cautious use of the 'public/

private domain' distinction. She suggests there is a danger of confusing an ideological statement with the underlying, interpenetrating relations of economic and social life. She also raises the problem of delineating and analyzing a distinct women's culture without romanticizing the mechanisms of oppression, a problem that 'raises political questions about identification with the culture of oppression.' (SH)

Register, Cheri (1979), 'Brief, A-Mazing Movements: Dealing with Despair in the Women's Studies Classroom,' *Women's Studies Newsletter*, vol. 7, no. 4, pp. 7-10.
From her own experience in the Women's Studies classroom, Register comes forward with a model for the development of feminist consciousness. After a period of 'compensating,' a negative period of 'criticizing' marked by bitter despair and frustration follows. But then the 'collecting and constructing' of facts on women leads us towards 'conceiving,' that is, developing a 'gynocentric vision.' But there is an 'abyss' to overcome . . . will we be able to make this leap?

Reinharz, Shulamit (1979), *On Becoming a Social Scientist*, San Francisco, Jossey-Bass,
In this detailed book, Shulamit Reinharz describes step by step three research projects which revealed to her the pitfalls of objective research. She became disillusioned with the principles and methodology of objective research and developed a new procedure which she calls 'experiential analysis.' The researcher is not aloof or 'elite' in this procedure; rather, s/he becomes a participant subject in the study and through self awareness and emotional involvement tries to unite and understand the environment. Reinharz's experiential analysis seriously challenges objective scientific research. (PA)

Reinharz, Shulamit (1983), 'Experiential analysis: a contribution to feminist research,' in G. Bowles and R. Duelli Klein (eds), *Theories of Women's Studies*, London, Routledge & Kegan Paul, pp. 162-91.
Shulamit Reinharz delineates the background of her departure from survey research and participant observation to the development of what she calls 'experiential analysis.' The first step in this undertaking consists of accepting the validity of one's own experience;

next we have to 'specify the assumptions of the traditional framework which are being challenged' and proceed to develop an alternative set of assumptions. Then, Reinharz advises us, we must connect
'the conventional and alternative assumptions into specific components of research procedures.' The key elements of experiential
analysis should be seen as a collection of interacting components:
assumptions, personal preparation, problem formulation, data
gathering and stopping, data digestion and presentation, policy questions. Reinharz elaborates on each of these components and concludes that the possibilities of creating more meaningful research
by using 'non-hierarchical, non-authoritative, non-manipulative'
research methods are well worth the many difficulties inherent in
working with these alternative research methods. (RDK)

Reinharz, Shulamit, Bombyk, Marti, Wright, Jan (1982), 'Feminist
Research Methodology in Sociology and Psychology: A Topical
and Chronological Selected Bibliography with Introductory Essays',
in *Women's Studies International Forum*, 1983, vol. 6, no. 4, forthcoming.
A 51-page bibliography on research and research methodology on
women in the social sciences and psychology. The chronological
order allows for easy identification of early papers on feminist research and the topical order includes such headings as 'Frameworks,'
'Who Has Access to Doing and Publishing?,' 'Uncovering Ignored
Topics and Data Concerning Women,' 'Critiques of Conventional
Methods from a Feminist Perspective,' 'Feminist Research Alternatives,' 'Women Discuss Their Experience as Researchers' and 'Bibliographies and Additional Resources' (RDK).

Rich, Adrienne (1975), 'Toward a Woman-Centered University,' in F.
Howe (ed.), *Women and the Power to Change*, New York, McGraw-
Hill, pp. 15-46.
This is Rich's plea for women in the university to work toward
changing the focus of the institution from men to people, which
means changing its hierarchical structure. Women's Studies helps
put an end to the fragmentation of knowledge because style and
content are new, anti-hierarchical and a response to women's whole-
ness. The questions we must ask are: How can misogyny be overcome to provide for women's 'nascence' instead of merely her

'renaissance' and how can we achieve a redefinition of 'human,'
that is, 'not merely for equal rights but for a new kind of being.'

Rich, Adrienne (1976), 'Women's Studies — Renaissance or Revolution?,' *Women's Studies*, vol. 3, no. 2, pp. 121-6.
Rich sees Women's Studies as 'a pledge of resistance'; she views
feminist culture and feminist politics as inseparable. Women's
Studies must strive to change our society, to end patriarchy, and to
continue to struggle until the division between politics and culture
in our society no longer exists.

Rich, Adrienne (1979a), 'Claiming an Education,' in *On Lies, Secrets
and Silence*, New York, W. W. Norton, pp. 231-5.
In this address to students at Douglass College, Rich advocates that
women involve themselves in diligent, challenging studies at the university. She stresses that women students must take responsibility
for their education, and that a women's college can provide the
environment for both teachers and students to achieve these goals.

Rich, Adrienne (1979b), 'Taking Women Students Seriously,' in *On
Lies, Secrets and Silence*, New York, W. W. Norton, pp. 237-45.
Addressing teachers of women, Rich discusses various circumstances
of society and education which devalue and alienate women
students. She briefly analyzes 'co-education,' sexist grammar,
physical and mental rape, and the nuclear family. Rich exhorts
women teachers (and students) to recognize their importance and
value as women and as women in academia.

Rich, Adrienne (1980), 'Compulsory Heterosexuality and Lesbian
Existence,' *Signs*, vol. 5, no. 4, pp. 631-61.
Rich discusses the marginal status of lesbians in most feminist
scholarship; she cites, for example, the work of Chodorow, Dinnerstein and Jean Baker Miller. She calls for an examination of the
dominance of heterosexuality, arguing that institutionalized heterosexuality helps to maintain male supremacy. Rich says that women
do not always have a choice about their sexual orientation, often for
economic reasons. She defines lesbian experience as more than
genital contact, as a 'lesbian continuum,' by which she means 'a
range . . . of woman-identified experience.' She goes on to distinguish

between the relationships of male homosexuals and of lesbians. The article challenges feminist scholars to participate in the work of 'unearthing and describing "lesbian existence." (LM)

Roberts, Helen (ed.) (1981), *Doing Feminist Research*, London, Routledge & Kegan Paul.
Doing Feminist Research is a collection of British papers on possibilities and problems when undertaking sociological research from a feminist perspective. Rather than discussing specifically what constitutes 'feminist research,' the contributors talk about their specific research projects. (The exception to this generalization is Ann Oakley's piece on feminist interviewing.) The influence of the researcher on the researched — her lifestyle, professional status, appearance, age — is discussed by Diana Woodward and Lynne Chisholm in a review of their research on housewives. Similarly, Joyce Pettigrew talks about her research in India as a white Western woman and the wife of an Indian man. Helen Roberts, in 'Women and their doctors: Power and powerlessness in the research process' and Christine Delphy in 'Women in stratification studies' discuss flaws and inadequacies in existing social science research for the investigation of women. Catriona Llewellyn presents findings from a feminist research project on women bankers and Dale Spender addresses the question of getting published, mercilessly exposing the persistence of male 'gatekeeping' which prevents women from getting research findings distributed. (RDK)

Rosaldo, Michelle Z. (1980), 'The Use and Abuse of Anthropology: Reflections on Feminism and Cross-cultural Understanding,' *Signs*, vol. 5, no. 3, pp. 389-417.
Rosaldo evaluates the way feminist writers have incorporated anthropology into their works, criticizes the search for the 'origins' of sexual inequality, and questions theories cast in universal, often dichotomous terms. She argues that 'universalizing' modes of thought lead to the reinstatement of traditional views that regard women's roles as primordial and unchanging. Asserting that gender roles in all cultures are social constructs, she argues that sexual asymmetry and women's subordination should be understood in social terms. Rosaldo evaluates her earlier use of the distinction between public and private domains as a heuristic device to better

describe and understand women's lives cross-culturally. After examining its uses and inadequacies, she suggests that such a dichotomy perpetuates the ideology of 'separate spheres' found in Victorian social science, that it fails to deal with the problematic nature of the relations between such domains, and that it creates a false separation between women and men who, after all, live in the world together. Rosaldo stresses the need for a theoretical perspective which analyzes the relations of women and men as aspects of a wider social context. Arguing that women's inequality must be seen as part of concrete historical and social realities, she asks that we remember 'that the individuals who create social relationships and bonds are themselves social creations.' (SH)

Rosenfelt, Deborah (1973), 'Going Strong: New Courses/New Programs,' *Female Studies*, vol. 7, New York, Feminist Press.
A comprehensive listing of new courses and programs in Women's Studies in 1973. Courses range from those in classics and speech to the arts and social work — eighteen sections in all. The structures and goals of twelve Women's Studies Programs close this volume.

Rosenfelt, Deborah (1979), 'Ethnic Studies and Women's Studies at UC Berkeley: A Collective Interview,' *The Radical Teacher*, Special California Issue — Proposition 13 and After, vol. 14, pp. 12-18.
Rosenfelt interviewed representatives from three programs at the University of California at Berkeley: Clara Sue Kidwell, Native American Studies, Ron Takaki, Asian-American Studies, and Gloria Bowles, Women's Studies. Topics include structure and origins, university support, student participation, majors, demands on coordinators and professors, and community involvement. A presentation of the functioning of programs at UC Berkeley, and of the structural contrasts between Women's Studies and Ethnic Studies.

Ross, Dorothy (1979), 'The Development of the Social Sciences,' in A. Oleson and J. Voss (eds), *The Organization of Knowledge in Modern America, 1860-1920*, Baltimore, Johns Hopkins University Press, pp. 107-37.
Ross discusses the factors that led the social sciences to take form as separate, academic, professional and scientific disciplines. Specifically, she first 'identifies groups of scholars concerned with social

science in the 1870s and the 1880s and discusses the emergence of academic and scientific disciplines within them.' In the next section she 'describes the young academics that appeared after 1880 and analyzes their impulse toward professionalization.' In a third section she discusses 'the conflicts and compromises within the institutions that shaped the disciplines.' In final section she 'talks about the scientific aspirations of the social sciences and notes some of the factors that led to the appearance of a more vigorous scientism after 1912.' (JH)

Rutenberg, Taly (1983), 'Learning Women's Studies,' in G. Bowles and R. Duelli Klein (eds), *Theories of Women's Studies*, London, Routledge & Kegan Paul, pp. 72-8.
An examination of the traditional disciplines and Women's Studies from a student's perspective in terms of intellectual development and personal and professional relevance. Because Women's Studies emerged from a social movement and is responsible to feminist principles, the author argues that it has characteristics which create the potential for a more rewarding and useful educational experience.

Salzman-Webb, Marilyn (1972), 'Feminist Studies: Frill or Necessity?,' *Female Studies*, vol. 5, pp. 64-76.
The author first presents a case for the necessity of Feminist Studies, and defines feminism as a philosophy of knowledge. She then proceeds to examine what and how feminist teachers teach, and concludes with a warning to Feminist Studies to be wary of co-optation.

Sapiro, Virginia (1979), 'Women's Studies and Political Conflict,' in J. A. Sherman and E. Torton Beck (eds), *The Prism of Sex; Essays in the Sociology of Knowledge*, Madison, University of Wisconsin Press, pp. 253-65.
Sapiro reaffirms the underlying political nature of Women's Studies and its research and discusses the political confrontation that Women's Studies presents to dominant values and methodologies. She develops an explanation for the exclusion of women from political science research by asserting that the discipline is defined in a way which limits the scope of its study, the questions it can ask and its vision of what is relevant. She specifically points to Robert

Dahl's *Who Governs?* as a 'clear example of the treatment of women in political science.' Her discussion of Dahl's work illuminates the contradictions in the assumptions and methods of his discipline. (JH)

Seller, Maxine (1980), 'Putting Women into American Jewish History,' *Frontiers*, vol. 5, no. 1, pp. 59-62.
As a professor of American Jewish History, Seller is determined to reveal the status of American Jewish women over time. Using the 'compensatory' approach, she added women previously ignored in the male-centered course. Next, she asked that '. . . the students consider women's activities, interests, and perceptions as an integral part of every topic, equal in importance to the activities, interests, and perceptions of men.' She discusses the dearth of material on American Jewish women and points out that even when they are referred to, their roles are underemphasized and treated from male perspectives. The use of poetry, fiction, and drama can be useful in obtaining information, as well as the work of journalists, social workers, and government commissions. (DB-A)

Sherwin, Susan (1972), 'Women's Studies as a Scholarly Discipline: Some Questions for Discussion,' *Female Studies*, vol. 5, pp. 114-16.
Sherwin raises four questions about Women's Studies and purposely provides only tentative answers. Her questions deal with the goals of programs, choice of curriculum materials, long-term aims, and whether ours is a scholarly discipline.

Showalter, Elaine (1971), 'Introduction: Teaching About Women, 1971,' *Female Studies*, vol. 4, pp. i-xii.
An introductory article on the history of Women's Studies. In addition, Showalter looks at the special difficulties of women students and professors, and at the problems of male students and professors in Women's Studies courses. She examines teaching techniques and the atmosphere of the Women's Studies classroom, control of programs and the course purposes.

Smith, Barbara (1977), 'Toward a Black Feminist Criticism,' *Conditions: Two*, vol. 1, no. 2, pp. 24-44.
Smith says that despite the abundance of gifted black writers, black literature is scarcely known and published black lesbian writing is

even more uncommon. This literature must be made available so that people can understand black, Third World and lesbian culture. White criticizes improperly handled reviews of black women writers and black male critics are often insensitive to the issue of sexism in the literature of black women. To ensure that black literature is not passed by, misunderstood or destroyed, critics are needed who understand black lesbians and black women's language. (ML)

Smith, Barbara (1979), *The Structure of Knowledge: A Feminist Perspective*, Proceedings of the 4th Annual GLCA Women's Studies Conference, pp. 11-16.
Smith believes that Black Women's Studies is a revolutionary new curriculum. It is an interdisciplinary and feminist examination of black women's lives emphasizing issues such as class, race and sexual violence. Black Women's Studies will 'transform knowledge as we know it' by introducing and expanding upon issues of interest to Women's Studies and Black Studies. Black Women's Studies is an extension of the Black Women's Movement; this 'knowledge that complements and makes possible political movement' will contribute to the transformation of existing disciplines. Smith maintains that objective scholarship — white male studies — changes nothing; the bias of Black Women's Studies must be toward the kind of knowledge that moves — and saves — black women's lives. (ML)

Smith, Barbara (1980), 'Racism and Women's Studies,' *Frontiers*, vol. 5, no. 1, pp. 48-9.
Smith challenges white feminists to 'fundamentally, organically and non-rhetorically' confront racism in their own lives, in Women's Studies and in the women's movement. She admonishes privileged white 'academic feminists' and professional women who 'hide from the oppression that undermines Third World women's lives' by isolating themselves from grass roots activism and politics. Homophobia and the de-emphasis of class and race analysis in white middle class feminism also prevent white women from overcoming their individual racism. Smith concludes that racism and sexism are fundamentally interrelated; racism must be eliminated before a non-sexist society can be realized. (TR)

Smith, Dorothy E. (1979), 'A Sociology for Women,' in J. A. Sherman and E. Torton Beck (eds), *The Prism of Sex: Essays in the Sociology of Knowledge*, Madison, University of Wisconsin Press, pp. 135-88. Smith proposes a 'Copernican shift in sociology' which would locate the knower within the everyday world of experience rather than, as at present, within the removed 'discourse' of the discipline. She identifies a 'line of fault' existing between women's experience and the forms of thought and action made available for its expression by social and ideological structures. This 'line of fault' forces women to view themselves as object; to become subject within the ideological relations of sociology or the 'ruling apparatus' of society, they must stand outside their own experience, examining it as phenomenon rather than as problematic, taking an overview not available to the knower located in a specific time and place. Drawing on Marx and Engels, she suggests that sociology begin its inquiry not from within the established framework of existing sociology, but from the standpoint of the individual, involved in everyday relations, acted upon in an apparently disorganized fashion by a 'ruling apparatus' of social and ideological organization beyond her control. (JA)

'Special Issue: Women and Education' (1982), *Off Our Backs*, May, vol. xii.
In this special issue on women and education, the section devoted to Women's Studies includes articles on: the theory and practice of Black Women's Studies, the integration of feminist teaching styles into the general curricula, the history of Women's Studies at SUNY Buffalo, and accounts of lesbian and Third World women who were fired — or 'not rehired' — due to their radical politics. (HK)

'Special Section: Women's Studies' (1982), *Change*, vol. 14, no. 3, April, pp. 12-46.
This issue includes: 'Feminist Scholarship — The Extent of the Revolution' by Florence Howe, 'New Knowledge or a New Discipline: Women's Studies at the University' by Judith Walzer, 'A Period of Remarkable Growth — Women's Studies Research Centers' by Miriam Chamberlain, 'Transforming the Academy: Twelve Schools Working Together' by Beth Reed, 'Toward a Balanced Curriculum: The Study of Women at Wheaton College' by Bonnie Spanier, 'Men's Studies and Women's Studies' by John Schilb and 'Wellesley's New President: The Right Woman for the Right Job' by Judy Foreman.

Florence Howe begins her essay with the reminder that traditional patriarchal education only maintains women's subordinate status and sex segregation in the workplace. The 'male-centered curriculum' must be changed into what it has never been, 'coeducational'; the major source for this transformation is Women's Studies. Howe concludes with a list of the resources and barriers facing Women's Studies today. Judith Walzer suggests that the existence of Women's Studies as a separate and distinct discipline may be decided upon practical grounds; universities may no longer be able to afford Women's Studies. Such a development would not conflict with Walzer's theoretical position. She believes that the work of Women's Studies can be accomplished from within the old disciplines by introducing the 'special perspective' of Women's Studies and thereby changing traditional disciplines. Finally, John Schilb discusses his position as a male teacher of Women's Studies at Denison University and makes a case for the importance of men teaching in Women's Studies. (NL)

Spender, Dale (ed.) (1981) *Men's Studies Modified. The Impact of Feminism on the Academic Disciplines*, Oxford and New York, Athene Series, Pergamon Press.
This book is concerned with the range of male control exercised within the construction of each discipline. It contains critiques of the disciplines and analyses of the changes that have been brought about in response to the feminist challenge. Contributors come from many countries and include Helen Baehr, Ruth Hubbard, Annette Kolodny, Cheris Kramarae, Joni Lovenduski, Helen Roberts, Sheila Ruth and Beverly Walker. Fifteen disciplines are examined and alternative feminist approaches to the respective fields discussed.

Spender, Dale (1982a), *Invisible Women. The Schooling Scandal* (1982), Writers and Readers Publishing Cooperative.
Spender exposes the myth of equal opportunities in education for women by drawing extensively on studies of classroom interaction. She demonstrates that 'equality' for young women is dependent upon their adjustment, rules and ideas instituted by men for the benefit of men. Therefore, our education system is founded upon half-truth. (RDK)

Spender, Dale (1982b), *Women of Ideas and What Men Have Done To Them. From Aphra Behn to Adrienne Rich*, London and Boston, Routledge & Kegan Paul.
Dale Spender looks at 150 women of our past and documents how they have been erased from the record of knowledgemaking as creative intellectual thinkers. In example after example she shows how those who control the production of knowledge — men — either 'use or lose' women's ideas and how little their methods have changed over the last three centuries. Because women still do not control the production of knowledge, Spender advocates going on a knowledge strike and stopping making our intellectual work available to men. The index of *Women of Ideas* demonstrates that working with a feminist perspective *is* different: by putting women at the center, entries such as 'harassment' (with well over 100 references), 'politics: male appropriation,' 'reasoning, male, limitations of,' 'theft of women's resources,' 'scholarship, male variety,' etc. differ radically from the standard male-centered ones. (RDK)

Spender, Dale (1983), 'Theorising about Theorising,' in G. Bowles and R. Duelli Klein (eds), *Theories of Women's Studies*, London, Routledge & Kegan Paul, pp. 27-31.
Drawing upon her own experience of becoming a feminist and a writer, Dale Spender meditates on how we come to know and to theorize. She reminds us of the arbitrary nature of all knowledge, asserting that since meaning is socially constructed, it is legitimate for us to advance our own feminist theories in order to create knowledge for women to end patriarchy. (RDK)

Stanley, Liz and Wise, Sue (1983), ' "Back into the personal" or: our attempt to construct "feminist research",' in G. Bowles and R. Duelli Klein (eds), *Theories of Women's Studies*, London, Routledge & Kegan Paul, pp. 192-209.
The doing of feminist research as advocated by Sue Wise and Liz Stanley, two British social scientists, must start with the researcher as a central part of her research project. Feminist research should be the doing of feminism, using the same approaches and procedures we use in 'doing' life. This means that we have to make ourselves vulnerable in the process of our research. By exploring how we construct our everyday lives as women and researchers (rather than 'interpreting'

in the conventional social science way) we will gain insights into the mechanisms of women's oppression so that we can challenge them. (RDK)

Stimpson, Catharine (1973a), 'The New Feminism and Women's Studies,' *Change*, September, pp. 43-8.
Stimpson's goal here is 'to dissipate the confusion and correct the contempt' provoked by the term Women's Studies. The article provides an overview of Women's Studies — its impetus and goals, its participants, and some of the issues and resistance encountered by those involved in Women's Studies.

Stimpson, Catharine (1973b), 'What Matter Mind: A Theory About the Practice of Women's Studies,' *Women's Studies*, vol. 1, no. 3, pp. 293-314.
An in-depth review of problems in Women's Studies and how to survive them. Stimpson examines internal disruptions as well as external opposition. Her strategy for surviving both internal and external problem stresses (1) freedom for individual programs to differ on issues, and (2) the necessity of a national organization to distribute information, conduct research, and sponsor projects in Women's Studies.

Stimpson, Catharine (1978), 'Women's Studies: An Overview,' *Ann Arbor Papers in Women's Studies* (Special Issue), May, pp. 14-26.
Stimpson sees Women's Studies as 'galvanizing marginality,' energetic and creative but still on the fringes of the academic community. She points to questions Women's Studies should ask and to changes which have occurred because of it. Stimpson then defines three major aims: deconstruction of false axioms, logic, and conclusions; reconstruction of reality; and finally the construction of new theories and ideas. She strongly recommends an interdisciplinary approach and continuing interactions between academic programs and the Women's Movement.

Stimpson, Catharine (1979), 'The Power to Name: Some Reflections on the Avant-Garde,' in J. A. Sherman and E. Torton Beck (eds), *The Prism of Sex: Essays in the Sociology of Knowledge*, Madison, University of Wisconsin Press, pp. 55-77.

Stimpson's article challenges the self-described avant-garde of literary criticism. Avant-garde critics tend to appreciate a radical approach to style but maintain a traditional notion of sex-roles in their criticism and in recognition of artists. To support her views, Stimpson explores the *MPLA* and the *Partisan Review*. The former claims to be free from the influences of any specific group or its ideologies. It has published few women, however, and has in the past portrayed art and artist as masculine. The *Partisan Review* is a politically based literary magazine which 'remains dedicated to an open inquiry that creates a climate for potentially and aesthetically radical activities.' It has also neglected the literature and criticism of women. Stimpson discusses the treatment of Gertrude Stein and James Joyce in each publication to further illustrate this masculine bias towards art and artists. Stimpson concludes that avant-garde criticism must be developed which is sensitive to both political and stylistic revolution and which generates new structures of the self and community. (RW)

Tobias, Sheila (1978), 'Women's Studies: Its Origins, Organization and Prospects,' in H. Astin (ed.), *The Higher Education of Women*, New York, Praeger, pp. 80-94. Also in *Women's Studies International Quarterly* (1978) vol. 1, no. 1, pp. 85-97.
Tobias documents Women's Studies' development with reference to various programs, courses, publications and organizations, as well as to the issues and conflicts in Women's Studies. She concludes with a brief look at the state of Women's Studies in 1978, future developments and difficulties, goals and possible alternative models.

Wallsgrove, Ruth (1980), 'The Masculine Face of Science,' in the Brighton Women and Science Group (eds), *Alice Through the Microscope*, London, Virago, pp. 228-46.
Wallsgrove argues that scientific rationalism is seen by most people in Western society as the clearest way of thinking because it is considered 'masculine' and 'masculine' is valued in our culture. At the same time, the traits of an oppressed group are seen as inferior and often despised by the oppressors. She sees three common characteristics of science — detachment, rationality and the desire for control — as a direct reaction to the caring, emotionality and 'mysterious' characteristics traditionally defined as feminine. (LM)

Watkins, Bari (1983), 'Feminism: A Last Chance for the Humanities?' in G. Bowles and R. Duelli Klein (eds), *Theories of Women's Studies*, London, Routledge & Kegan Paul, pp. 79-87.
A lively paper delivered at the first meeting of the National Women's Studies Association which asserts that the bereft humanities have a good deal to gain from the lesson of Women's Studies — if they will only learn. Watkins says that for people in Women's Studies the 'liberal arts education holds a promise and a sense of purpose sadly lacking in much of the university' and that, in fact, Women's Studies offers a 'model of intellectual revolution which may well prove to be most effective for all of the humanities.'

Westkott, Marcia (1979), 'Feminist Criticism of the Social Sciences,' *Harvard Educational Review*, vol. 49, no. 4, pp. 422-30.
Westkott argues that social science has failed women because of its 'happy functionalist assumption of a mutually supportive relationship between personality and culture;' the methodological separation of researcher and researched; and its study of women as part of a kind of academic fad. Moreover, she challenges the idea that once conscious, people act — since women are most often powerless. On the other hand, feminist social science describes female alienation from the world, depends on intersubjectivity as a method, and creates a scholarship for women that reflects the tension and contradiction in our lives.

Westkott, Marcia (1983), 'Women's Studies as a Strategy for Change: Between Criticism and Vision,' in G. Bowles and R. Duelli Klein (eds), *Theories of Women's Studies*, London, Routledge & Kegan Paul, pp. 210-18.
Marcia Westkott reminds us that Women's Studies is not a mere academic exercise but work to induce social change. She says that we must keep the dialectic of criticism and vision constantly in mind as we teach and write. She points out that vision is more apparent in our classrooms than in our publications, since survival in the academy encourages us to be cautious. She warns against this lack of risk-taking and points to feminist poets and writers outside the academy who are 'shattering . . . old forms and creating new ones.' Women in academe must do this, too, cutting ourselves free from the 'false-categories and promises' of conventional scholarship and teaching. (GLB)

'Women's Studies in 1977: Going Forward' (1977), *The Radical Teacher*, Special Issue, December.

This issue is entirely devoted to Women's Studies. Of the fifteen articles, eight are personal histories and reviews by instructors of Women's Studies classes at different colleges. Three others deal with women's literature (Afro-American Literature, Poetry by Women in Prison, and the 'Bawdy Lore of Southern Women') and one relates the story of a lesbian culture study group. Additionally, Stimpson tells of 'The Making of Signs,' and Nancy Hoffman reviews Florence Howe's report on Women's Studies Programs.

'Women's Studies' issue (1980), *The Radical Teacher*, no. 17, November, 64 pages.

This issue focuses on two recent directions in Women's Studies: (1) teaching, researching and theorizing about the lives and work of black women, and (2) the development of lesbian studies and the perpetuation of heterosexual bias within Women's Studies. Authors include Mary Helen Washington on a theoretical framework for a literary history of black women; Linda Berry and Judith McDaniel on teaching contemporary black women writers; an annotated bibliography on Black Lesbian Literature/Black Lesbian Lives by J. R. Roberts. In addition, Peg Cruishank discusses Lesbian Studies ('Some Preliminary Notes') and Bonnie Zimmerman's essay 'Lesbianism 101' talks about some of the problems and joys of teaching a lesbian studies class, while Elly Bulkin explores the phenomenon of homophobia in 'Heterosexism and Women's Studies.' In a reflection on the limitations of Women's Studies, Marilyn Frye is particularly worried about training our students to be reformists rather than revolutionaries and suggests that we carefully reexamine the ways we teach Women's Studies. Paraphrasing Emma Goldman, she says that the way we make our revolution determines how and who we shall be after it: 'We suffered a single flash of vision . . . and set about to institutionalize it.' (RDK)

Zangrando, Joanna S. (1975), 'Women's Studies in the United States: Approaching Reality,' *American Studies International*, vol. 14, no. 1, pp. 15-36.

Zangrando discusses the development of Women's Studies — its interdisciplinary aspects, methodologies, communication networks and resource centers. She then continues with an extensive list and a brief description of Women's Studies and women's movement literature, from early documentaries and personal writings to current collections and analytical works.

Zihlman, Adrienne L. (1978), 'Women in Evolution, Part II: Subsistence and Social Organization Among Early Hominids,' *Signs*, vol. 4., No. 1, pp. 4-20
Presenting an overview of the evidence on hominid evolution, Zihlman discusses the development of social organization as an adaptive strategy and, in contrast to traditional interpretations of prehistory, she places the female at the center of the analysis. The article focuses on the question: 'How did human males evolve so as to complement the female role?' Using evidence from archaeology, primate studies, and biochemical dating, Zihlman provides a convincing and well documented argument for the creation and transmission of social organization and culture based on a mother-centered group. Kinship bonds, food sharing, and the development of tools are linked to the necessities of childcare in a foraging economy which would emphasize strategies for enhanced mobility.

Editors' Note Whilst *Theories of Women's Studies* was in the process of publication, the following important work for Women's Studies was published:
Cruikshank, Margaret (ed.) (1982), *Lesbian Studies: Present and Future*, Old Westbury, New York, The Feminist Press.
'The contributors to *Lesbian Studies* believe that our past invisibility has been harmful not only to us, but to all students and teachers, to anyone, in fact, who trusts education to "lead out" to comprehensive views and a tolerance for diversity.' This statement from the introduction summarizes the main aim of *Lesbian Studies*: to start compensating for Women's Studies's lack of incorporating lesbian perspectives as experienced by a wide range of women of different colours, classes, ages and religious beliefs in its research and teaching. The book opens with five essays on 'Lesbians in the Academic World: The Personal/Political Experience', among them Doris Davenport's paper 'Black Lesbians in Academia: Visible Invisibility' and Toni McNaron's ' "Out" At the University: Myth and Reality'. The next section comprises nine

essays on what happens in the classroom when lesbian issues are introduced. These papers range from Carolyn Fontaine's proposed conceptual framework based on an analysis of patriarchy, hetero-sexism and woman-identification to Jane Gurko's 'Sexual Energy in the Classroom' which discusses the power imbalances and consequent romantic fantasies with which the lesbian tutor has to deal, 'Teaching About Jewish Lesbians in Literature' by Evelyn Torton Beck and 'Lesbian Literature: A Third World Feminist Perspective' by Cherrie Moraga and Barbara Smith. Discussions on 'New Research/New Perspectives' are compiled in the third section providing a multitude of examples of the dimensions that Lesbian Studies brings to Women's Studies by asking different questions, or by understanding existing questions differently. It includes essays on science, literary criticism, history, sport and physical education, lesbians of colour, older lesbians, etc. Estelle Friedman's short essay 'Resources for Lesbian History' suggests the study of personal papers, literature, newspapers, legal records, oral history and photographs in order to fill in the gaps in our history. The syllabi of nine courses in *Lesbian Studies* taught in the US are put together in the appendix and a bibliography as well as a list of other resources such as audio-visual materials, archives, publishers, centres etc. make this book strengthening and encouraging for lesbians and challenging for heterosexual Women's Studies practitioners, but above all it is an important contribution to Women's Studies/feminism's aim to be accountable to and in the interest of all women. (RDK)

Notes

1 The bibliography was compiled by the members of the Women's Studies 110 (Theories of Women's Studies) seminars at the University of California, Berkeley, Fall 1979, Fall 1980 and Spring 1982. Annotations were written by Jane Appling, Paulina Azocar, Danit Ben-Ari, Ann Ben-Porat, Gloria Bowles, Renate Duelli Klein, Wendy Gilmore, Susan Hensley, Marie Langly, Nancy Lindsley, Lillian McDonnel, Karen Minardi, Marie Paris, Taly Rutenberg and Robin Winn. Annotations without initials were written by Ericka Heckscher, Gloria Bowles and Renate Duelli Klein. The bibliography was edited by Taly Rutenberg.

2 Single copies of this monograph may be requested from: Social Processes/ Women's Research Team, National Institute of Education, Mail Stop 7, 1200 19th Street, NW Washington, DC 20208, USA.

3 Ibid.

4   Ibid.
5   Single copies of this monograph may be requested from: Mary Ann Millsap, Program on Teaching and Learning, Testing, Assessment and Evaluation Program, National Institute of Education, 1200 19th Street, NW, Washington, DC 20208, USA.

Index

Psychology Today, 149, 170
public opinion, use of 'objective'
  research to manipulate, 155-6

qualitative research, 20-1, 140-1,
  144-5, 153-4, 155, 186n
quantitative research, 17, 20-1, 140-61;
  feminist criticism of process and
  analysis, 145-52; generalizing with,
  157-8; objective appearance of
  data, 154-7; process, 141-5;
  simplistic and superficial nature of,
  152-8
questionnaires, 48, 143, 144, 178
Questions féministes, 42
Quinn, R.P., 141

racism, 5, 10, 66, 91
rap groups, 167
rape, 117, 150
Rawlings, E., 170
Reason, P., 173
reciprocity, 123
Reinharz, Shulamit, 17, 21, 37, 140,
  141, 145, 150, 162-91
research: abundance of 'quick and
  dirty', 151-2; concept of linking
  praxis and, 124; experiential,
  162-91; humanities funded
  projects, 79-80; method and theory
  preferences, 164-5; qualitative,
  140-1, 144-5, 153-4; quantitative,
  17, 20-1, 140-61; underutilization
  of, 147-9; see also feminist research
research collectives/communes, 176,
  180, 181
researcher: conscious partiality of, 19;
  decision-making by, 147-8; Mies's
  methodological postulates for,
  19-20, 93, 94-5; obedience to the
  authority of, 180-1; vulnerability
  of, 196-7; see also feminist research
researcher-subject (researched)
  relations, 17, 37, 94, 119, 120,
  123, 126-7, 150-1, 176-7, 180-2,
  183, 194-5
response effects, 177
Rich, Adrienne, 25n, 108, 114n, 215,
  217
Riesmann, L., 185
Roche, Maurice, 174, 175
role-specific behavior, 127

Ross, Dorothy, 33
Roth, Julius, 179
Rothschild-Whitt, Joyce, 180
Rowan, J., 173
Rowbotham, Sheila, 222
Rubin, Lillian, 37
Ruble, D.N., 140
Rutenberg, Taly, 16, 72-8

sampling, revised notion of, 176-7
Schatzman, L., 144
Schmidt, Ruth, 4
Schmitz, Betty, 3
Schwab, J.J., 48
science, history of, 164
science-making, 105-13
scientific revolutions, Kuhn's model
  of, 50-1, 67-8, 69n
scientism and the modern disciplines,
  35-6, 43n
Scully, Malcolm, 37
'seeing things complexly, contextually', 110-11
Segal, Lynn, 222
selective perception, 156
sex differences, 70n, 92, 152-3, 165
Sex Roles: A Journal of Research, 55,
  147
sexism, 17, 53, 54, 57, 66, 77, 91-2,
  117, 118, 120, 121, 122, 126, 142,
  146-7, 149, 210; feminine/
  masculine stereotypes, 92, 93;
  inherent biases in methodology,
  91-2; obscene phone callers,
  197-200
shared feedback loops, 182
shared topic formulation, 182
Sharff, Jagna W., 170
Shattuck, Roger, 43n
Sherif, Carolyn, 167
Shils, E., 185n
Signs, 56-7, 69n
Simmons, J.L., 144
SIROW (Southwest Institute for
  Research on Women), Dinnerstein
  report, 8-9
Smircich, L., 174-5
Smith, Barbara, 52
Smith, Dorothy, 165, 166
social construction of reality theories,
  174
social pathology, Mills's study of, 163